CAREER COUNSELING:
Contemporary Topics in Vocational Psychology

CAREER COUNSELING:
Contemporary Topics in Vocational Psychology

Edited by
W. Bruce Walsh
Samuel H. Osipow
Ohio State University

LEA LAWRENCE ERLBAUM ASSOCIATES, PUBLISHERS
1990 Hillsdale, New Jersey   Hove and London

Lawrence Erlbaum Associates, Inc., Publishers
365 Broadway
Hillsdale, New Jersey 07642

Library of Congress Cataloging-in-Publication Data

Career counseling: contemporary topics in vocational psychology /
  edited by W. Bruce Walsh, Samuel H. Osipow.
      p. cm.
  Includes bibliographical references.
  ISBN 0-8058-0266-5
    1. Vocational guidance. 2. Counseling. 3. Vocational guidance —
Psychological aspects. I. Walsh, W. Bruce, 1936- . II. Osipow,
Samuel H.
  HF5381.C26523 1990
  158.6 — dc20   89-28357
                                                        CIP

Printed in United States of America
10 9 8 7 6 5 4 3 2 1

Contents

Introduction: Approaches to Career Counseling

W. Bruce Walsh
Samuel H. Osipow
Ohio State University

The original approach to formal vocational counseling is generally traced back to Frank Parsons (1909). Parsons became interested in unemployed school leavers and developed a counseling service in the Boston Civic House, a social settlement. In 1909 he published a book (*Choosing a Vocation*) in which he structured the three steps of vocational counseling as he viewed them in practice: self-analysis, occupational analysis, and true reasoning or counseling to relate personal and occupational information. Since Parsons' original contribution, a variety of approaches to career counseling have been developed representing a rich range of intellectual perspectives. Differential, developmental, social learning, cognitive, sociological, economic, and mathematical models have all been used. It is the purpose of this volume to link the past and the present and look to the future in reviewing contemporary approaches to career counseling. Thus, this book is for vocational counselors practicing in the field. We hope it will assist their awareness of the practical and applied aspects of the approaches to career counseling and help them maintain a databased objectivity about the approaches.

The book presents seven contemporary approaches to career counseling: trait-and-factor approach, person-centered approach, psychodynamic approach, developmental approach, social learning approach, social psychological approach, and computer-assisted career counseling. The final chapter attempts to summarize, and to some extent, integrate the different approaches to career counseling.

The chapter on the trait-and-factor approach to career counseling by Rounds and Tracey makes the point that trait-and-factor counseling is viable and useful. In this chapter the authors argue that person–environment fit theories of vocational behavior have replaced trait-and-factor theories as the dominant focus of inquiry; Williamson's trait-and-factor counseling can be seen as an earlier version of what is now generally subsumed under the rubric of problem solving theories of counseling; and the person–environment fit premise of trait-and-factor counseling can be applied to the client–counselor interaction itself using current conceptions of problem solving and information processing. Thus, the model proposed by Rounds and Traccy involves applying the person–environment fit premise of trait-and-factor counseling to the client–counselor interaction itself using current conceptions of problem solving and information processing. Information-processing skill occupies a central place in this model. Key ingredients of information processing used in the model include encoding skills, pattern matching skills, and breadth/narrowness of these skills. According to Rounds and Tracey, the label *trait-and-factor theory*, when applied to career counseling, is best thought of as a problem-solving approach that emphasizes diagnosis, assessment, and actuarial methods guided by one or more person–environment fit models of occupational choice and work adjustment.

The chapter by Bozarth and Fisher presents a person-centered career counseling model. The model is an attempt to integrate the person-centered approach with the specific needs of the career counseling relationship. The focus in the model is the person-to-person interaction that promotes self-discovery by the client. The locus of control remains with the client and there is a lack of treatment planning. The relationship is collaborative and emergent. The counselor assists exploration of self-identity, assists in the formulation of vocational expression of that identity, and participates in the planning and execution of methods to implement that expression. The focus in the model is the person-to-person interaction that promotes self-discovery by the client and implementation of the personal identity (self-concept) in a fulfilling occupational role.

The chapter by Watkins and Savickas on psychodynamic career counseling is divided into two main sections. In the first half of the chapter, the authors consider vocational theory and research derived from the Psychodynamic theories of Freud, Erikson, and Adler. In the second half, the authors consider the use of the psychodynamic model and associated methods for career counseling. The authors note that psychodynamic theories typically have not been well applied to career counseling practice. However, some psychodynamic theories and concepts can be used to inform one's thinking about vocational behavior. In general, psychodynamic theories conceptualize people as somewhat neurotic and consider overcoming neurosis to be the most important life problem that faces each person. People develop by turning symptoms into strengths and strengths into social contributions. Understanding self deals with turning neurotic symptoms into strengths and understanding how the client is like others deals with turning personal strengths into social contributions. The counselor seeks to explain the client to the client by making intelligible interconnections among the episodes of the client's life. Stated differently, the counselor helps clients find socially viable and personally suitable vocational opportunities to develop their life themes and grow through work. In summary, as noted by Watkins and Savickas, psychodynamic theory has a distinct contribution to make to the practice of career counseling.

The chapter by David Jepsen on developmental career counseling builds on the earlier work of Crites by summarizing and integrating recent published work about the broadened notion of developmental career counseling. The chapter is divided into three sections, each built around a problem arising from the recent expansions to developmental career counseling. The first section addresses the problem of what distinguishes the developmental approach from other approaches to career counseling. The second section reviews the expansion in theoretical models, specifically ideas derived from developmental psychology that are useful to developmental career counselors. The third section considers the counseling methods commonly identified with the developmental approach. Jepsen notes that the theoretical and empirical advances in developmental psychology during the past three decades have not as yet been translated completely into models that career counselors can readily apply in daily work. The ideas in developmental theory seem to have considerable promise for enriching career counselors' understanding of the dynamics of careers and the impact of counseling interventions, but the translation is very difficult primarily because the ideas are so abstract.

The chapter on social learning theory of career decision making by Krumboltz and Nichols initially discusses the functions of a theory. Second, the authors review the basic concepts of the social learning theory of career decision making (SLTCDM). Third, the authors compare the SLTCDM with three other career development theories. Finally, a broader living systems view of career decision making essentially consistent with the SLTCDM is discussed. The authors note that the purpose of social learning theory in career decision making is to explain how people come to be employed in a variety of occupations and to suggest interventions that might help people make satisfactory career decisions. Decision making is the process of selecting goals, determining strategies to attain them, and maintaining progress toward those goals.

In career counseling, understanding client goals and helping the client clarify goals and resolve goal conflicts is an important part of information giving and problem solution. Krumboltz and Nichols suggest that we all need to learn that the process of career development never ends. It is a lifelong task to refine one's perceptions of self, to relate one's own self-perceptions to career demands, and to make some sense out of the world in which we live and interact.

The chapter by Fred Dorn on the social psychological approach, presents a rationale for utilizing social influence theory in career counseling. An emphasis is placed on how the career counseling process can be examined from a social psychological perspective and how career counseling practice and research can be enhanced. Dorn indicates that from a social psychological perspective, the process of assisting clients in abandoning existing attitudes and formulating new attitudes about career development is one of persuasion. Motivated clients are influenced by counselors perceived to be expert, trustworthy, and socially attractive. Counselors are also influenced by self-presentational strategies that clients employ. They are face work, ingratiation, supplication, self-promotion, and intimidation. According to Dorn, client attitudes lead to specific behaviors and if these attitudes are ineffective then it becomes necessary for new attitudes to be formulated so that new behaviors can be utilized. The integration of social influence theory in career counseling offers some intriguing possibilities for both practitioners and researchers.

The chapter on computers and career counseling by Jack Rayman was written to provide both the counseling practitioner and the counseling services administrator with an integrated update on the status of the use of computers in support of the career counseling process. This chapter is divided into six sections. The first section provides a brief history of the development of computer-assisted career guidance (CACG). The second section provides a sketch of the theoretical basis for the content of CACG systems now available. The third section outlines the content necessary for a CACG system, describes the content of available systems, and provides some comparisons. Following that is a review of the evaluation studies that have been made of existing systems. The fifth section reviews the difficult issue of integrating CACG systems into the career counseling process. Finally, in the last section, the author discusses current issues related to the use of computers in career counseling, and comments on the significant contributions that CACG has made to the profession. In general, Rayman notes that CACG systems promote a greater awareness of the need for career planning, increase the concern with vocational choice, and facilitate user's ability to relate information about themselves to potential occupations.

Common sense and some research suggest that integrating CACG as one component part of a comprehensive career counseling and guidance system is probably the best and most powerful way to utilize such a system.

The final chapter of the book by Walsh is an attempt to summarize and, to some extent, integrate the career counseling approaches. To organize the approaches a classification schema used by Crites in 1981 was implemented. This classification schema elaborates the significant features along which the career counseling approaches may be described and differentiated. The schema consists of a model and methods. The model may be broken down into three major stages: diagnosis, process, and outcomes. The model defines the theoretical framework. In the first phase of counseling, a diagnosis of the client's problem is typically made. In the middle phase, the process of intervention with the client is carried out. In the third and ending phase of career counseling, the outcomes of the counseling experience are reviewed and evaluated by the client and counselor.

The methods of career counseling are more pragmatic than theoretical and attempt to translate the model into operational terms. The methods include the interview techniques used by the counselor, the test-interpretation procedures engaged in by the client and counselor, and the acquisition and use of occupational information. The model is operationalized by the methods of career counseling and both serve to define the significant characteristics of a given approach to career counseling. In combination, the model and methods of career counseling serve to effectively summarize the unique parameters of the career counseling approaches. It is within this context that we have attempted to summarize and, to some extent, integrate the career counseling approaches presented in this volume.

REFERENCES

Crites, J. O. (1981). *Career counseling: Models, methods, and materials.* New York: McGraw-Hill.
Parsons, F. (1909). *Choosing a vocation.* Boston: Houghton Mifflin.

1

From Trait-and-Factor to Person–Environment Fit Counseling: Theory and Process

James B. Rounds
Terence J. Tracey
University of Illinois at Urbana-Champaign

What's in a name? That which we call a rose
By any other word would smell as sweet
  —William Shakespeare (*Romeo and Juliet*, Act II, Scene ii, lines 43–44)

Rose is a rose is a rose.

  —Gertrude Stein

Without an explicit theory of vocational behavior or a theory of vocational behavior change, and with only a rudimentary notion of counseling process, trait-and-factor counseling becomes an approach, hardly a theory, that emphasizes the virtues of assessment and actuarial prediction to generate alternative options for vocational choice and adjustment problems. Indeed, Williamson himself (Williamson & Biggs, 1979) suggested that trait-and-factor counseling needs to be grounded in both a general vocational behavior theory, citing two such theories — theory of work adjustment (Dawis, Lofquist, & Weiss, 1968) and Super's (1977) model of vocational maturity, and a more fully developed model of counseling process. Pace the common wisdom, we contend that Williamson's formulations about vocational counseling are as viable today as they were in the 1930s — when, that is, they are articulated with current psychotherapy and counseling theory; pace Williamson himself, we argue that trait-and-factor counseling has evolved from its atheoretical (i.e., not based on an explicit vocational behavior theory) beginnings to a sufficiently theorized state — as it has come to be informed by person–environment fit theories.

Our discussion of the evolving nature of trait-and-factor counseling and practices is grounded in several ideas about the nature of career counseling. Our central idea, informing the approach we take to trait-and-factor counseling (or for that matter to any type of vocational counseling), is that vocational counseling is a form of psychotherapy. In this position, not acceptable in all quarters (for example, see Borgen, 1986; Crites, 1981; Spokane & Oliver, 1983), we do not stand alone, as the collection of chapter presented in this book, recent practitioner texts (Gysbers & Moore, 1987; Yost & Corbishley, 1987), and other theoretical writings (for example, see Patterson, 1959, 1973; Strupp, 1978; Urban & Ford, 1971) attest. We subscribe to the basic assumptions set forth by Rounds and Tinsley (1984):

> career intervention is simply a form of psychological intervention de-
> signed to affect vocationally related feelings, attitudes, cognitions, and
> behaviors. Thus, it is a form of *psychotherapy* and should be viewed as a
> method of behavior change and tied to psychotherapy theory . . . career
> interventions can be practiced and evaluated within the context of more
> general behavior theories that provide models of behavior change . . . a
> conceptual shift in which career interventions are understood as psycho-
> logical interventions (and career counseling as psychotherapy) would
> foster advances in the understanding of vocational behavior change
> processes. (pp. 138–139)

Given these assumptions, the practice of vocational counseling is usually accomplished within a context of a general vocational behavior theory, a classificatory schema of vocational problems, a theory of vocational problems, and a theory of vocational behavior change. Theories of vocational behavior explain the process of normal occupational choice and work adjustment. A vocational problem classification identifies (labels) and describes the parameters (attributes) of these problems: the signs and symptoms and the severity, intensity, frequency, and duration of vocational problems. Once a problem is identified one needs a theory of vocational problems to understand or be able to conceptualize how and why the problem functions as it does. Such a theory explains the source of or causal relationships among the events of concern: what accounts for how vocational difficulties are acquired and maintained. Answers to these questions are the basis on which intervention tactics are brought to bear on the vocational problem. A given theory of vocational behavior change—that is, a theory of vocational counseling—will, if not explicitly then implicitly, rely on or incorporate a general theory of vocational behavior.

We take the unpopular and, for some, counterintuitive approach, that trait-and-factor counseling is viable and useful. In this chapter we argue

that: (a) person–environment fit theories of vocational behavior, although traceable to Parsons' model, have replaced trait-and-factor
theories as the dominant focus of inquiry; (b) Williamson's trait-
and-factor counseling can be seen as an earlier version of what is now
generally subsumed under the rubric of problem-solving theories of
counseling; and (c) the person–environment fit premise of trait-
and-factor counseling can be applied to the client–counselor interaction
itself using current conceptions of problem solving and information
processing. (It will perhaps be noticed that we leave to one side a
discussion of assessment and actuarial methods, hallmarks of Williamson's approach, which, whether theory-determined or not, continue to
inform practice no matter what theoretical orientation is taken; these
matters have been sufficiently addressed in the literature and are rarely
points of contention. For recent reviews of vocational assessment, see
Walsh & Betz, 1985, and Zytowski & Borgen, 1983, on a person–environment perspective; Borgen, 1986, on interest assessment; Betz, 1988,
on career development and maturity; and Slaney, 1988, on career
decision making. The best review of clinical versus actuarial judgment
continues to be Wiggins, 1973; for updates of Meehl's, 1954, monograph, see Wiggins, 1981, and Dawes, Faust, & Meehl, 1989.) Thus, it is
our contention that the label *trait-and-factor theory* when applied to career
counseling is best thought of as a problem-solving approach that
emphasizes diagnosis, assessment, and actuarial methods guided by
one or more person–environment fit models of occupational choice and
work adjustment.

WHAT IS TRAIT-AND-FACTOR COUNSELING?

It is customary to ascribe the historical antecedents of trait-and-factor
counseling to Parsons's tripartite model of vocational advising in
Choosing a Vocation, posthumously published in 1909, and D.G. Paterson's studies of individual differences and test development during the
1930s at the Minnesota Employment Stabilization Research Institute
(Paterson & Darley, 1936). It is also customary to identify trait-and-factor
counseling with E.G. Williamson's *How to Counsel Students* (1939a) and
the subsequent writings (Williamson, 1939b, 1950, 1965a, 1965b, 1972;
Williamson & Biggs, 1979; Williamson & Bordin, 1941; Williamson &
Hahn, 1940) that spanned the next 40-odd years (Williamson authored
some 400 publications). And it is equally customary to make such claims
as trait-and-factor counseling "has gone into an incipient decline"
(Crites, 1981, p. 49), and "is in decline, if not moribund" (Zytowski &
Borgen, 1983, p. 9), or, "Currently, the trait-factor model has been

absorbed into many other approaches to career counseling, though few practitioners of vocational counseling today are pure trait-factor adherents" (Osipow, 1983, p. 9).

It probably is fair to characterize the trait-and-factor counseling of Williamson's 1939 formulation in the following ways. It made use of the case history method. Williamson proposed that counseling proceeds along six steps of analysis, synthesis, diagnosis, prognosis, counseling or treatment, and follow-up (see discussion here). The first four steps were the province of the professional. The counselor engages in a tutorial or advisor relationship with the client, assisting the client in obtaining data or providing the client with necessary information, presenting and discussing alternative options and actions, and attempting to aid the client to reach the best choice, decision, or solution. Overall, the emphasis is on a rational, problem-solving counseling process. When viewed from the perspective of current help-seeking models, Williamson's counselor role and process formulations are akin to discussions of behavioral consultation relationships and process (Dustin & Blocher, 1984). Modern-day equivalents can also be found in Goodyear and Healy's (1988) description of the career counseling at University of California, Los Angeles Career Counseling Center (CCC) or Dawis and Lofquist's (1984) description of practices at the University of Minnesota, Department of Psychology Vocational Assessment Clinic (VAC). (It is interesting to note in passing that both CCC and VAC are fee-based services, primarily serving an adult clientele; the CCC uses a clinical synthesis, whereas VAC uses an actuarial combination of data.) Williamson's major contribution is the proposal that tests and actuarial methods be brought to bear on the counseling process. It should be noted, some critics to the contrary, that although Williamson's approach is actuarial when it comes to test data and its interpretation, the combination of data from multiple sources (synthesis) and its interpretation is clinical.

It should also be noted that the approach has not failed to evolve from its Depression-era inception and motivations. Williamson (1965a, 1965b; Williamson & Biggs, 1979) modified his trait-and-factor formulations (quotes are from Williamson & Biggs, 1979) in the following ways:

It is still rational but "The interview involves cognitive and affective processes. The counselor uses the interview to assist the client in considering how these factors play roles in effective decision making" (p. 107).

Use of valid and reliable information continues to be stressed but:

It is especially important that nonquantitative clinical information be collected to make a complete picture of the individual who is being counseled. We hold that, before visiting a counselor, clients have learned much about their own characteristics by comparing their behaviors with the behaviors of other individuals. . . . Thus, a counselor needs to help clients to understand how their social comparison history is related to their past and present self-evaluations. (pp. 105–106)

It relies less on direct methods (advising and teaching) as a form of influence: "The counseling interview also involves interpersonal influence processes (Strong, 1968). . . . In the counseling interviews, the counselor uses his or her influence power to achieve desired changes in the client's cognitive framework and behaviors" (p. 107).

The counseling process continues to be neglected: For the most part, trait-and-factor counselors have sorely neglected making theoretical and empirical investigations of the counseling process. . . . The importance of the client in the interpretation and acceptance of counseling information has not been emphasized fully enough. To be sure, trait-and-factor counselors still need to pay more attention to the processes by which clients attribute meaning to counseling information. (p. 126)

It continues to be atheoretical: "making no pretense of being a comprehensive theory of personality or of counseling. . . . For us, the trait-and-factor approach is an abstract model that counseling activities will approximate to some degree" (p. 125).

These statements also suggest a basis for the remarks just cited of Crites, of Zytowski and Borgen, and especially of Osipow about the status of trait-and-factor counseling. That the trait-and-factor approach has not quite attained the status of full-fledged theory is not in contention here; that there is more to say about it we hope to demonstrate. The rest of this chapter is divided into three major sections—In Defense, Person-Environment Fit, and Counseling Process—throughout which we pursue the main points of our argument as outlined earlier.

IN DEFENSE

Trait-and-factor counseling, whether it is dated from Parsons or from Williamson, is one of the earliest forms of vocational assistance: it is one of the few counseling approaches that developed from the study of vocational behavior. For at least the last 20-odd years, however, as the aforementioned comments on its demise suggest, trait-and-factor counseling has been criticized (if not declared dead and not quite buried) for one reason or the other. Some of the criticism has been justifiable, but most simply isn't. We do not intend a blanket endorsement of Williamson's ideas or trait-and-factor counseling as it is currently envisioned; there are serious unresolved and undeveloped theoretical issues in this area that need to be addressed. But we are going to argue that reports of the death of trait-and-factor counseling have been greatly exaggerated, that much of the current criticism is poorly thought out and weak in form. We begin with some of the criticism of trait-and-factor counseling, making such rejoinders as strike us as appropriate, and in the course of this discussion a preliminary outline of our own perspective takes shape.

Criticism

Because, when it comes to trait-and-factor approaches, critics and defenders alike rarely view theory, practice, and assessment as distinct areas of inquiry, these areas get tangled together—criticism of one area by implication tarring the others with the same brush, all of which makes it difficult to begin to answer such an unwieldy body of misconceived readings and misbegotten analyses. We approach extant criticism, therefore, by dividing (not to say conquering) it, and deploying representative reproaches and rejoinders in order to build our case for our own perspective. We have found that critical discussions of trait-and-factor counseling invariably commit some combination of misreading Williamson's text, and/or setting up a straw figure and calling it trait-and-factor counseling.

Misreadings of Williamson's Text

Much of the criticism across the last 20 or so years has been aimed at what authors believe to be typical trait–factor practices and their assumptions without even any corresponding documentation of what these theories, practices, or assumptions are. It seems to be something of a popular sport to make up an assumption that is obviously false and attribute it to one or more theoretical positions.

It is rare to find responses to the criticism, much less a defense of trait-and-factor counseling. One exception has been Brown's (1984) recent review and spirited defense. Brown made two points: He suggested that reviewers (e.g., Crites, 1974, 1978, 1981, whose writings about career counseling have been particularly influential) have misinterpreted Williamson's writings, stating that "those counselors who followed the three-interviews-and-cloud-of-dust approach never really understood the approach, for Williamson never advocated a test-and-tell approach" (p. 14). He argued furthermore that reviewers have "incorrectly concluded" that trait-and-factor ideas and counseling are no longer viable, contending that "no theory or approach has yet been developed that has satisfactorily replaced trait-oriented thinking, whether the concern be work adjustment, career counseling, or personnel selection" (pp. 14–15).

Straw Man Arguments

Misreadings of Williamson's texts are generally accompanied by misconstrual of basic assumptions of trait-and-factor theory and/or unfairly holding the practice of trait–factor counseling to the letter of the 1939 text—failing, that is, to consider the possibility that it has evolved in the last 50 years. One version of the misconstrual of basic assumptions is produced by the textbook mirage effect. The textbook mirage is an effect of critics of the approach taking the part for the whole: The writer's main task is to distinguish it from other vocational counseling approaches and to discuss its major contributions. These distinguishing factors and contributions (e.g., diagnosis, psychometric information, occupational classification, and information) in turn are taken for the whole of trait-and-factor counseling. The critics fail to include the obvious—that the trait-and-factor approach is delivered within a general counseling and psychotherapeutic framework, by counselors relying on cognitive and social influence techniques.

When critics do write about trait-and-factor counseling techniques, they have continued to rely on Williamson's (1939a, 1939b) early statements and descriptions (e.g., pupil–teacher relationship, "test them and tell them approach to test interpretation," directive advice giving). That reliance results in the distorted view of current practice that holds it to the letter of the 1939 text. To illustrate the latter error, we turn to Crites (1981), who in a sense has stereotyped trait-and-factor practices along with other career counseling practices. (Crites's agenda is to introduce his comprehensive career counseling.) But Crites did not per se misrepresent Williamson's *theory*. The important distinction here is between counseling theory and practice. Although theory is occasionally revised in response to new ideas and developments in a field, practices emanating from a theory change much more rapidly, especially in a relatively new field such as counseling psychology. Williamson (1964) has commented that during the 1930s and 1940s therapy was restricted to psychiatrists and the role of clinical psychologists was only as "mental testers." Thus, concluding that trait-and-factor *practices* from the 1930s, 1940s, and the 1950s are in decline, as Crites has, seems to be stating the obvious. But to go on, as Crites does, and suggest that because practices from the 1930s are not in current vogue, the theory is outmoded is at best begging the issue.

A genealogical search for the source of one important line of criticism based on misconstrual of the basic assumptions of trait-and-factor theory leads us to Jones, Stefflre, and Stewart's (1970) text on principles of guidance. Much of the criticism of the Williamson position and trait–factor models in general (and there has been considerable criticism) has evolved from a series of assumptions suggested by Stefflre and Stewart's revision and update of the Jones et al. (1970) text on principles of guidance. We briefly dwell on these assumptions because they have been frequently cited verbatim (see Isaacson, 1986, p. 38) and paraphrased (see Miller, 1974, pp. 238–239; Weinrach, 1979, p. 66–67; Zytowski & Borgen, 1983, p. 7; also see Herr & Cramer, 1979, p. 70; 1984, p. 90, verbatim citation of Miller). Depending on who you read, Jones et al. proposed four or five assumptions. (It is instructive to read the paraphrases of Jones et al.; several of the authors obviously began to paraphrase each other.) Actually, Jones et al. (1970) proposed that the following five assumptions underlie the trait-factor conception of vocational development:

1. Vocational development is largely a cognitive process in which the individual uses reasoning to arrive at his decision.
2. Occupational choice is a single event.
3. There is a single right goal for everyone making decisions about work.
4. A single type of person works in each job.
5. There is an occupational choice available to each individual. (pp. 182–183)

As a number of writers have taken some effort to disagree with the validity of these assumptions, it suffices here simply to point that these statements are, *prima facie*, reductive generalizations. The last four, in addition, posit an impossible and simplistic universality: Surely no conception of vocational development, even the least satisfactory, would ever declare, for example, that only one "type" of person works in each job. With the exception of Parsons's three-step statement of occupational choice, none of the authors mentioned here cited a particular theorist or theory, trait–factor or otherwise, when discussing these assumptions. The scarcity of this type of "trait–factor theorist" reminds us of Jackson and Paunonen's (1980) rejoinder to current criticisms of trait concepts that are based on the early view of traits as fixed, unchanging, and so on. They wrote, "Like witches of 300 years ago, there is confidence about their existence, and even possibly their sinister properties, although one is hard pressed to find one in the flesh or even meet someone who has" (p. 523).

Rejoinders

In addition to overall defenses of Williamson's basic formulations (as we have previously indicated, see Brown, 1984), rejoinders to the conclusion that the practice of trait-and-factor counseling has been in decline and to criticism (and caricatures) of trait–factor practices take a second form: the description of modern versions of trait–factor counseling practices and theories (Betz, Fitzgerald, & Hill, 1989; Borgen, 1986; Holland, 1974; Spokane, 1985; Zytowski & Borgen, 1983).

Modern-Day Versions

The oversimplification of trait-and-factor counseling is due in part to a paucity of attempts to update and describe the evolving nature of trait-and-factor theory and counseling practices since the 1960s. In a response to Crites' review of trait–factor counseling, Holland (1974, 1978; also see Holland, Magoon, & Spokane, 1981), calling himself an adherent of a modified trait-and-factor view of vocational assistance, nevertheless refused to refute Crites on trait-and-factor counseling issues per se, intimating that, after all, nothing comes of such conflicts (incidentally thus repudiating the historically agonistic structure of academic discourse). Instead, Holland (1974) fashioned a rebuttal of sorts grounded in the additional advantages offered by what he called these new approaches, among which were the following:

> (3) emphasize information, experience, and immediate reinforcement rather than insight, talking, and remote reinforcement; (4) encourage experience and exploration; . . . (6) emphasize levels and varieties of treatment (If this doesn't help, how about this module?); and (7) make use of structural theories and classifications. (p. 25)

The specificity of the body of practices and theory traditionally labeled *trait-and-factor* are thus lost in a discussion grounded more or less generally in assertedly "modern" versions thereof, rather than theories of behavior change. But Holland's last point about structural theories and classifications does acknowledge that trait-and-factor counseling now has a general vocational theory to identify pertinent variables and their measures (in Holland's case, personality types and work environments), a structure within which to view these variables (hexagonal model), and a prediction system to identify satisfying alternatives. Such a system can easily be explained to clients and can be used to guide client's decision-making processes.

From Zytowski and Borgen (1983) perspective, Holland's (1973) research and conceptualizations have expanded and clarified the core Parsonian assumption of matching people and occupations leading to current trait–factor practices that are more flexible, efficient, and effective. They contend that the assumptions of vocational assessment from a historical, paradigmatic, and conceptual view are linked to trait-and-factor conceptions of vocational counseling. Furthermore, modern day assessment practices continue to be informed by the Parsonian matching assumption. They report, however, that the Parsonian assumption has evolved to a congruence model. The central assumptions of the congruence model are:

1. The well-adapted individuals within an occupation share certain psychological characteristics.
2. There are measurable and practical significant differences in people and in occupations.
3. Individual differences interact differentially with occupational differences. In other words, outcome is a function of individual-environment fit (Pervin, 1968).
4. Person and job characteristics show sufficient temporal and situation consistency to justify prediction of outcome over the longer term. (p. 9)

Zytowski and Borgen believe that "refurbished" trait-and-factor practices guided by the congruence model is "eminently appropriate to counseling for decision making" (p. 9). In a further elaboration of the congruence model, Borgen (1986) highlighted the differences between the congruence model and developmental model, stating that the congruence model is best understood as a matching and choice process while a change process underlies a developmental model.

From Congruence Models to PE Fit Theories

The Zytowski and Borgen chapter is important to vocational psychology because it is one of the first attempts to acknowledge and describe the shift in concepts and ideas that underlie what is called a trait-and-factor model (see also Katz & Shatkin, 1983). Although they may be criticized (unfairly) for their "relocating of bones from one academic graveyard to another followed by capping them off with a new headstone" (Horan, 1979, p. 154, anticipating criticism of his synthesis of problem solving, decision making, and counseling literature). Notwithstanding the obvious similarities to Parsons' "true reasoning," the congruence model makes it explicit that a class of vocational behavior theories has been developed and is currently informing trait-and-factor counseling practices. For Williamson's counseling theory or for that matter, any counseling approach, a general behavior theory is needed to guide the analysis of the vocational problem (what went wrong in the normal course of development and how to identify the behavioral difficulty) and the selection of counseling objectives and types of interventions.

Our point of departure from the congruence model is that it does not completely capture the recent shifts (post-1983) in thought of trait-and-factor theorists, especially those trained by Paterson and Darley—Dawis, Holland, Lofquist, and those theorists, French, Moos, and others, working on issues with direct relevance to vocational psychology. These theorists have conceptualized behavior as a function of the person and the environment, developing what is called person–environment (PE) fit theories (the generic term *fit* is used here because congruence implies a specific process hypothesized by certain theories and not others). The initial PE fit theories (Pervin, 1968) were fairly straightforward matching models, what Zytowski and Borgen called congruence models. Recent proposals (Lazarus & Launier, 1978; Pervin, 1987), theoretical revisions (e.g., Dawis & Lofquist, 1984; Holland, 1985), and introduction of life-span developmental approaches to vocational psychology (Vondracek, Lerner, & Schulenberg, 1986) represent efforts to develop PE fit models that are dynamic and process oriented as opposed to matching models that are descriptive. But we must not lose sight of the practical. Dynamic PE fit theories, not unlike their developmental counterparts, anchor vocational behavior in the change process but have yet to contribute meaningfully to the practice of vocational counseling.

There are notable continuities and considerable discontinuities in a historical and conceptual sense from Parsons's true reasoning model to matching models to models that emphasize reciprocal interaction. Because there are a number of useful ways to conceptualize PE fit and because the term *trait-and-factor* is anachronistic, we suggest that PE fit, broadly conceived, be used to refer to current approaches and theories and that PE fit counseling be used instead of trait-and-factor counseling. (For the sake of continuity with Williamson's formulations and our elaborations thereof, we continue to use his terminology in this chapter).

PERSON-ENVIRONMENT FIT

Person-Situation Controversy

During the same year that Pervin (1968) published his *Psychological Bulletin* review on individual–environment literature, Mischel published his well-known anti-trait critique, setting off a person–situation debate that has occupied center stage in personality psychology for the past two decades. The controversy has had considerable influence on personality and social theory and research, affecting what questions are being investigated and how they are being studied. It has had important repercussions for applied psychology and direct implications for trait-and-factor theory and counseling: the consistency controversy strikes at the heart of the trait-and-factor (congruence model) assumptions described by Zytowski and Borgen (1983). We briefly outline the debate and try to convey its implications for the status and nature of traits in vocational theory.

When client abilities, interests, and values are assessed, whether with standard measures or in nonstandard ways (e.g., counselor–client discussions), the counselor assumes cross-situational consistency in traits and behaviors and assumes reliable and stable individual differences between clients. From this perspective, it seems difficult to believe that Mischel (1968, 1983, 1984) and others (e.g., Nisbett & Ross, 1980; Shweder, 1975) not only questioned the trait assumption but suggested that traits are based more on illusion than reality.

Kenrick and Funder (1988) Review

Kenrick and Funder, two active participants in the discussion (from both sides of the aisle), have recently summed up the consistency debate, reviewing the main issues, how these issues were resolved, and how psychology has profited from the debate. To advance their analysis, seven hypotheses are offered as having arisen during the trait-consistency debate. The hypotheses are alternatives to the view that traits are real and important; they are arranged in a hierarchical order in the sense that if an earlier hypothesis is true the later hypotheses will be of no consequence to the debate. Kenrick and Funder (1988) conclude that the available data *fail* to support all of the following seven hypotheses:

1. Personality is in the eye of the beholder.
2. Agreement between raters is an artifact of the semantic structure of the language used to describe personality.
3. Agreement is an artifact of base-rate accuracy (rater's tendency to make similar guesses about what people in general are like).
4. Differential agreement is an artifact of the shared use of invalid stereotypes.
5. Observers are in cahoots with one another; that is, their agreement results from discussion rather than accurate observation.

6. Raters see targets only within a limited range of settings and mistake situational effects for traits.
7. Compared with situational pressures, cross-situational consistencies in behavior are too weak to be important. (p. 24)

Tellegen (in press), after reviewing Kenrick and Funder's analysis, said, "The dismissal of these trait-dismissive hypotheses does not leave us empty-handed: it leaves us with traits." Tellegen defined a trait as "an inferred relatively enduring organismic (psychological, psychobiological) structure underlying an extended family of behavioral dispositions." (See also Lubinski & Thompson, 1986; Meehl, 1986, for discussions of trait concepts.) Tellegen's position on the relation of traits and situations is worth repeating here because of its centrality to PE fit thinking. Responding to criticisms that trait conceptions lack reference to situations, he sketched out Murray's (1938) and Allport's (1937, 1961) theoretical positions showing that trait constructs have often implied (explicitly or implicitly) the particular circumstance in which behavioral manifestations of the trait are likely to occur. Tellegen then advanced the argument, citing similar positions (e.g., Snyder, 1981), that trait dispositions "inherently include a tendency to search for situations that enable trait expression" and that individuals can create trait-congruent situations through how they construe and interpret situations. This process leads to trait-situation matching.

Size and Stability of Trait Relationships

Among vocational psychologists, Kenrick and Funder's Hypothesis 7, that the relationship between traits and behaviors is too small to be of practical importance, is the most widely accepted. It is frequently accompanied by the explicit or implicit hypothesis that traits are too unstable to be of value for purposes of forecasting future vocational behavior. When these two hypotheses are uncritically accepted, they usually form the basis for suggestions that trait measures should not be used to inform the career counseling process.

But in fact the relationships between personality traits and behaviors are large enough to be of practical value. Accumulated evidence has shown that:

1. The often quoted ".30 ceiling" (the upper limit for correlations between trait scores and behaviors) is usually found when single behavioral instances (a poor criterion measure) rather than aggregates of behavior are used (e.g., Epstein & O'Brien, 1985; Jackson & Paunonen,

1985). With aggregate behavior measures, the correlations are usually larger (i.e., .50 to .60).

2. The correlation coefficient of .30 has often been misinterpreted as signifying that it accounts for 9% of the variance between the relevant variables, when in most cases, it accounts for 30% of the variance (Ozer, 1985; Wiggins, 1973). Another way of clarifying the practical usefulness of correlations within the range of .20 to .30 is Rosenthal and Rubin's (1979; see also Rosnow & Rosenthal, 1988) binomial effect size display: a .30 coefficient, approximately the size of the effects of psychotherapy (Smith & Glass, 1977) and of the effects of career interventions (Oliver & Spokane, 1988), with a dichotomous criterion is equivalent to a success rate increase from .35 to .65, hardly a trivial effect.

Given the recent emphasis on hypothesizing developmental disturbances in adulthood—for example, a midlife crisis (Levinson, Darrow, Klein, Levinson, & McKee, 1978)—and applying discrete stages of development to adulthood (Super, 1980), some readers may be surprised that accumulated evidence shows that personality traits are stable in adulthood. McCrae and Costa (1984), in *Emerging Lives, Enduring Dispositions: Personality in Adulthood*, presented a detailed summary of the evidence on personality stability in normal adult development and aging. The evidence brought to bear on the question of "whether, how much, and in what ways personality changes in adulthood" includes retrospective, cross-sectional, and longitudinal studies. Although on the whole the different investigative strategies are consistent with the position of stability in personality, the longitudinal studies many completed in the 1970s using a variety of measures (e.g., California Psychological Inventory, Sixteen Personality Factor Questionnaire), methods (e.g., self-report, trait ratings), samples (females and males), age cohorts (18 to 76 years), and retest intervals (2 to 30 years) are the foundation for McCrae and Costa's major conclusions: (a) There is little change with age in the average level of personality traits. Thus, age does not seem to bring about normative increases or decreases in personality traits. (b) Personality scales show long-term retest correlations of .30 to .80 over intervals of up to 30 years. Thus, individual differences in personality are relatively stable in adulthood. Costa and McCrae (1986) also speculated that the constancy of personality suggests that supportive and reeducative therapies—two major forms of trait-and-factor counseling (see the discussion here of counseling process)—are more likely to produce successful outcomes than reconstructive therapies. As is shown here, the findings presented about the predictability and stability of personality traits are mirrored by the variables typically assessed in vocational counseling.

Although this is not the forum for a comprehensive review of the stability of vocational constructs and the size of the relationships typically found among vocational constructs that are relevant to trait-and-factor counselors, the data from a few prototypical studies are briefly provided to dispel notions that vocational traits are either too unstable or that their relationships with vocational behaviors are too small to be of practical value.

Vocational Interests

Vocational interests are probably the most frequently assessed traits in career counseling. Most of the benchmark interest stability studies, for example, Strong's (1951) test–retest data over 22 years for 220 Stanford University students and Campbell's test–retest data over 36 years for 1,214 California teenagers, are summarized by Campbell (1971). Hansen (1984) reviewing the evidence stated, "by age 20 considerable stability of interests is obvious even over test-retest intervals of 5 to 10 years, and by age 25 interests are very stable over intervals of more than 20 years" (p. 116). More recently, Swanson and Hansen (1988) reported intraindividual stability coefficients for the Strong–Campbell Interest (SCII) scales. Results across gender and types of SCII scales showed median coefficients ranging from: .73 to .85 for the college period (age 18–22), .72 to .86 for the post-college period (age 22–30), and .63 to .78 for late adolescence to adulthood (age 18–30). In summary, measured interests by age 18 show sufficient temporal stability to justify predictions over the longer term.

Although these stability coefficients are large enough for most counseling uses, how well are interest scores tied to vocationally relevant concepts? One such relevant issue for most clients is satisfying work. Recent meta-analytic studies on findings from 80 studies (Rounds, 1988b) and 41 studies (Assouline & Meir, 1987) come to similar conclusions that mean congruence-satisfaction correlations range from .21 to .35. In summary, measured interests are substantially related to satisfaction of employed workers.

Work Values

Similar conclusions can be drawn about work values. Although they are less often assessed in counseling, work values are tied to major theoretical approaches (e.g., Dawis & Lofquist, 1984) and constitute an important cornerstone of computer-assisted guidance (Taylor, 1988). Research using the Minnesota Importance Questionnaire (Rounds, Henly, Dawis, Lofquist, & Weiss, 1981), for example, has shown that median intraindividual stability coefficients for nine samples

range from .70 to .95 across time periods of up to 1 year. Work values
have also been shown to be related in substantial ways to job satisfaction. Rounds, Dawis, and Lofquist (1987), for example, evaluated work
value-satisfaction relationships with 225 adult vocational counseling
clients in 98 different occupations 1 year after initial contact. Results
showed that correspondence-satisfaction correlations varied from .16 to
.55, depending on type of occupational classification and client's gender.
When compared to vocational interests, work values for adult clients are
better indicators of how satisfying they will find future occupations
(Rounds, 1988a). In summary, measured work values show sufficient
temporal stability for counseling purposes and can be used to identify
satisfying work environments.

Cognitive Abilities

Although Mischel (1968) made an exception for abilities in his anti-
trait claims, several propositions about cognitive abilities similar to
Kenrick and Funder's (1988) anti-trait hypotheses were advanced during
the 1960s and widely accepted until a few years ago. As summarized by
Schmidt (1988) and paraphrased here, these propositions are:

1. Test validity for cognitive ability measures is situationally specific: an ability measure that is valid for a job in one organization
   or setting may be invalid for the *same* job in another organization
   or setting.
2. Test validity for cognitive ability measures is job specific: an
   ability measure that is valid for one job may be invalid for
   another job.
3. Valid cognitive ability measures are of little practical value for
   predicting job performance.

A series of studies by Schmidt and Hunter (e.g., Schmidt, Gast-
Rosenberg, & Hunter, 1980; Schmidt, Hunter, & Caplan, 1981; Schmidt,
Hunter, & Pearlman, 1981) and others (e.g., Callender & Osburn, 1980)
have shown that these propositions are false. Schmidt and Hunter's
(1977) arguments are based on a type of meta-analysis called *validity
generalization*. Validity generalization is a procedure that estimates the
validities of a test for performance on new jobs from a meta-analysis of
the criterion-related validities of the test for studied jobs. In practice, the
observed validities are usually adjusted for sampling error, restriction of
range, and criterion unreliability to estimate the distribution of true
validities across a population of jobs. If after adjustments to validity
coefficients, the variance of the validity parameters is estmated to be

small, then it is assumed that validities are generalizable. Validity generalization, therefore, addresses the issue of test validities across situations, populations of applicants, and jobs.

Although some of the claims resulting from the applicaiton of validity generalization are controversial (Fitzgerald & Rounds, 1989), the basic premise seems sound. A panel of the National Academy of Sciences (NAS; Hartigan & Wigdor, 1989) evaluated validity generalization in the context of the use of the General Aptitude Test Battery (GATB) and issues of fairness of employment testing. The NAS's report supports "the general thesis of the theory of validity generalization, that validities established for some jobs are generalizable to some unexamined jobs" (p. 132). The conclusions of the NAS panel members support, in general, assertions that the above anti-ability testing propositions are false and, in particular, that the GATB is a valid predictor of approximately 30% of job performance variance, performing better than other predictor data—interviews, educational background, skills, and job experience. In summary, the validity of cognitive ability tests is neither specific to situations nor specific to jobs, and are sufficient, in most cases, to predict outcomes over the longer term.

All in all, vocational interests, work values, and cognitive abilities are stable and show valid relationships with criteria that counselors and clients believe are important career counseling outcomes. Counselors who do not avail themselves and their clients of this valuable information do a disservice to their clientele.

PE Fit Theory and Assumptions

Pervin (1987) and Kenrick and Funder (1988), reflecting on how psychology has profited from the person–situation controversy, come to several similar conclusions. First, the debate has served to focus attention on the person actively selecting and shaping environments and environments in turn shaping the person. Second, theory and research has begun to refocus on the processes of person–environment interactions. As Osipow (1987) stated, "person–environment is what vocational psychology is all about" (p. 333). Thus, it is not surprising that person–environment interactions have been a focus of considerable theory and research in vocational psychology and a recurrent theme in psychology (Walsh, 1987). (We note in passing that it is somewhat ironic that until recently contributions from various fields of psychology that represent major views on person-environment fit and work have rarely been acknowledged; Spokane, 1987).

We now take up the central assumptions of PE fit theory. PE fit theories have various perspectives and theoretical positions on work but several assumptions are shared:

1. Individuals seek out and create environments (used in a generic sense, e.g., occupations, jobs, situations, positions) that provide and/or allow for behavioral trait manifestation; for example, extroverts seek out and/or create stimulating environments, dominant individuals may choose occupations that offer possibilities of leadership and managerial roles and may structure situations such that they are in charge.

2. Degree of fit between the person and environment is associated with significant outcomes that can substantially affect the individual and environment; for example, performance, productivity, satisfaction, turnover, and stress. The better the PE fit, the better the outcomes.

3. The process of PE fit is reciprocal, involving the individual shaping the environmental context and the environmental context influencing the individual.

Among PE fit approaches and theories (e.g., Buss, 1984; French, Rodgers, & Cobb, 1974; Kulik, Oldham, & Hackman, 1987; Lerner, Baker, & Lerner, 1985), a wide array of functional units of behavior and environment units are proposed encompassing a variety of time frames (cf. Lubinski & Thompson, 1986; Moos, 1987) with different explanatory mechanisms and objectives. Most PE fit theories propose that reciprocal P and E change processes occur over time; the different models and systems posit various paces of influence and change depending on the person and environment units under investigation. Take Meehl's (1986) source and surface trait distinction with, for example, abilities representing source traits and skills representing surface traits. A similar distinction can be made on the environment side: ability requirements representing source units and skill requirements representing surface units. It would be expected according to the surface–source construct that an individual's skills and an occupation's skill requirements would more rapidly change within brief time spans (months) through a process of reciprocal interaction than would the individual's abilities and the occupation's ability requirements. Hence, for long-term career planning purposes, it would be best to rely on P and E source traits and units, a more stable reference dimension, than on surface traits and units.

Our next objective is to briefly introduce four exemplary PE fit theories, discussing two aspects of each theory: the functional units hypothesized to be determinants of the "fit" and the ways by which the person and environment influence each other (reciprocal interaction). We have chosen these four theories to serve as touchstones to indicate the kinds of contributions that PE fit theory can make to trait-and-factor counseling. For each theory, the reader is referred to appropriate citations for further details.

Dawis and Lofquist (1984)

The trait-and-factor counselor who chooses to be guided by the theory of work adjustment (Dawis, Dohm, Lofquist, Chartrand, & Due, 1987; Dawis & Lofquist, 1984; Lofquist & Dawis, 1969) takes on the point of view that (a) person–environment *correspondence* involves negotiating between, on the one hand, the client's work *personality* structure (work values and abilities), and on the other hand, the work *environment* structure (reinforcer classes and ability requirements), and that (b) a client's adjustment style together with the work environment's adjustment modes influence the process of person–environment correspondence. The four adjustment style dimensions described from the individual's perspective are:

Flexibility. Tolerance for discorrespondence with the environment before doing something to reduce the discorrespondence.

Activeness. Reducing discorrespondence by acting to change the environment.

Reactiveness. Reducing discorrespondence by acting on self to change expression of personality structure.

Perseverance. Tolerance of discorrespondence with the environment before leaving it, as indicated by length of stay. (Dawis & Lofquist, 1984, p. 65)

These four adjustment styles are also basic to describing how the environment maintains correspondence with the individual (see Dawis & Lofquist, 1978, for a description of these adjustment modes from an environment standpoint). Flexibility, for example, is used to describe how much tolerance the environment displays before it acts to reduce discorrespondence. Thus, correspondence describes not only the degree of fit, for example, between an individual's work values and the work environment's reward system but also the ongoing *reciprocal interaction* by which the individual and the environment seek to achieve and maintain work adjustment.

The surface–source distinction on which theory of work adjustment rests is that work values and abilities are considered source traits or reference dimensions to describe vocational needs and skills, respectively. A similar surface–source distinction is applied to the work environment: ability requirements are reference dimensions for skill requirements and reinforcer factors are reference dimensions for need reinforcers.

Holland (1985)

The trait-and-factor counselor who chooses to be guided by the theory of vocational personalities and work environments (Holland, 1973, 1985) takes on the point of view that (a) person–environment *congruence* involves negotiating between, on the one hand, the client's personality type (preferences, competencies, self-perceptions, and values), and on the other hand, the environmental models (demands and opportunities), and that (b) the differentiation and consistency of a client's personality pattern as well as identity influences the process of person–environment congruence. Holland hypothesized that persons with differentiated and consistent personality patterns and clear identity are more prone to change (remake) the environment to achieve greater congruence, whereas persons with the opposite personality patterns (undifferentiated, inconsistent, and diffuse identity) tend to adapt to incongruent environments by changing their behavior and personality pattern to achieve greater congruence. (Notice the similarity to Dawis and Lofquist's idea of active–reactive adjustment styles.) In a sense, a reciprocal interaction between P and E is hypothesized because environments are defined by the type of people in them.

The surface–source distinction on which the theory of vocational personalities and work environments rests is that personality and environment types are considered source traits or reference dimensions to describe preferences, competencies, self-perceptions, and values. (Holland clearly endorsed a dimensional view of types rather than the existence of true discrete categories.)

Vondracek, Lerner, and Schulenberg (1986)

The trait-and-factor counselor who chooses to be guided by the goodness-of-fit model of person–context relations (Vondracek et al., 1986) takes on the point of view that person–environment *fit* involves negotiating between, on the one hand, the client's characteristics of individuality, and on the other hand, the contextual demands. The contextual demands take the form of (a) attitudes and expectations held by others in the context regarding the client's physical or behavioral attributes, (b) the behavioral attributes of others in the context, and (c) physical characteristics or presses of the setting. The goodness-of-fit model of person–context relations relies on Lerner and Lerner's (1986) circular function idea of an ongoing act-reaction-act-reaction between the person and context (see Vondracek, 1987). The goodness-of-fit concept describes the status of the individual and context at one point in time only; this time point influences future fit.

French, Rodgers, and Cobb (1974)

The trait-and-factor counselor who chooses to be guided by the French and associates PE fit theory of adjustment (Caplan, 1987; French, Caplan, & Harrison, 1982; French et al., 1974) takes on the point of view that: (a) the degree of adjustment is the amount of improvement over time in the goodness of fit (discrepancy) between demands–abilities and between needs–supplies. Demands–abilities fit refers to whether the individual has the abilities that fit demands of his work role. Needs--supplies fit refers to whether the individual's needs fit what can be supplied by the work environment. (b) Fit is to be assessed both by subjective and objective methods making it possible to define accuracy of perception as a discrepancy between objective and subjective fit.

French and associates have not proposed PE units or characteristics and the theory makes no assumption about how adjustment is to be achieved. Their theory has been primarily used as a heuristic device to study issues of commensurate measurement of P and E, the role of past, present, and anticipated fit on well-being, the relation of PE fit to strain and depression, and who brings about the adjustive change (self or others) in PE fit.

Applications to Counseling

All of these theories when applied to trait-and-factor counseling assume that: (a) the reciprocal ongoing nature of person–environment fit is central to career planning, (b) the client learns the PE fit model as a basis for present and future problem solving and decision making, (c) the main theoretical constructs for both the individual and the environment are assessed and the resulting information taken account of in the counseling process, and (d) the question of the quality of the assessment has to do with the dependability and accuracy of the information, rather than with the form or method of obtaining it. Trait-and-factor counseling can be informed by one or a combination of PE fit theories depending on the concepts that are most salient to a client's presenting problems. We recommend that counselors selectively use relevant aspects of these and other PE fit theories, tailoring them to the situation at hand.

These theories per se do not take a position on how information is obtained and communicated (although Dawis and Lofquist and Holland have well-developed measures and occupational classifications) or on the client–counselor interaction. These are all issues of counseling process, which are the focus of the next section.

COUNSELING PROCESS

The counseling process of trait-and-factor counseling is largely unexplicated and unexplored. Unlike other theories that have been updated from their origins to keep pace with the times (e.g., client-centered, psychodynamic, behavioral), the potential of the trait-and-factor model to accommodate and profit by newer approaches and current research has not been recognized. Williamson and Biggs (1979) have lamented that, "In far too many instances, trait-and-factor counselors seem to assume that the counseling process is information-centered rather than meaning centered" (p. 126).

An implicit assumption in the trait-and-factor approach is that the provision of information about the client and the world of work will result in behavior change (for example, increased certainty of choice, improved decision-making skills and so on). The trait-and-factor approach has focused mostly on the quality—reliability and validity—and type of information (i.e., types of vocationally relevant variables) provided rather than on how the information is processed to ensure that it will be used and understood. (The literature usually labeled test interpretation research, pertinent but not directly relevant to our approach in this section, is not reviewed here.) The "how" of process is trait-and-factor's black box, as it were: how counseling occurs remains out of sight. The historically pragmatic focus of the trait-and-factor counseling approach leaves its operating assumptions (i.e., what accounts for the behavioral change process) open to analysis—and, unfortunately, also to inaccurate inference and misprision. Williamson and Biggs (1979) have called for theoretical investigation of the counseling process in trait-and-factor counseling. Our intent in this section is to illuminate trait-and-factor's black box of process in the context of the counseling and psychotherapy literature.

In order to do so we: (a) argue that the trait-and-factor approach is the progenitor (and beneficiary) of modern problem-solving models of counseling; (b) update trait-and-factor concepts with more recent formulations in the areas of problem solving and information processing.

Trait-and-Factor as Problem Solving

Two important underlying assumptions in the trait-and-factor model are that the client is capable of rational decision making (Williamson, 1965a) and that the goal of counseling is to provide the client with information to assist this process. The emphasis on this goal has often led to the rejection of Williamson's work on the grounds of its being overly cognitive and authoritarian (Crites, 1981; Weinrach, 1979). But Williamson talked repeatedly about how trait-and-factor counseling not only directs the client to an educational or career choice but also teaches the client more generally how to independently make important life decisions. That this attitude anticipates at the very least current problem-solving and decision-making views of process is confirmed by Crites (1981) and Patterson (1973), who have referred to trait-and-factor approaches as essentially problem-solving approaches. Problem-solving approaches do tend to be largely cognitive and this is very much in line with Williamson's (1961) "sovereignty of reason" idea that counseling focuses on helping the client reason out the issues. As noted earlier, Williamson is somewhat vague about how this counseling is to be conducted. We first provide a brief review of theories of problem solving and then go on to demonstrate how recent advances in problem-solving models could be applied to trait-and-factor approaches via conceptions of information processing.

Theories of Problem Solving

Problem-solving literature spans many disciplines; early references in the behavioral sciences can be found in the work of Thorndike (1911, 1913) on trial and error learning, and Kohler (1917/1925) on insight. But Dewey's (1933) five-phase model of reflective thought has had the most profound effect on contemporary problem-solving literature in counseling. Dewey's phases of problem solving (which he called "reflective activity") are preceded by a state of mind he called "*pre*-reflective," in which the individual is in a confused, perplexed state. The five phases are paraphrased here:

1. Suggestion: The mind "leaps forward to a possible solution."
2. Intellectualization: The resolution of the "*felt* (directly experienced)" difficulty into a "problem to be solved."
3. Hypothesis: Raising suggestions "to initiate and guide observation and other operations in collection of factual material."
4. Reasoning: Depends "upon the store of knowledge" the individual is "already in possession of," and transforms the idea to "a form in which a problem can be dealt with most expeditiously and effectively."
5. Testing: Consists of "testing the hypothesis by overt or imaginative action." (Dewey, 1933, p. 106–113)

Recently, the problem-solving process has been integrated with models of decision making. Horan (1979) reviewed the major counseling applications of both problem-solving and decision-making models. (It is interesting to note that Horan, 1979, in his review of problem-solving models, omitted Williamson or any other trait-and-factor approaches despite his inclusion of Parson's, 1909, work.) Although he noted important differences between problem-solving and decision-making models, he saw a predominance of overlap. His composite of the many models found in these literatures is as follows:

1. Conceptualization: definition of the problem and construction of a cognitive model of the troubling portions of the environment.
2. Enlargement of the Response Repertoire: generation of alternatives or solutions.
3. Identification of Stimuli Discriminative of Positive or Negative Consequences for Each Response: effects of each alternative and its actual effect assessed. (Horan, 1979, p. 175)

Compare Williamson's (1939b) model of trait-and-factor counseling:

1. Analysis: Collecting data from many sources about attitudes, interests, family background, knowledge, educational progress, aptitudes, etc., by means of both subjective and objective techniques.
2. Synthesis: Collating and summarizing the data by means of case study and techniques and text profiles to "highlight" the student's [client's] uniqueness or individuality.
3. Diagnosis: Describing the outstanding characteristics and problems of the student [client], comparing the individual's profile with educational and occupational ability profiles, and ferreting out the causes of the problems.
4. Prognosis: Judging the probable consequences of problems, the probabilities for adjustments, and thereby indicating the alternative actions and adjustments for the student's [client's] consideration.
5. Counseling or treatment: Cooperatively advising with the student [client] concerning what to do to effect a desired adjustment now or in the future.
6. Follow-up: Repeating the steps just given as new problems arise and further assisting the student [client] to carry out a desirable program of action. (Williamson, 1939b, p. 215)

What the models referred to here have in common is their reliance on rational evaluation of: the definition and diagnosis of the problem, provision of information, alternative search and selection, and finally action. Our view is that the trait-and-factor approach is an ancestor of current problem-solving models. Williamson, in his last statement on trait-and-factor counseling, recognized the similarity of his approach to decision making theories:

> The goals of the trait-and-factor counselor are very similar to those described by Krumboltz (1966a) as "learning the decision-making process." Krumboltz also thinks that the central purpose of counseling is to help clients resolve those problems for which they seek help, and that the criteria for evaluation should be tailored to particular clients' problems. (Williamson & Biggs, 1979, p. 104)

Information-Processing Applications to Problem Solving

None of the problem-solving approaches (including trait-and-factor) discussed here are very specific about how we are to intervene to facilitate effective problem solving. Therefore we propose to look to another area to explore this question: information processing. A precedent for this view of counseling has been established: Heppner and Krauskopf (1987) and Dixon and Glover (1984) have used information-processing concepts to help explain the problem-solving process and to integrate it with counseling practice.

Although there is a wealth of different models of information processing in the literature (e.g., Carver & Scheier, 1982; Miller, Galanter, & Pribram, 1960; Neisser, 1967; Newell & Simon, 1972; Powers, 1973), Anderson's (1982, 1983, 1985) ACT theory (Adaptive Control of Thought) is of primary assistance in our attempt to update trait-and-factor counseling process (the reader is referred to Heppner and Krauskopf for a more detailed presentation); we use the elaboration likelihood model to discuss attitude change in the counseling process.

Anderson's ACT Model. In Anderson's model there are three types of knowledge bases: working, declarative, and procedural. Working knowledge is similar to active, conscious thought. Declarative knowledge consists of facts. In procedural knowledge the relations among different pieces of knowledge become apparent and are integrated (via the working knowledge base) into a procedure. In general, novices in any area use more trial-and-error declarative knowledge, whereas experts use more complex procedural knowledge. It is important to assess these different knowledge bases (especially the declarative and procedural) to know how a person is processing any incoming information and how he or she is approaching a decision. With respect to vocational problems, it appears safe to assume that most clients will be novices; thus our vocational interventions should be directed at facilitating the compilation of declarative knowledge into procedural knowledge in this area.

This process of compiling declarative knowledge into procedural knowledge follows a four-step process of information processing: (a) encoding, (b) goal setting, (c) development of plans and pattern matching, and (d) action.

Encoding involves both the perception of information and the appraisal of its meaning. According to Heppner and Krauskopf (1987), the encoding process can vary in its speed or its accuracy and completeness. Lazarus and Folkman (1984) have demonstrated that in ill-defined problem areas (i.e., where there is no right answer, as in career choice) both the speed and accuracy of the encoding are negatively affected. Following the encoding, the person sets goals for solving the problem. A good job of goal setting involves the establishment of concrete, realistic goals that are organized into sequential processes. Poor goal setting results in unrealistic or vague goals that may not be organized into a coherent set. Once goals have been established, the problem solver searches his or her knowledge bases, both declarative and procedural, for past information that resembles the current problem as it was encoded. Heppner and Krauskopf (1987) see three different types of thinking involved in this pattern matching: solution thinking, means–end thinking, and consequential thinking. The knowledge patterns found should result in a variety of alternative solutions (solution thinking), have a variety of means of reaching the goals (means–end thinking), and should take account of the consequences of any action (consequential thinking). Deficits in any of these three types of thinking could result in poor pattern matching, and consequently poor problem solving.

The final step involves implementation of action. The problem solver selects a behavior or action to remedy the problem based on the previous steps. If the steps have been adequately completed, the action selected and implemented should result in the amelioration of the problem. However, this does not necessarily guarantee a successful conclusion, as even if the steps just listed have been well executed, it could be possible that the individual just does not have the necessary behaviors in his or her repertoire. Further complications can arise with the crucial variable of emotional arousal. When it is present, especially in the form of anxiety, it results in: (a) less flexibility attached to both declarative and procedural knowledge bases (Everall, 1935); (b) less ability to retrieve information from long-term memory (involved in pattern matching) (Feather, 1959); and (c) less ability to enact a variety of behaviors in ones repertoire.

This model of information processing makes the steps involved in problem solving much clearer; more importantly, it can provide the counselor with information about how to intervene. It is obviously important to assess client knowledge bases (both declarative and procedural), goal setting, pattern-matching informational processing skills, the behavioral repertoire, and the presence and degree of emotional arousal.

Elaboration Likelihood Model. The elaboration likelihood model (Petty & Cacioppo, 1981) is important for thinking about information processing and problem solving with reference to counseling process. (The literature on attitude change contains extensive material on this model; the reader is referred to Petty & Cacioppo, 1981, or Heesacker's, 1986, and Stoltenberg's, 1986, application of this model to counseling for more extended presentation than is possible here.) Petty and Cacioppo theorized that influence varies depending on how information is processed and propose two different types of information processing: central and peripheral. Central processing involves active, conscious deliberation, whereas peripheral processing involves more associative learning. In peripheral processing, the person is influenced by persuasion cues (e.g., the social influence of variables of counselor expertness, trustworthiness, and warmth) associated with the presentation of information rather than with the information itself; it involves minimal encoding and pattern matching (to put it in terms of Anderson's ACT model). Central processing, on the other hand, involves extensive encoding and evaluation of pattern matching in the working memory.

Central processing results in longer term attitude change than does peripheral processing (Cialdini, Levy, Herman, Kozlowski, & Petty, 1976; Cialdini, Petty, & Cacioppo, 1981). Cialdini et al. (1981) found that people use central processing only when they are highly motivated and able to grasp the information presented. When they are not, peripheral processing is more persuasive. Consequently, when the vocational client is not motivated or shows problems in the information-processing steps listed here, we should focus on enhancing our persuasion cues in order to induce our clients to attend and adopt beneficial career exploration or decision-making behaviors. Highly motivated and capable information processors, on the other hand, should be presented with cogent information; packaging will be less important for this group.

Given the aforementioned, assessment of motivation and information-processing skills provides a good basis for designing vocational interventions. The combination of problem solving, information processing, and elaboration likelihood models provides some guidance for how vocational problem-solving (trait-and-factor) counseling could be approached by the practitioner. The question of type of intervention is addressed next. We then discuss how to apply the combined model (as outlined earlier) of problem solving, information processing, and attitude change models to trait-and-factor interventions.

Type of Intervention

Although career counseling has often been regarded as much more circumscribed than personal–emotional counseling (compare the also arbitrary distinction between vocational counseling and "real" psychotherapy), requiring little more than the pro forma information dispensing so often negatively associated with the trait-and-factor approach, in practice such a division of labor is only sometimes appropriate. Sometimes all clients need, for example, is some additional information about themselves and about possible vocational choices; this is a situation that calls for a circumscribed intervention. Often enough, however, vocational clients need more. The issue of a career is central, and it is not uncommon for it to become a source of major difficulty linked to personal–emotional issues and resulting in varying degrees of emotional arousal and distress. In fact, the centrality of vocational and career issues is underscored by the growing emphasis psychotherapists place on dealing with such concerns (Blustein, 1987; Lowman, 1987).

Thus, the counselor must be prepared to choose an appropriate type of intervention. One useful way to conceptualize this kind of choice is offered by Weiner (1978), who makes a distinction between insight (also called uncovering, intensive, and depth) therapy and supportive therapy—the crucial difference being the extent to which the unconscious motivations of behavior are the focus of work. In insight work, the personality style of the client as well as the content of what is said are brought into play; whereas in supportive work, the focus is only on content and the personality style of the client is accepted as is (i.e., it is not challenged or focused on).

The aim of supportive therapy is to help augment the client's ability to deal with the world by adding to client skills; the term *supportive* refers to the acceptance of the current personality, not necessarily the behaviors exhibited by the therapist. The term is sometimes misleading: Many tend to associate supportive interventions with a warm and accepting counselor. In fact, being warm and accepting is central to all treatments.

An example may help to clarify this distinction. If one were to work with a client who had a dependent decision-making style and who was mired in making a career decision, one could use either approach. In an uncovering or insight model, the counselor would focus on the decision-making style in general and the career issue as an example of it; the personality style of the client would be the focus. In supportive work, the counselor would work with the client to make a sound decision within the dependent decision-making style. The counselor is equally warm and accepting of the person in each intervention. The important difference between the two interventions is the extent to which the client's underlying personality style is the focus.

Traditional notions of distinctions between career counseling, personal counseling, and psychotherapy rest not so much on the content of the focus (career concerns could be involved in all three) but rather on the type of intervention. Our contention is that career counselors, personal counselors, and psychotherapists must all be prepared to use an appropriate type of intervention. For our purposes in the ensuing discussion, the insight-supportive distinction described by Weiner will be representative of choice of type of intervention in general.

Correspondence of Client and Intervention

Ironically, although trait-and-factor models focus so much on the fit of person with an optimal career, little focus is devoted to fitting the client with the optimal type of counseling intervention. It stands to reason that, if the fit of a person to a vocation is important, the fit of an intervention to the client would also be important (for similar suggestions, see Fretz, 1981; Oliver & Spokane, 1988; Osipow, 1983; Rounds & Tinsley, 1984). Although researchers across diverse areas (e.g., Cronbach & Snow, 1977) have called for matching client attributes with treatments, few specific suggestions have been made about what client and treatment variables to use in the matching process. The only theoretical work in the vocational field that we are aware of is the intervention classification system used by Tyler (1969), but we have seldom seen it used either in practice or research. Holland, Daiger, and Power (1980) have called for differential treatment based on *My Vocational Situation*. They proposed that the counselor use the Vocational Identity (stability of choice) scale, the need for vocational information, and the presence of choice barriers to assign the client to one of three treatments: (a) personal counseling or career seminars, (b) information and/or reassurance provision, or (c) a combination of the two. Few details, however, were provided of how the fit between intervention and diagnostic signs is accomplished. In a recent review, Slaney (1988) noted that no studies were located that examined the effects of differ-ential intervention on the antecedents of career indecision.

The need for matching client to treatment mirrors the challenge made by Paul (1967; also see Krumboltz, 1966b) in the psychotherapy area: We need to know what the best interventions are for particular client characteristics and problems. Some helpful work has been done: Hos-ford, Burnett, and Mills (1984), for example, reviewed the issues involved in making counseling/psychotherapy treatment prescriptions using depression as an example; Beutler (1983) has proposed a relatively comprehensive model for treatment–client matching. However, in gen-eral, there is little research on these issues, and the specifics regarding how this information should be delivered (i.e., the counseling process) have not been adequately covered in either the psychotherapy or vocational literature.

We are proposing that in determining what treatment to use the trait-and-factor counselor use a person-environment fit approach similar to that used in attempting to fit the person with an occupation. The counselor, that is, would adapt his or her intervention (the counseling environment) to fit with the client. Because of its focus on actively providing self and environmental information to influence the client in resolving vocational problems, the person–environment fit perspective is especially appropriate for conceptualizing the trait-and-factor process. Updated as suggested by the previous discussions on problem solving, information processing, type of intervention choice, and person–envi-ronment fit assumptions, trait-and-factor approaches can provide the modification of the counseling process to fit with the client.

We contend that the selection of the type of treatment intervention should be a function of: (a) level of client information processing, (b) client motivation, and (c) relative progress in the counseling process. Our hypothesis is that the more each of these dimensions is taken into account in treatment provision, the better the outcomes. We briefly review each in sequence.

Fitting Level of Client Information Processing to Intervention

An important variable in the selection of the type of intervention (i.e., support vs. insight) is the client's level of information processing. Those with high levels of information-processing skills are presumed to have the requisite skills to benefit from straight information without the need to receive extensive help in integration and decision making. This assumption is depicted in Table 1.1.

As represented in Table 1.1, we propose that those "very high" in information-processing skills would benefit from simple presentation of

TABLE 1.1
Types of Treatment and Interventions Recommended as a Function of Level of
Information Processing

Level of information processing	Treatment characteristics	Sample intervention
Very high	*Little needed*	Assessment (e.g., MIQ, SDS)
	Brief, information	Occupational information
	focused	Computer-assisted guidance
High	*Weak supportive*	Assessment, brief counseling
	Mentor	Occupational information
	Short-term	Brief discussion either
	information and	individual or group based
	decision focused	Career workshops
Medium	*Insight*	Analysis of coping/problem
	Longer term	solving skills
	Broad focus	Individual counseling
		Career course
Low	*Strong supportive*	Teach, instruct, guide
	Active guide	Individual counseling
	Longer term	
	Remedial	
	Narrow focus	

Note: See text for explanation of levels of information processing. Abbreviations: MIQ = Minnesota Importance Questionnaire; SDS = Self-Directed Search.

information (either about themselves through test results or about the world of work through occupational information, or both). These clients have demonstrated these skills (encoding, goal setting, pattern matching, and action selection) in a variety of contexts in their lives and appear to be able to apply these skills with respect to the career choice area. Clients of this sort are very appropriate for career-planning systems (Taylor, 1988): computer-assisted career guidance (e.g., DISCOVER and SIGI PLUS); standardized paper–pencil programs such as Vocational Interest, Experience, and Skill Assessment (VIESA; American College Testing Program, 1988); self-help career materials (Bolles, 1986); and occupational information (e.g., *Guide for Occupational Exploration*). They require little intervention as they already have the requisite information-processing skills.

Those with "high" levels of information-processing skills are assumed to have generally sound information-processing skills in most contexts of their lives; they may, however, lack adequate pattern-matching knowledge bases for career choice, given the ill-defined nature and novelty of this problem. The intervention type should be supportive, attempting to provide the client with ways of integrating the information to reach a decision. As the client's ability to encode the information is not in question, the counselor should provide information (about both client and work) but focus more on how to use the information. This is the kind of intervention that has been characterized as "three sessions and a cloud of dust," and it can be done individually or in groups. This supportive intervention should resemble a mentor relationship, where there is some guidance and information provided; we label this sort of supportive intervention *weak support*.

Those clients who have more difficulty integrating information in general, or who have difficulty processing certain types of information are viewed as having medium information-processing skills. These clients have deficits in encoding information (for example, the client will only encode information relating to relative status of an academic major or an occupation) or in goal setting and pattern matching. These information-processing difficulties may be exhibited only with respect to career choice, but more commonly they arise in a variety of contexts. For this kind of client, provision of information will probably not be of much value. It could even be detrimental because the client may use the information to make poor decisions. The focus with this client is on aiding him or her to do a better job of encoding. The intervention must then be of a depth or insight type, where, as noted earlier (Weiner, 1978), the focus is the personality style of the client (i.e., how is it that she or he characteristically misses this information?). Obviously, this type of intervention, with its breadth of focus, would take more time.

Finally, with clients who have low-level information-processing skills, we are advocating the use of supportive counseling. These clients are assumed to have significant deficits in their information-processing and problem-solving skills. These information-processing deficits are clear in a variety of life contexts, not just the career choice area. They are unable to encode much of what is presented to them and are unable to process any of this information. These clients need intensive, active, remedial counseling, which is different from the less active, mentor role of the supportive counseling provided to clients with high information-processing skills. Focus for clients with low information-processing skills is placed on directly providing needed skills and knowledge to the client. The counselor needs to become an instructor, actively guiding and teaching the client the needed pieces of information and decision-making skills. Given the skills of these clients, it may even be appropriate to tell these clients where they should be going. We label this type of supportive intervention as *strong supportive* counseling, which can only be provided individually.

It is important to note that the level of information-processing skills presented here refers to current skills. A client who typically has a high level of information processing may encounter temporary, situational strains that decrease her or his ability to process information and to cope. It is this current level of processing that should be used in determining the type of treatment to provide. In our assessment of level of information-processing skills, we need to be aware of the emotional arousal level of our clients, keeping in mind such suggestions as Mitchell and Krumboltz' (1984) who concluded in a review of career decision making that inability to make career decisions is often related to anxiety (also see Slaney's, 1988, review on the relationship of anxiety to the indecision–indecisiveness distinction). It may well be that, with time, the situation remedies itself and the client returns to the previous level of information processing. When this occurs the treatment should be changed accordingly. This model thus does not assume static matching of clients to treatment. We need to change the treatments according to the client's current functioning.

It is assumed that the provision of the wrong type of intervention will result in a poor outcome. For example, attempting to provide insight treatment to someone very high in information-processing skills could result in premature termination. Providing an exclusively supportive intervention (guidance, direct instruction on decision making) to one who is dependent (having deficit information-processing skills and medium level of adjustment) would be expected to result in poor outcome because the underlying problematic information-processing style (the dependence) is still in place.

We realize that it is often difficult to establish a cutoff in information-processing skills (e.g., is a particular client "high" or "medium" in information-processing skills). Given that it is generally easier and more cost effective to provide weak supportive interventions (provision of information and limited reassurance and instruction), in borderline situations it may be best to provide these interventions and then assess their success. (For a similar recommendation, see Holland, 1974.) If it is found that the weak supportive interventions are insufficient, the counselor can then adopt an insight approach or a strong supportive one, whichever is more appropriate. In keeping with this cost-effectiveness model, we hypothesize that if the optimal client-intervention match is not selected (for whatever reason), it is better to select another intervention that is associated with slightly higher information-processing skills than an intervention that is associated with lower level information-processing skills. The lower level intervention is assumed to be viewed as less valuable and less helpful by the client.

We also see client problem diagnosis as a variable that could affect the type of treatment proposed. Although *diagnosis*, as defined in the more common career diagnostic or taxonomy models, is not independent of level of information-processing skills, there is some unique information available that could help in the selection of the optimal client-treatment fit. For example, if we decided a client fit Bordin's (1946) classification of "lacks information," it would be clear that the provision of straight information is what is called for. Similarly, if the client fit the "self-conflict" classification, it would be clear that insight interventions would be appropriate. However, many diagnostic classifications have less clear translation into intervention selection (e.g., Bordin's "choice anxiety" or Crites', 1969, "undecided" or "unrealistic" categories). None of the current career diagnostic models, however, provide the specificity to enable one to make differential treatment decisions of the sort we are proposing (Oliver & Spokane, 1988; Rounds & Tinsley, 1984).

Fitting Intervention to Client Motivation

The attitude change literature (specifically the elaboration likelihood model of Petty and Cacioppo, 1981) provides some further guidance on treatment selection. The level of client motivation affects the extent of client information processing. People with high levels of motivation or interest are most influenced by the content qualities of the information presented. Presumably they actively attend to the information (central processing) and the resulting attitude changes are relatively longstanding. People with low levels of motivation or interest are most influenced by the persuasion cues associated with the information, not the quality of the information itself. These low motivated people are assumed to process the information peripherally and this results in less outstanding attitude change.

Dixon and Claiborn (1981) have found that there is a fair amount of variance in motivation among career clients. The implications of the elaboration likelihood model are that we assess motivation level and adjust our approach accordingly. If clients are highly motivated, we can focus more on clear presentation of information. With low-motivated clients, we need to attend to how the information is presented or packaged. Specifically, the research (Corrigan, Dell, Lewis, & Schmidt, 1980; Heppner & Dixon, 1981; Strong & Claiborn, 1982) on the social influence dimensions (warmth, trustworthiness, and expertness) support the need to attend to these dimensions. We suggest that these persuasion cue dimensions are especially important with this low-motivation client group.

Progress of Counseling

As Williamson (1965b) noted, counseling is "successive approximations of self-understanding and self-management by means of helping [the client] to assess assets and liabilities in relation to the requirement of progressively changing life goals and [the client's] vocational career" (p. 198). The key element is the successive approximation aspect. The counselor starts his or her intervention close to the client's level of processing and slowly moves the client toward more appropriate information processing. This requires a very acute understanding of how the client processes and how much discrepancy to introduce. The appropriate dose of discrepant information will enable the client to attend to and integrate it. It is beyond the scope of this chapter to go into the various possible explanations for this change process. Indeed there are several models that propose the same process of change (incremental change initiated by the counselor), yet start from very different conceptual bases. Strong and Claiborn (1982) used a cognitive dissonance model to explain this change process. Tracey (1986; Tracey & Ray, 1984) used a systems model. Peterfreund (1971) applied information processing and psychoanalysis. We believe that the central issue is that the counselor needs to be aware of where the client is at all times with respect to how the client is processing the information. With close monitoring, the counselor can stay slightly ahead of the client's progress, thereby helping the client to learn to use the material presented and to improve in information-processing skills.

Client-Intervention Fit Hypotheses

We have made several claims regarding the appropriate prescriptive choice of intervention to fit with the client. By way of summary and to stimulate research in this area, we list specific hypotheses. All the hypotheses involve more and less successful intervention outcomes. There are many outcomes that can be included in this set (see Rounds & Tinsley, 1984, for discussion of outcome levels, i.e., instrumental, target, and referent). Examples of instrumental outcomes are accuracy of self-knowledge, career-related knowledge, and decision-making skills; target outcomes are certainty/decidedness and appropriateness of choice; and referent outcomes are satisfaction and satisfactoriness. The following hypotheses should be judged with these outcomes in mind.

Hypotheses Relating to Client Information-Processing Skills

1. The success of direct, remedial interventions (strong support) is inversely related to client information-processing skills.
   A. Clients with low or poor information-processing skills will have the best outcomes with interventions of a strong supportive type.

2. The success of straight information provision interventions is positively related to client information-processing skills.

A. Clients with very high information-processing skills will have the most successful outcomes with interventions that are brief and focus only on information transmission.

B. Clients with high information-processing skills will have the best outcomes with interventions that are of a weak supportive type.

3. The success of broad band, insight interventions is related to client information-processing skills in a curvilinear manner.

A. Clients with high or low information-processing skills will have poor outcomes with broad band, insight interventions.

B. Clients with medium information-processing skills will have the best outcomes with interventions of a broad focused, insight nature.

Hypotheses Relating to Client Motivation

1. The success of interventions that focus on high quality, logical presentation of information is positively related to client level of motivation.
2. The success of interventions that focus on the social influence cues (e.g., expertness, trustworthiness, and warmth) is inversely related to client motivation.

Summary of Proposed Trait-and-Factor Client-Treatment Fit Model

Extrapolating from 1939 into the present, we have offered a model of the counseling process of trait-and-factor counseling. Our model involves applying the person–environment fit premise of trait-and-factor counseling to the client–counselor interaction itself using current conceptions of problem solving and information processing. Information-processing skill occupies a central place in this model; key aspects of information processing used in this model include encoding skills, pattern-matching skills, and breadth/narrowness of these skills. Finally, we suggest that sequential analysis of the career counseling process itself would provide information on the extent to which successful counseling is related to the successive approximation of information-processing skills. Further research on the function of information-processing skill in this model requires instrument derivation work, and further research is needed to verify the several recommendations and hypotheses we have presented.

CONCLUSION

A colleague of ours remarked apropos of the first author's complaint about the sheer bulk of critical attacks on trait-and-factor counseling, "What else is there?" Whatever else there is may well smell as sweet by another name: much of trait-and-factor counseling's usefulness comes from its affinities with problem-solving formulations. Tracing the vicissitudes of trait-and-factor counseling from Williamson's original formulations to its current manifestations, we find further that, lacking a theory of vocational behavior change to call its own, trait-and-factor counseling is now informed by person–environment fit theories of vocational behavior. It was left to us only to fill the remaining significant lacuna: We supplemented the extremely rudimentary notion of counseling process with models of information processing and applied a person–environment fit hypothesis to differential intervention selection. The proposed client-intervention fit model is a current extrapolation of trait-and-factor counseling that awaits further investigation, examination, and operationalization.

It remains only to point out that trait-and-factor counseling remains without a significant body of proponents interested in reaping its possible empirical and theoretical rewards as an object of study. We find this curious: What is it about this approach that provokes ire and contention but no theoretical progress? We suspect its close ties to assessment makes it a touchstone for what the field of counseling psychology as a whole would prefer to avoid—but that is an altogether different chapter.

ACKNOWLEDGMENT

We thank Lynda Zwinger for her editorial assistance.

REFERENCES

Allport, G.W. (1937). *Personality: A psychological interpretation.* New York: Holt.
Allport, G.W. (1961). *Pattern and growth in personality.* New York: Holt.
American College Testing Program. (1988). *Interim psychometric handbook for the 3rd edition ACT career planning program.* Iowa City, IA: Author.
Anderson, J.R. (1982). Acquisition of cognitive skill. *Psychological Review, 89,* 396–406.
Anderson, J.R. (1983). *The architecture of cognition.* Cambridge, MA: Harvard.
Anderson, J.R. (1985). *Cognitive psychology and its implications* (2nd ed.). San Francisco: Freeman.
Assouline, M., & Meir, E. (1987). Meta-analysis of relationship between congruence and

well-being measures. *Journal of Vocational Behavior, 31,* 319–332.

Betz, N.E. (1988). The assessment of career development and maturity. In W.B. Walsh & S.H. Osipow (Eds.), *Career decision making* (pp. 77–136). Hillsdale, NJ: Lawrence Erlbaum Associates.

Betz, N.E., Fitzgerald, L.F., & Hill, R.E. (1989). Trait-factor theories: Traditional cornerstone of career theory. In M.B. Arthur, D.T. Hall, & B.S. Lawrence (Eds.), *Handbook of career theory* (pp. 26–40). New York: Cambridge University Press.

Beutler, L.E. (1983). *Eclectic psychotherapy: A systematic approach.* New York: Pergamon.

Blustein, D.L. (1987). Integrating career counseling and psychotherapy: A comprehensive treatment strategy. *Psychotherapy, 24,* 794–799.

Bolles, R.N. (1986). *What color is your parachute?? A practical manual for job hunters and career changers.* Berkeley, CA: Ten Speed Press.

Bordin, E.S. (1946). Diagnosis in counseling and psychotherapy. *Educational and Psychological Measurement, 6,* 169–184.

Borgen, F.H. (1986). New approaches to the assessment of interests. In W.B. Walsh & S.H. Osipow (Eds.), *Advances in vocational psychology: Vol. 1. The assessment of interests* (pp. 83–125). Hillsdale, NJ: Lawrence Erlbaum Associates.

Brown, D. (1984). Trait and factor theory. In D. Brown, L. Brooks, and Associates (Eds.), *Career choice and development* (pp. 8–30). San Francisco: Jossey-Bass.

Buss, D.M. (1984). Toward a psychology of person-environment (PE) correlation: The role of spouse selection. *Journal of Personality and Social Psychology, 47,* 361–377.

Callender, J.C., & Osburn, H.G. (1980). Development and test of a new model of validity generalization. *Journal of Applied Psychology, 65,* 543–558.

Campbell, D.P. (1971). *Handbook for the Strong Vocational Interest Blank.* Stanford, CA: Stanford University Press.

Caplan, R.D. (1987). Person-environment fit theory and organizations: Commensurate dimensions, time perspectives, and mechanisms. *Journal of Vocational Behavior, 31,* 248–267.

Carver, C.S., & Scheier, M.F. (1982). Control theory: A useful conceptual framework for personality-social, clinical, and health psychology. *Psychological Bulletin, 92,* 111–135.

Cialdini, R.B., Levy, A., Herman, P., Kozlowski, L., & Petty, R.E. (1976). Elastic shifts of opinion: Determinants of direction and durability. *Journal of Personality and Social Psychology, 34,* 663–672.

Cialdini, R.B., Petty, R.E., & Cacioppo, J.T. (1981). Attitudes and attitude change. *Annual Review of Psychology, 32,* 357–404.

Costa, P.T., Jr., & McCrae, R.R. (1986). Personality stability and its implications for clinical psychology. *Clinical Psychology Review, 6,* 407–423.

Corrigan, J.D., Dell, D.M., Lewis, K.N., & Schmidt, L.D. (1980). Counseling as a social influence process: A review. *Journal of Counseling Psychology, 27,* 395–441.

Crites, J.O. (1969). *Vocational psychology.* New York: McGraw-Hill.

Crites, J.O. (1974). Career counseling: A review of major approaches. *The Counseling Psychologist, 4,* 3–23.

Crites, J.O. (1978). Career counseling: A review of major approaches. In J. Whiteley & A. Resnikoff (Eds.), *Career counseling* (pp. 18–56). Monterey, CA: Brooks-Cole.

Crites, J.O. (1981). *Career counseling: Models, methods, and materials.* New York: McGraw-Hill.

Cronbach, L.J., & Snow, R.E. (1977). *Aptitude and instructional materials.* New York: Wiley.

Dawes, R.M., Faust, D., & Meehl, P.E. (1989). Clinical versus actuarial judgment. *Science, 243,* 1668–1674.

Dawis, R.V., Dohm, T.E., Lofquist, L.H., Chartrand, J.M., Due, A.M. (1987). *Minnesota Occupational Classification System III: A psychological taxonomy of work.* Minneapolis, MN: Vocational Psychology Research, Department of Psychology, University of Minnesota.

Dawis, R.V., & Lofquist, L.H. (1978). A note on the dynamics of work adjustment. *Journal of Vocational Behavior, 12,* 76–79.

Dawis, R.V., & Lofquist, L.H. (1984). *A psychological theory of work adjustment: An individual differences model and its applications.* Minneapolis, MN: University of Minnesota Press.

Dawis, R.V., Lofquist, L.H., & Weiss, D.J. (1968). *A theory of work adjustment (a revision). Minnesota Studies in Vocational Rehabilitation.* (Vol. XXIII). Minneapolis, MN: Work Adjustment Project, Department of Psychology, University of Minnesota.

Dewey, J. (1933). *How we think.* New York: D.C. Heath.

Dixon, D., & Claiborn, C. (1981). Effect of need and commitment on career exploration behavior. *Journal of Counseling Psychology, 28,* 411–415.

Dixon, D., & Glover, J.A. (1984). *Counseling: A problem solving approach.* New York: Wiley.

Dustin, D., & Blocher, D.H. (1984). Theories and models of consultation. In S.D. Brown & R.W. Lent (Eds.), *Handbook of counseling psychology* (pp. 751–781). New York: Wiley.

Epstein, S., & O'Brien, E.J. (1985). The person-situation debate in historical and current perspective. *Psychological Bulletin, 98,* 513–537.

Everall, E. (1935). Perseveration in the rat. *Journal of Comparative Psychology, 19,* 343–368.

Feather, N.T. (1959). Subjective probability and decision under uncertainty. *Psychological Review, 66,* 150–164.

Fitzgerald. L.F., & Rounds, J.B. (1989). Vocational behavior, 1988: A critical analysis. *Journal of Vocational Behavior, 35,* 105–163.

French, J.R.P., Jr., Caplan, R.D., & Harrison, R.V. (1982). *The mechanisms of job stress and strain.* Chichester: Wiley.

French, J.R.P., Jr., Rodgers, W., & Cobb, S. (1974). Adjustment as person-environment fit. In G.V. Coelho, D.A. Hamburg, & J.E. Adams (Eds.), *Coping and adaptation.* New York: Basic Books.

Fretz, B.R. (1981). Evaluating career interventions. *Journal of Counseling Psychology, 28,* 77–90.

Goodyear, R.K., & Healy, C.C. (1988). UCLA's Career Counseling Center: A dialogue about a unique service. *Journal of Counseling and Development, 67,* 49–53.

Gysbers, N.C., & Moore, E.J. (1987). *Career counseling: Skills and techniques for practitioners.* Englewood Cliffs, NJ: Prentice-Hall.

Hansen, J.C. (1984). The measurement of vocational interests: Issues and future directions. In S.D. Brown & R.W. Lent (Eds.), *Handbook of counseling psychology* (pp. 99–136). New York: Wiley.

Hartigan, J.A., Wigdor, A.K. (1989). *Validity generalization, minority issues, and the General Aptitude Test Battery.* Washington, DC: National Academy Press.

Heesacker, M. (1986). Extrapolating from the elaboration likelihood model of attitude change to counseling. In F. Dorn (Ed.), *The social influence process in counseling and psychotherapy* (pp. 43–54). Springfield, IL: Charles C. Thomas.

Heppner, P.P., & Dixon, D. (1981). A review of the interpersonal influence process in counseling. *Personnel and Guidance Journal, 59,* 542–550.

Heppner, P.P., & Krauskopf, C.J. (1987). An information processing approach to personal problem solving. *The Counseling Psychologist, 15,* 371–447.

Herr, E.L., & Cramer, S.H. (1979). *Career guidance through the life span: Systematic approaches.* Boston: Little, Brown.

Herr, E.L., & Cramer, S.H. (1984). *Career guidance and counseling through the life span: Systematic approaches* (2nd ed.). Boston: Little, Brown.

Holland, J.L. (1973). *Making vocational choices: A theory of careers.* Englewood Cliffs, NJ: Prentice-Hall.

Holland, J.L. (1974). Career counseling: Then, now, and what's next. *The Counseling Psychologist, 4,* 24–26.

Holland, J.L. (1978). Career counseling: Then, now, and what's next. In J. Whiteley & A.

Resnikoff (Eds.), *Career counseling* (pp. 57–62). Monterey, CA: Brooks-Cole.

Holland, J.L. (1985). *Making vocational choices: A theory of vocational personalities and work environments* (2nd ed.). Englewood Cliffs, NJ: Prentice-Hall.

Holland, J.L., Daiger, D.C., & Power, P.G. (1980). *Manual for my vocational situation.* Palo Alto, CA: Consulting Psychologists Press.

Holland, J.L., Magoon, T.M., & Spokane, A.R. (1981). Counseling psychology: Career interventions, research, and theory. *Annual Review of Psychology, 32,* 279–305.

Horan, J.J. (1979). *Counseling for effective decision making: A cognitive-behavioral perspective.* North Scituate, MA: Duxbury Press.

Hosford, R.E., Burnett, G.F., & Mills, M.E. (1984). Toward prescription in counseling: Problems and prospects. In S.D. Brown & R.W. Lent (Eds.), *Handbook of counseling psychology* (pp. 334–396). New York: Wiley.

Isaacson, L.E. (1986). *Career information in counseling and career development* (4th ed.). Boston: Allyn & Bacon.

Jackson, D.N., & Paunonen, S.V. (1980). Personality structure and assessment. *Annual Review of Psychology, 31,* 503–551.

Jackson, D.N., & Paunonen, S.V. (1985). Construct validity and the predictability of behavior. *Journal of Personality and Social Psychology, 49,* 554–570.

Jones, A.J., Stefflre, B., & Stewart, N.R. (1970). *Principles of guidance* (6th ed.). New York: McGraw-Hill.

Katz, M.R., & Shatkin, L. (1983). Characteristics of computer-assisted guidance. *The Counseling Psychologist, 11,* 15–31.

Kenrick, D.T., & Funder, D.C. (1988). Profiting from controversy: Lessons from the person-situation debate. *American Psychologist, 43,* 23–34.

Kohler, W. (1925). *The mentality of apes* (E. Winter, Trans.). New York: Harcourt, Brace. (Originally published 1917)

Krumboltz, J.D. (1966a). Behavioral goals for counseling. *Journal of Counseling Psychology, 13,* 153–159.

Krumboltz, J.D. (Ed.). (1966b). *Revolution in counseling.* Boston: Houghton Mifflin.

Kulik, C.T., Oldham, G.R., & Hackman, J.R. (1987). Work design as an approach to person-environment fit. *Journal of Vocational Behavior, 31,* 278–296.

Lazarus, R.S., & Folkman, S. (1984). *Stress, appraisal, and coping.* New York: Springer.

Lazarus, R.S. & Launier, R. (1978). Stress-related transactions between person and environment. In L.A. Pervin & M. Lewis (Eds.), *Perspectives in interactional psychology* (pp. New York:). Plenum.

Lerner, J.V., Baker, N., & Lerner, R.M. (1985). A person-context goodness-of-fit model of adjustment. *Advances in Cognitive-Behavioral Research, 4,* 278–296.

Lerner, R.M., & Lerner, J.V. (1986). Contextualism and the study of child effects in development. In R.L. Rosnow & M. Georgoudi (Eds.), *Contextualism and understanding in behavior sciences: Implications for theory and research* (pp. 89–104). New York: Praeger.

Levinson, D.J., Darrow, C.N., Klein, E.B., Levinson, M.L., & McKee, B. (1978). *The seasons of a man's life.* New York: Knopf.

Lofquist, L.H., & Dawis, R.V. (1969). *Adjustment to work.* New York: Appleton-Century-Crofts.

Lowman, R.L. (1987). Occupational choice as a moderator of psychotherapeutic approach. *Psychotherapy, 24,* 801–808.

Lubinski, D., & Thompson, T. (1986). Functional units of human behavior and their integration: A dispositional analysis. In T. Thompson & M.D. Zeiler (Eds.), *Analysis and integration of behavioral units* (pp. 275–314). Hillsdale, NJ: Lawrence Erlbaum Associates.

McCrae, R.R., & Costa, P.T., Jr. (1984). *Emerging lives enduring dispositions: Personality in adulthood.* Boston: Little, Brown.

Meehl, P.E. (1954). *Clinical versus statistical prediction: A theoretical analysis and a review of the evidence.* Minneapolis, MN: University of Minnesota Press.

Meehl, P.E. (1986). Trait language and behaviorese. In T. Thompson & M.D. Zeiler (Eds.), *Analysis and integration of behavioral units* (pp. 315–334). Hillsdale, NJ: Lawrence Erlbaum Associates.

Miller, C.H. (1974). Career development theory in perspective. In E.H. Herr (Ed.), *Vocational guidance and human development* (pp. 235–262). Boston: Houghton Mifflin.

Miller, G.A., Galanter, E., & Pribram, K.H. (1960). *Plans and the structure of behavior.* New York: Holt, Rinehart, & Winston.

Mischel, W. (1968). *Personality and assessment.* New York: Wiley.

Mischel, W. (1983). Alternatives in the pursuit of the predictability and consistency of persons: Stable data that yield unstable interpretations. *Journal of Personality, 51,* 578–604.

Mischel, W. (1984). Convergences and challenges in the search for consistency. *American Psychologist, 39,* 351–364.

Mitchell, L.K., & Krumboltz, J.D. (1984). Research on human decision making: Implications for career decision making and counseling. In S.D. Brown & R.W. Lent (Eds.), *Handbook of counseling psychology* (pp. 238–282). New York: Wiley.

Moos, R.H. (1987). Person-environment congruence in work, school, and health care settings. *Journal of Vocational Behavior, 31,* 231–247.

Murray, H.A. (1938). *Explorations in personality.* New York: Oxford.

Neisser, U. (1967). *Cognitive psychology.* New York: Appleton-Century-Crofts.

Newell, A., & Simon, H.A. (1972). *Human problem solving.* Englewood, NJ: Prentice-Hall.

Nisbett, R.E., & Ross, L.D. (1980). *Human inference: Strategies and shortcomings of social judgment.* New York: Prentice-Hall.

Oliver, L.W., & Spokane, A.R. (1988). Career-intervention outcome: What contributes to client gain? *Journal of Counseling Psychology, 35,* 447–462.

Osipow, S.H. (1983). *Theories of career development* (3rd ed.). Englewood Cliffs, NJ: Prentice-Hall.

Osipow, S.H. (1987). Applying person-environment theory to vocational behavior. *Journal of Vocational Behavior, 31,* 333–336.

Ozer, D.J. (1985). Correlation and the coefficient of determination. *Psychological Bulletin, 97,* 307–315.

Parsons, F. (1909). *Choosing a vocation.* Boston: Houghton Mifflin.

Paterson, D.G., & Darley, J.G. (1936). *Men, women, and jobs: A study in human engineering.* Minneapolis, MN: University of Minnesota Press.

Patterson, C.H. (1959). *Counseling and psychotherapy: Theory and practice.* New York: Harper & Row.

Patterson, C.H. (1973). *Theories of counseling and psychotherapy.* New York: Harper & Row.

Paul, G.L. (1967). Strategy in outcome research in psychotherapy. *Journal of Consulting Psychology, 31,* 109–118.

Pervin, L.A. (1968). Performance and satisfaction as a function of individual-environment fit. *Psychological Bulletin, 69,* 56–68.

Pervin, L.A. (1987). Person-environment congruence in the light of the person-situation controversy. *Journal of Vocational Behavior, 31,* 222–230.

Peterfreund, E. (1971). *Information, systems, and psychoanalysis.* New York: International Universities.

Petty, R.E., & Cacioppo, J.T. (1981). *Attitudes and persuasion: Classic and contemporary approaches.* Dubuque, IA: William C. Brown.

Powers, W.T. (1973). *Behavior: The control of perception.* Chicago: Aldine.

Rosenthal, R., & Rubin, D.B. (1979). A note on the percent variance explained as a measure of the importance of effects. *Journal of Applied Social Psychology, 9,* 385–396.

Rosnow, R.L., & Rosenthal, R. (1988). Focused tests of significance and effect size estimation in counseling psychology. *Journal of Counseling Psychology, 35,* 203–208.

Rounds, J.B. (1988a, April). *The comparative and combined utility of work values and interest data in career counseling with adults.* Paper presented at the annual meeting of the American Educational Research Association, New Orleans, LA.

Rounds, J.B. (1988b, April). *Meta-analysis of research on the relationship of vocational interests and job satisfaction.* Invited paper presented at the annual meeting of the American Educational Research Association, New Orleans, LA.

Rounds, J.B., Dawis, R.V., & Lofquist, L.H. (1987). Measurement of person-environment fit and prediction of satisfaction in the theory of work adjustment. *Journal of Vocational Behavior, 31,* 297–318.

Rounds, J.B., Henly, G.A. Dawis, R.V., Lofquist, L.H., & Weiss, D.J. (1981). *Manual for the Minnesota Importance Questionnaire: A measure of needs and values.* Minneapolis, MN: Vocational Psychology Research, Department of Psychology, University of Minnesota.

Rounds, J.B., & Tinsley, H.E.A. (1984). Diagnosis and treatment of vocational problems. In S.D. Brown & R.W. Lent (Eds.), *Handbook of counseling psychology* (pp. 137–177). New York: Wiley.

Schmidt, F.L. (1988). The problem of group differences in ability test scores in employment selection. *Journal of Vocational Behavior, 33,* 272–292.

Schmidt, F.L., Gast-Rosenberg, I., & Hunter, J.E. (1980). Validity generalization results for computer programmers. *Journal of Applied Psychology, 65,* 643–661.

Schmidt, F.L., & Hunter, J.E. (1977). Development of a general solution to the problem of validity generalization. *Journal of Applied Psychology, 62,* 529–540.

Schmidt, F.L., Hunter, J.E., & Caplan, J.R. (1981). Validity generalization results for two jobs in the petroleum industry. *Journal of Applied Psychology, 66,* 261–273.

Schmidt, F.L., Hunter, J.E., & Pearlman, K. (1981). Task differences and validity of aptitude tests in selection: A red herring. *Journal of Applied Psychology, 66,* 166–185.

Smith, M.L., & Glass, G.V. (1977). Meta-analysis of psychotherapy outcome studies. *American Psychologist, 32,* 752–760.

Shweder, R.A. (1975). How relevant is an individual-difference theory of personality? *Journal of Psychology, 43,* 455–485.

Slaney, R.B. (1988). The assessment of career decision making. In W.B. Walsh & S.H. Osipow (Eds.), *Career decision making* (pp. 33–76). Hillsdale, NJ: Lawrence Erlbaum Associates.

Snyder, M. (1981). On the influence of individuals on situations. In N. Cantor & J.F. Kihlstrom (Eds.), *Personality, cognition, and social interaction* (pp. 309–329). Hillsdale, NJ: Lawrence Erlbaum Associates.

Spokane, A.R. (1985). A review of research on person-environment congruence in Holland's theory of careers. *Journal of Vocational Behavior, 26,* 306–343.

Spokane, A.R. (Ed.). (1987). Conceptual and methodological issues in person-environment fit research [Special issue]. *Journal of Vocational Behavior, 31,* 217–221.

Spokane, A.R., & Oliver, L.W. (1983). The outcomes of vocational intervention. In W.B. Walsh & S.H. Osipow (Eds.), *Handbook of vocational psychology* (Vol. 2, pp. 99–136). Hillsdale, NJ: Lawrence Erlbaum Associates.

Stoltenberg, C. (1986). Elaboration likelihood model and the counseling process. In F. Dorn (Ed.), *The social influence process in counseling and psychotherapy* (pp. 55–64). Springfield, IL: Charles C. Thomas.

Strong, E.K., Jr. (1951). Permanence of interest scores over 22 years. *Journal of Applied Psychology, 35,* 89–91.

Strong, S.R. (1968). Counseling: An interpersonal influence process. *Journal of Counseling Psychology, 15,* 215–224.

Strong, S.R., & Claiborn, C.D. (1982). *Change through interaction: Social psychological processes of counseling and psychotherapy.* New York: Wiley.

Strupp, H.H. (1978). Psychotherapy research and practice: An overview. In S.L. Garfield & A.E. Bergin (Eds.), *Handbook of psychotherapy and behavior change: An empirical analysis* (2nd ed.). New York: Wiley.

Super, D.E. (1977). Vocational maturity in mid-career. *Vocational Guidance Quarterly, 25,* 294–302.

Super, D.E. (1980). A life-span, life-space, approach to career development. *Journal of Vocational Behavior, 16,* 282–298.

Swanson, J.L., & Hansen, J.C. (1988). Stability of vocational interests over 4-year, 8-year, and 12-year intervals. *Journal of Vocational Behavior, 33,* 185–202.

Taylor, K.M. (1988). Advances in career-planning systems. In W.B. Walsh & S.H. Osipow (Eds.), *Career decision making* (pp. 137–211). Hillsdale, NJ: Lawrence Erlbaum Associates.

Tellegen, A. (in press). Personality traits: Issues of definition, evidence, and assessment. In D. Cicchetti & W. Grove (Eds.), *Thinking clearly about psychology: Essays in honor of Paul Everett Meehl.* Minneapolis, MN: University of Minnesota Press.

Thorndike, E.L. (1911). *Animal intelligence.* New York: McMillan.

Thorndike, E.L. (1913). *Educational psychology.* New York: Teacher's College.

Tracey, T.J. (1986). The stages of influence in counseling and psychotherapy. In F. Dorn (Ed.), *The social influence process in counseling and psychotherapy* (pp. 107–116). Springfield, IL: Charles C. Thomas.

Tracey, T.J., & Ray, P.B. (1984). Stages of successful time-limited counseling: An interactional examination. *Journal of Counseling Psychology, 31,* 13–27.

Tyler, L. (1969). *The work of the counselor* (3rd ed.). Englewood Cliffs, NJ: Prentice-Hall.

Urban, H.B., & Ford, D.H. (1971). Some historical and conceptual perspectives on psychotherapy and behavior change. In A.E. Bergin & S.L. Garfield (Eds.), *Handbook of psychotherapy and behavior change* (pp. 3–35). New York: Wiley.

Vondracek, F.W. (1987). Comments with a focus on Pervin's paper. *Journal of Vocational Behavior, 31,* 341–346.

Vondracek, F.W., Lerner, R.M., & Schulenberg, J.E. (1986). *Career development: A life-span developmental approach.* Hillsdale, NJ: Lawrence Erlbaum Associates.

Walsh, W.B. (1987). Person-environment congruence: A response to the Moos perspective. *Journal of Vocational Behavior, 31,* 347–352.

Walsh, W.B., & Betz, N.E. (1985). *Tests and assessment.* Englewood Cliffs, NJ: Prentice-Hall.

Weiner, I. (1978). *Principles of psychotherapy.* New York: Wiley.

Weinrach, S.G. (1979). Trait and factor counseling: Yesterday and today. In S.G. Weinrach (Ed.), *Career counseling: Theoretical and practical perspectives* (pp. 59–69). New York: McGraw-Hill.

Wiggins, J.S. (1973). *Personality and prediction: Principles of personality assessment.* Reading, MA: Addison-Wesley.

Wiggins, J.S. (1981). Clinical and statistical prediction: Where are we and where do we go from here? *Clinical Psychology Review, 1,* 3–18.

Williamson, E.G. (1939a). *How to counsel students: A manual of techniques for clinical counselors.* New York: McGraw-Hill.

Williamson, E.G. (1939b). The clinical method of guidance. *Review of Educational Research, 9,* 214–217.

Williamson, E.G. (1950). *Counseling adolescents.* New York: McGraw-Hill.

Williamson, E.G. (1961). Value commitment and counseling. *Teacher's College Record, 62,* 602–608.

Williamson, E.G. (1964). An historical perspective of the vocational guidance movement. *Personnel and Guidance Journal, 42,* 854–859.

Williamson, E.G. (1965a). *Vocational counseling.* New York: McGraw-Hill.

Williamson, E.G. (1965b). Vocational counseling: Trait-factor theory. In B. Stefflre (Ed.),

Theories of counseling (pp. 193–214). New York: McGraw-Hill.

Williamson, E.G. (1972). Trait-and-factor theory and individual differences. In B. Stefflre & W.H. Grant (Eds.), *Theories of counseling* (2nd ed., pp. 136–176). New York: McGraw-Hill.

Williamson, E.G., & Biggs, D.A. (1979). Trait-and-factor theory and individual differences. In H.M. Burks, Jr. & B. Stefflre (Eds.), *Theories of counseling* (3rd ed., pp. 91–131). New York: McGraw-Hill.

Williamson, E.G., & Bordin, E.S. (1941). A statistical evaluation of clinical counseling. *Educational and Psychological Measurement, 1,* 117–132.

Williamson, E.G., & Hahn, M.E. (1940). *Introduction to high school counseling.* New York: McGraw-Hill.

Yost, E.B., & Corbishley, M.A. (1987). *Career counseling: A psychological approach.* San Francisco: Jossey-Bass.

Zytowski, D.G., & Borgen, F.H. (1983). Assessment. In W.B. Walsh & S.H. Osipow (Eds.), *Handbook of vocational psychology* (Vol. 2, pp. 5–40). Hillsdale, NJ: Lawrence Erlbaum Associates.

2

Person-Centered Career Counseling

Jerold D. Bozarth
University of Georgia

Ron Fisher
Center for Professional and Personal Growth, Inc., Atlanta, GA

Carl R. Rogers (1942, 1951, 1957, 1959) developed a theory of psychotherapy that impacted the fields of counseling and psychotherapy in an unprecedented way. He was the first psychotherapist to extensively tape record counseling interviews, and the first psychologist to thoroughly investigate the process of psychotherapy using the scientific method of research. His efforts revolutionized the field of psychotherapy by de-mystifying it, and by opening up psychotherapeutic practice to professionals other than psychiatrists. The work of Rogers, however, had a penetrating influence. The principles that he hypothesized, first, in the field of psychotherapy were applied to a wide span of areas that included group work, education, international conflict mediation, and career counseling.

This chapter reviews the historical dimensions and the principles of person-centered career counseling. A person-centered career counseling model is proposed; and several examples of career counseling from the person-centered perspective are given.

HISTORICAL DIMENSIONS

Client-centered vocational counseling was in vogue during the 1940s and 1950s. The application of this approach began with Rogers' (1942) book, *Counseling and Psychotherapy*, that introduced the nondirective or client-centered approach in counseling and psychotherapy. At this time, he expressed the view that it was only when the counselor assumed a

nondirective approach that the client would feel able to explore underlying difficulties and not be tied into counselor driven actions. This
approach conflicted with other theories of career counseling and involved a different approach to handling problems of vocational choice
and adjustment problems (Super, 1988). It was an approach that
contrasted with the approach of analyzing the individual, studying
occupations, and the counselor applying "true reasoning" as the counseling mode.

Bixler and Bixler (1946) approached vocational counseling with a faith
in the basic integrity of their counselees. Others (Bordin & Bixler, 1946;
Grummon, 1972; Patterson, 1964) discussed, among other things, the
use of tests and occupational information from the client-centered
perspective.

Seeman (1948) discussed the use of tests and other aspects associated
with vocational and career counseling as they related to client-centered
counseling. These authors and others (Bown, 1947; Combs, 1947;
Covner, 1947) discussed at length the relative merits of "directive" and
"nondirective" orientations. In a more recent article, Miller (1988)
developed a modified psychometric measure that is directed toward
client-centered career counselors. Other than this, the recent literature
concerning client-centered or person-centered career counseling is quite
sparse.

It is, perhaps, not surprising that Rogers did not specifically attend
much to the area of career counseling. He was interested in the core
principles of constructive personality change as applied to multiple
areas; and, especially as applied to psychotherapy. Rogers expressed
little interest in any attempt to apply the approach to career counseling;
whereas others (Arbuckle, 1961; Doleys, 1961) argued that when clients
improve psychologically they increase their capacities to deal with
vocational and career problems. Rogers and advocates of the client-
centered persuasion did not seem to have a need for a model for
client-centered career counseling. Super (1950) was the first writer in
career counseling to bring the contrasting views of "directiveness" and
"nondirectiveness" together by offering a model that focused on the
self-concept (Super, 1951, 1957). However, after the 1950s the client-
centered approach waned in vocational/career counseling as a clearly
definable approach.

The assumptions of Rogers and the identifiable client-centered techniques (e.g., reflection, empathic understanding responses) became a
more integrated and pervasive phenomena with other approaches to
career counseling in a manner similar to that which occurred in the
general field of psychotherapy. Few individuals identified themselves as
specifically client-centered in either psychotherapy or career counseling

even though Rogers's work had a major impact on them.

C.H. Patterson (1964) wrote one of the most complete and comprehensive statements concerning client-centered career counseling. He noted that there was no difference in the way the client-centered counselor dealt with a client who had a vocational problem than with one with another type of problem. He viewed the difference between career counseling and other counseling as career counseling focused on the particular area of work of the client's life. Patterson (1973) offered a cogent summary of the essence of the approach when he discussed the highest stage of client development.

> The client experiences new feelings with immediacy and richness and uses them as referents for knowing who he is, what he wants, and what his attitudes are. . . . Since all of the elements of experience are available to awareness, there is the experiencing of real and effective choice. (p. 394)

It is the experience of the person becoming available to awareness that results in the person being able to make real and effective vocational and career choices.

Patterson (1964) was also one of the first writers to note that the client-centered approach to career counseling was more concerned with the attitudes of the counselor than that of the techniques used by the counselor. The focus on the expertise of the counselor and on external authority of other career counseling approaches rather than on the attitudes of the counselor were the critical differences of the client-centered stance with other approaches. Crites suggested that a client-centered approach might encourage clients to decide to take tests whenever they deem appropriate during counseling rather than at the beginning of counseling, and that clients would be encouraged to participate in the test-selection process. The focus on the concept of the self and the phenomenological aspects of client-centered theory was taken up by Rusalem (1954) who indicated that the presentation of occupational information becomes a process that involves an assumption of selective perception of the client; by Samler (1964), who stated that the occupational information process is psychological from the stance that the perceptions of the client are important; and by Grummon (1972), who emphasized the phenomenological part of client-centered theory by noting that the client's reality is determined by his or her perception. Crites (1974) described this in the following manner:

> The counselor describes the kind of information the client can gain from the various tests available, and the client decides which behaviors he/she wants to assess. The counselor then usually designates the most appro-

priate measures with respect to their psychometric characteristics (applicability, norms, reliability, validity). (p. 9)

The counselor's role is then to report the results to the client within the context of the attitudinal qualities.

Patterson (1964) commented in a less circumscribed manner than Crites by suggesting that "The essential basis for the use of tests in career counseling is that *they provide information which the client needs and wants*, information concerning questions raised by the client in counseling" (p. 449).

Authors who have considered the client-centered influence on career counseling have often followed Super's formulations that focus on the self-concept. Grummon (1972), for example, suggested that information supplied by tests can be integrated into the self-concepts of clients and be consistent with the client-centered approach in career counseling.

Crites' review aptly summarizes the fact that the principles underlying the client-centered approach to career counseling are much the same whether focusing on test interpretation or occupational information. Four of these basic principles are cited by Patterson (1964) while discussing the use of occupational information in client-centered career counseling. These are noted in Crites' review and worth quoting from the original source:

1. Occupational information is introduced into the counseling process when there is a recognized need for it on the part of the client . . .
2. Occupational information is not used to influence or manipulate the client . . .
3. The most objective way to provide occupational information and a way which maximizes client initiative and responsibility, is to encourage the client to obtain the information from the original sources, that is, publications, employers, and persons engaged in occupations . . .
4. The client's attitudes and feelings about occupations and jobs must be allowed expression and be dealt with therapeutically (pp. 453–455).

These principles are considered later in this chapter when a more defined model for person-centered career counseling is presented.

In summary, the client-centered approach has had a penetrating influence on the development and practice of career counseling in a way similar to that in the field of psychotherapy. It has not, however, been defined in relation to the specific function of career counseling.

THE PERSON-CENTERED MODEL

This section summarizes the basic principles of the person-centered approach and notes several of the general issues of applying the approach to areas outside of psychotherapy.

Rogers first used the term *person-centered approach* to refer to the applications of the principles of the client-centered approach to areas outside of psychotherapy. He used the term most emphatically in his book, *Carl Rogers On Personal Power* (1977). The term was later used interchangeably with *client-centered therapy* (Corey, 1988; Raskin & Rogers, 1989). Rogers (1987) did not differentiate between the terms *client-centered* and *person-centered*, stating that he believed himself to be doing the same thing whether he was doing client-centered therapy with a client, or working as a person-centered facilitator with a group. The term *person-centered* communicates at least two things that seem to us to bear on career counseling. First, the term itself communicates even more than the term *client-centered* an emphasis on the importance of the egalitarian and interactive relationship of the counselor with the client. Second, it suggests the importance of the person to person encounter of the counselor and client.

Hart and Tomlinson (1970) when referring to the experiential period (1957–current) offered a view that is close to the concept of person-centered therapy. They suggested that the counselor of this period engages in a wide repertoire of interview behaviors to express the basic attitudes. This era includes, according to them, the counselor, as a person who relates personal experiences to the client in order to facilitate the client's experiencing. We believe that it is a mistaken notion that the therapist is relating such experiences for the purpose of facilitating client experiencing. Rather, the therapist is not relating such experiences to obtain designated responses but only to promote his or her understanding of the person; and as a way of spontaneously being in the other person's world. The evolution of the term *client-centered* to *person-centered* is noted as important within the context of the review of the person-centered career counseling model.

Patterson's observation that the attitudes of the counselor are more important than the techniques to be employed by the counselor is the crux of the person-centered approach. However, the basis for the importance of the attitudinal qualities as counselor values has received less attention than the extensive attention to the attitudes. This basis is that of the importance of the full commitment of the counselor to trust in the client and in the client's own way of going about dealing with his or her problems and life. Although Rogers placed greater emphasis on emotional factors than did other approaches, a careful reading of even his early statements finds clear communications of his trust in the growth tendency for the cognitive rational as well as for emotional development (Rogers, 1940).

The foundation block of the theory is the actualizing tendency (Rogers, 1980); the crux of the theory is trust in the client "for the direction of movement in the process" (Rogers, cited in Kirschenbaum,

1979, p. 89); and the essence of the therapy "is the therapist's dedication to going with the client's direction, at the client's pace, and with the client's unique way of being" (Bozarth, in press). These elements are included in the following definition of person-centered therapy (PCT):

> When a psychological climate is experienced by the client, family, or couple who assume the locus of control for their own lives, the actualizing and formative tendencies are promoted. (Bozarth & Shanks, 1989, p. 281)

The attitudes of the therapist promote the actualizing process of the client. These attitudinal conditions are identified as the therapist being genuine, and experiencing unconditional positive regard, and empathy toward the client. Rogers (1957) hypothesized that therapeutic personality change would occur if the therapist was genuine, experienced unconditional positive regard and empathic understanding toward the client while endeavoring to communicate this to the client, and if this was successfully accomplished to some degree.

Rogers postulated that if six conditions existed over a period of time that no other conditions are necessary and that these conditions are sufficient to induce constructive personality change. The six conditions postulated by Rogers (1957) are:

1. Two persons are in psychological contact.
2. The first, whom we term the *client*, is in a state of incongruence, being vulnerable or anxious.
3. The second person, whom we term the *therapist*, is congruent or integrated in the relationship.
4. The therapist experiences unconditional positive regard for the client.
5. The therapist experiences an empathic understanding of the client's internal frame of reference and endeavors to communicate this experience to the client.
6. The communication to the client of the therapist's empathic understanding and unconditional postive regard is to a minimal degree achieved. No other conditions are necessary. If these six conditions exist, and continue over a period of time, this is sufficient. The process of constructive personality change will follow. (p. 96)

The attitudinal qualities can be defined for purpose of this chapter in the following ways:

Genuineness (or congruency): being integrated in the relationship; being real within the relationship;

Unconditional Positive Regard: prizing the individual in a nonjudgmental way;

Empathic Understanding: understanding the person's world as if you were the other person.

The approach in therapy offers a functional premise that includes wide therapist personality differences, unique ways of doing things, and idiosyncratic ways of responding as far as therapists are dedicated to the client's direction, the client's pace, and the client's unique way of being. The approach is one of total open inquiry with no intentions of treatment plans, treatment goals, or interventive strategies to get the client somewhere, or for the client to do a certain thing. The idea that there are no goals for the client in PCT is one that is alien to other approaches of either therapy or career counseling.

The authors believe that this functional premise can be offered within a context of career counseling wherein there is wide flexibility for what one does while maintaining the attitude of complete dedication to the client's direction, pace, and way of being.

There are other values that are implicit in the person-centered approach that are often not explicitly considered. These are the supporting assertions of the approach. Several of these assertions are the following (Brodley & Bozarth, 1986):

1. Human nature is basically constructive. It is not destructive.
2. Human nature is basically social.
3. Self-regard is a basic human need and self-regard, autonomy, and individual sensitivity are to be protected in helping relationships.
4. Persons are basically motivated to perceive realistically and to pursue the truth of situations.
5. Perceptions are a major determinant of personal experience and behavior, and, thus, to understand a person one must attempt to understand them empathically.
6. Individuals, not groups, are participants in a relationship.
7. Belief in the concept of the whole person.
8. Persons are realizing their potentialities and protecting themselves as best they can at any given time and under the internal and external circumstances that exist at that time.
9. Belief in abdication of the pursuit of control or authority over other persons and, instead, a commitment to share power and control.

These supporting assumptions are integral aspects of the core values of the person-centered approach that are: (a) the belief in the inherent growth principle and a "profound regard for the wisdom and construc-tive capacity inherent in the human organism (Rogers, 1986, p. 3); and (b) the theory of attitudinal facilitative conditions that create "a safe climate where persons can gain insight, can change and grow and expand (and) empower themselves" (p. 5). The most basic person-centered value has implications for person-centered career counseling (i.e., that authority about the person rests in the person not in an outside expert). As Brodley and Bozarth (1986) stated:

> It is when, no matter how subtly, the helping person begins to presume the authority of knowing better than the person being helped—what hurts, what directions the person should go, or what problems are crucial to be solved—that the fundamental person-centered values are violated. It is, from our perspective, when the helping person assumes authority over the experience and autonomy of the helped person that the foundation of the approach is distorted and lost. (p. 9)

When the approach is discussed in terms of the authority and expertise of the counselor, it is easy to understand why the PCA is not readily applicable to career counseling in the context of other models. The issues concerning vocational diagnosis and the counselor as the expert who can match client characteristics and work world require-ments emerge again.

A PERSON-CENTERED CAREER COUNSELING MODEL

This section postulates a model for career counseling that is predicated on person-centered principles. Super's (1988) definition of vocational guid-ance and occupational adjustment is used as a foundation for this development:

> Vocational adjustment is the process of helping a person to develop and accept an integrated and adequate picture of himself and of his role in the world of work, to test this concept against reality, and to convert it into a reality, with satisfaction to himself and benefit to society. (p. 90)

Person-centered career counseling, therefore, is similar to person-centered therapy, in that both deal with the formulation of a unique personal identity. Career counseling focuses on the public manifestation of that identity in the choice and implementation of vocational goals. This model of person-centered career counseling is based on certain axioms.

Axiom 1: *The person-centered career counselor has attitudes and behaviors that focus on promoting the inherent process of client self-actualization.*

The locus of control is within the client, whereas the counselor manifests genuineness, unconditional positive regard, and empathy. In this premise, person-centered career counseling is no different than person-centered therapy.

Axiom 2: *There is an initial emphasis on a certain area of client concern, that of work.*

Patterson (1964) made this distinction. This choice of emphasis is made by the client, not the counselor or the "career counseling" situation. As the career counseling relationship develops, various areas may be explored, depending on the self-actualizing process that develops from the interactive relationship. In this fashion, person-centered career counseling might evolve into individual psychotherapy, group psychotherapy, family therapy, job-change counseling, or preparation for return to school. The evolutionary nature of person-centered career counseling is examined at length through examination of two instances of career counseling.

Axiom 3: *There are opportunities for the client to test his or her emerging concept of personal identity and vocational choice with real or simulated work activities.*

This might involve actions with the counselor such as testing as well as encouraging relationships with other clients in a group, or with family and friends, and with persons from whom the client can obtain vocational information first-hand.

Axiom 4: *The person-centered career counselor has certain information and skills available to the client through which a career goal can be implemented.*

This is the area in which person-centered career counseling most seems to be different from person-centered therapy, for there is a large informational component not present in therapy. The career counselor must be aware of career information such as educational and experience requirements, aptitude and ability necessities, local, regional and national employment outlooks, job-seeking skills such as interviewing and resume-writing, and so forth. However, the necessity for the person-centered career counselor to possess and make available this information to the client does not vitiate the principles of the person-centered approach, if the locus of control remains with the client.

The third and fourth axioms vary from counselor to counselor, depending on the counseling setting, the needs of the client, and the financial and time resources of the counselor. The counselor may use techniques as limited as paper-and-pencil assessment or as elaborate as videotaped interviewing preparation, but the person-centered principles guide their usage. The tools and techniques employed by the career counselor are a source of information and reality testing for the client, but the meaning and implication of that information is left to the client to decide, within their unique process of self-actualization. Thus, the information-laden nature of career counseling and the emphasis on tools and techniques need not preclude a person-centered approach, as long as the counselor's attitudes and behaviors are congruent with the respectfulness of the person-centered approach.

The counselor's demeanor is that of relating to the client as a person rather than as an authority. In this sense, the counselor is consistent with that aspect of person-centered therapy. Likewise, the counselor who meets a client who brings a "vocational problem" is intent on following the client's direction, pace, and way of being with trust in the client's process but free to include his or her own spontaneous comments within this context.

A proposed definition of person-centered career counseling is:

> Person-centered career counseling is a relationship between a counselor and a client, arising from the client's career concerns, which creates a psychological climate in which the client can evolve a personal identity, decide the vocational goal that is fulfillment of that identity, determine a planned route to that goal, and implement that plan. The person-centered career counselor relates with genuineness, unconditional positive regard, and empathy; the locus of control for decisions remains with the client out of the counselor's trust in the self-actualizing tendency of the individual. The focus in person-centered career counseling is that of attitudes and beliefs that foster the natural actualizing process rather than on techniques and goals.

Person-centered career counseling, as stated under the second underlying axiom, may remain strictly job focused or it may evolve into other forms of counseling, depending on the client's needs, as they become apparent to client and counselor. Because of the collaborative nature of person-centered career counseling, the client may discover career or personal problems that he or she is unclear how to resolve. The counselor can offer information on his or her own experience of the client's issues, helping the client to define choices, which the client can then enact.

EXAMPLES

One of the authors (Ron Fisher) is the director of a private counseling center that has offered person-centered psychotherapy and career counseling for 10 years in a large urban setting. He has experienced working with clients on career concerns that have evolved into family therapy, individual or group psychotherapy, job-seeking skills training, and "personal growth groups" (which focus on career issues more than the traditional psychotherapy group.) From records of his sessions, we present edited transcripts of sessions with two different clients to illustrate principles of person-centered career counseling. The counselor's internal reaction is presented contemporaneous with his responses, as well as a summary observation following each session.

Harry

Harry is a 53-year-old who came in for career counseling after being terminated from his job as director of a nonprofit social service agency. He has been unsuccessfully looking for work in a nonprofit or government agency for 6 months. On the telephone he said that he was feeling depressed and desperate.

Harry's First Session

Harry: I don't know what I'm supposed to do here. I brought you my resume and my reports of performance. . . . Is that what you want? I didn't bring letters of reference, because I didn't know. . . . I guess I don't know where to start.

Ron: [He's brought a lot of written material, but I don't want to get so involved in reading that we don't get acquainted.] Harry, you brought a lot of material in today. Are you feeling that if I read these things it would help me to get to know you more quickly?

Harry: Well, I didn't know how you work, since I've never done this before. I'm not sure if this is what I need—maybe I need therapy . . . I've been feeling so rotten since I've been unemployed. But I really think the problem is being out of a job—do you think that I need to get help with my depression before you can help me?

Ron: [He's concerned about whether he needs therapy or not. I really can't answer that at this time.] It sounds like you've been feeling depressed since you lost your job and that worries you. Right now, I'm not sure whether you need psychotherapy or whether career counseling alone can resolve how bad you're feeling. You did ask me what we should talk about and how we were going to proceed. What seems to work out well for my clients is if you'd think about what you would like me to know about you and your life this evening, whatever you'd like to tell me—then I can tell you my thoughts and feelings as I listen to you.

Harry: I'm not sure where to start. It would really be easier if you could just ask me questions . . . you've been doing this for a long time, I'm sure you know what you need to ask me so that you can help me get a job.

Ron: Well, I'm sure your specific situation is unique and [pause] it's hard to be unemployed and you'd like me to be able to quickly help you.

Harry: That's right. Joe [his friend, a former client who referred him] said you helped him find a new career and he's real happy. He said you gave him tests and some books to read . . . [pause of 90 seconds—Harry looks at the floor dejectedly, seems sad] . . . I wish I'd come to see you when Joe told me about you. I knew this was going to happen. [Looks up] Maybe I *should* have known this was going to happen. This is the third time I've worked for an agency, they get in a new board, priorities change, money gets short, there's some problem, and then—bam!—heads roll . . . [bangs fist into his thigh]

Ron: [He seems both angry and depressed. Also, he's more angry at himself for not foreseeing this than he is angry at his board for laying him off.] You seem real angry when you remember this happening before—and you seem to blame yourself, like you should have seen this coming.

Harry: Of course I should have known it was going to happen.

Ron: Has this happened at *every* agency you've ever worked at?

Harry: No, of course not. I've been doing this kind of stuff for . . . for about 25 years, ever since I got my Masters. I've worked at seven agencies, four of them in [city]. This is the first time I've been let go here. But it just goes with the territory. I was stupid for ever going into social work. I should have gotten an M.B.A., like everybody else, instead of doing this idealistic social work bit.

Ron: [He's blaming himself for something that seems endemic to his field. He rejects the life-preserver I threw him by saying that it's his fault for not realizing this and avoiding the field.] It sounds like you've had a lot of turmoil working for nonprofits. Or at least, you've been let go from about half of your jobs. Yet you've stayed in that line of work. I wonder why.

Harry: [laughing] Well, when I'm not out of work it's great! I really do enjoy managing folks . . . I *really* know how to inspire them, really get the most from them. I know people would tell you that everybody was very loyal to me, that I went to bat for them. It's just so disappointing . . . we do great things for a few years, then a sponsor dries up or—one time it was a conflict a board member's brother had with me over something entirely different—I was renting a house from him and it was in terrible shape—anyway, this fellow turned his brother against me—I didn't even know it—and he turned the board against me. [sighs as he remembers] . . . I think what I want to do is find something that I'd like as much but more secure. This is hard on me, my wife, our kids . . . nobody's pressuring me, but it's just so embarrassing – and this just isn't the way I want my career to be going. If I put my energy into a job, I want to get some security out of it . . . [becomes self-conscious] . . . Boy! I'm really covering everything here. Whatta you think?

Ron: It sounds to me that this has been very important, very fulfilling work to you, but you're really having serious doubts about the price you have to pay. I'm also hearing that you're real hard on yourself – you seem to me to be more angry at yourself than at your board for firing you.

Harry: It's real hard for me to get angry. I've been going to Al-Anon for a long time and they're always telling me that I need to get my anger out, but I just stuff it, just like my old man. . . . Do you think I need to find a new career? This happens to everybody in my field, it seems. But I'm worried – you know, I'm 53 years old. It's not that I'm not willing to go back to school or whatever I need to do, but will anybody hire me? Besides, I need to make a lot of money in a hurry, for my retirement – my kids are almost finished with college, so those expenses are coming down. But I don't want myself and my wife to have to look to them when we retire. That's the question that stops me every single time I start to look at other jobs. It seems like I'd have to take a really big salary cut, but maybe I could make more in the long run. The pay is fairly good at what I've been doing, now that I'm up to the director level, but . . . [thinks a moment] . . . you know, I just thought – I bet if I averaged out my salary over the last few years, including these gaps, that it really hasn't been that great. So maybe I could take a job at a lower salary . . . Yeah . . . So how could I find out what I'd be good at? Can you give me some tests like you gave Joe?

Ron: [If he insists on testing, I will certainly give it to him and hope that he doesn't think that testing is a magical shortcut. But I'd prefer to help him find his answers internally.] Harry, I don't like to test people initially, because I believe that most people know themselves a lot better than they realize. And if I test you right now, then you'll put a lot of faith in the test and think that you couldn't have figured out things by yourself. If we get stuck, I can test you, but I'd prefer to use some exercises first, which will help you decide what your options are.

Harry: You know, I think this is going to be helpful. Just talking to you . . . I've been trying to hide all this from Mary and the boys. I didn't want them to think I was upset. I was kinda – I've been ashamed that I can't find something and I didn't want to tell them that I was half-hearted in looking for another agency job. Some days I go out and drink coffee, afraid to go on an interview. And I'm not sure if I'm more afraid of the rejection or whether they might actually offer me a job. 'Cause now I'm feeling like a job is just a period of time leading up to another layoff. It's like I couldn't even enjoy it, no matter how good it was, because I'd be waiting for the axe to fall. Or, I didn't tell you this—it's not just *my* being laid off. If other people have to go, guess who has to do the dirty work? I'm tired of being the Terminator, I'm tired of being the Terminatee.

Ron: You wrestle a lot with the pros and cons—you like your work but the working conditions make it very unpleasant for you. Over the next few weeks, we'll look at your past work as well as alternatives, you can talk to people in different occupations that interest you, then you can decide—you may choose to put up with the problems of your field or you may choose to change.

Harry: It does help to talk to you because you're not involved and I feel like you'll be able to see things more objectively than I can.

Ron: Well, I don't know about more "objectively," but—let's say, I can look at things from outside your situation and give you a different perspective which will clarify your feelings. But *you're* really the expert on Harry—what I can do is help you make things a little less muddy . . . [noticing clock] Harry, we're almost out of time for today. I'd like to give you an exercise for next time. It's called the Fantasy Want Ad exercise. I want you to get a copy of the Sunday Classified section . . .

Harry: [mock groan] Oh, I'm so sick of reading the Want Ads!

Ron: [This is a typical response for a discouraged job-seeker. I want him to know that I can teach him more effective ways to look for work, later. Right now, we're going to examine his career preferences. This will stop the reactive-style job search he's pursuing.] Well, this time you're not looking for a job—of course, if you see anything that interests you and you want to apply, that's fine. But the Want Ads are actually not a very good source of job leads—80% of jobs are never advertised—no, we're going to use the Want Ads just as a handy list of typical jobs. What I want you to do is to pretend that you're qualified for every single job in the paper—you have all the education, all the experience, you're the right age, gender, strength—there's no reason that you'd be turned down. I want you to ignore *any* kind of obstacle. If it requires French, you speak like a native.

Harry: Sounds like it could be fun. What am I supposed to do?

Ron: I want you to look at only three factors in each ad: the job title—it just leaped off the page and grabbed you; the duties—something about them was appealing or exciting; and the employer—maybe the job wasn't so great, but you'd really like to work for that employer. Go through with something like a red felt tip and circle any ad which attracts you. Try to do it like a fantasy. For example, if you were attracted to "Architect," but then you thought about going back to graduate school, so you didn't circle it—we'll lose some valuable information.

Harry: O.K., then what do I do?

Ron: I'd like you to spread the ads out on a table, or on the floor, whatever's comfortable. Then see if you can find some themes, some clusters of jobs.

Harry: I'm not sure what you mean.

Ron: Well, for example, one cluster might be "Jobs in Social Work." A different cluster might be "Jobs in the Corporate Sector which Make Use of My Social Work and Administrative Background." There's no right or wrong to the clusters; it's just a way to break the jobs down into manageable groups.

Harry: O.K., is that it?

Ron: Not quite. The third step, after you've arranged the ads into three or four or five clusters, then take each cluster, and tape them to a sheet of paper, running them down the leftside margin like this [demonstrating]. You might have 5 or 6 or 10 ads in each cluster, running down the leftside. Finally, at this point you've been doing this exercise for, oh, probably 5 or 6 hours total. A lot of ferment and thought is going on inside you. I don't want you to lose that information. So the final step is to write something next to each of the ads, whatever you think or feel as you re-read the ad.

Harry: Could you give me an example?

Ron: Sure. [gesturing to sample sheet] Once a woman cut out an ad for "flight attendant," among others. And next to that particular ad she wrote: "I've always wanted to be a flight attendant. I even applied twice, but I got scared and didn't follow through. But tonight, as I think about it, I realize that a flight attendant is nothing more than a waitress in an airplane."

Harry: I see. And does this need to be typed?

Ron: No, these comments are for yourself, so don't worry about form or grammar or anything like that. Just write whatever comes to your mind, there is no right or wrong. I'll go over the ads and comments with you, but the sheets are yours to keep. [this reassures clients and allows them to not regard the homework as a school assignment]

Harry: Anything else?

Ron: Bring the ads in and we'll talk about them and figure out what they mean. Also, we'll go over your work history next time, so that you can tell the desirable and undesirable parts of each of your jobs.

Harry: Sounds good. I feel better after talking to you. Do you think you can help me?

Ron: Harry, you seem really motivated to change things. My job is the easy part—you've got to do most of the hard work. What do you think?

Harry: Well, I know how much you helped Joe. And you do seem to understand how bad this unemployment has affected me. O.K. Let's give it a shot. When should I come back?

Ron: Well, you're going to use this Sunday's paper. How long do you think it might take you to go through it?

Harry: I could be finished by Tuesday afternoon—no later than Wednesday morning. [stops self] No, I changed my mind—I was going to do some chores around the house Monday, but that's what I've been doing to avoid job-seeking. Why don't we say Monday afternoon or Tuesday morning?

Ron: Fine, how would Tuesday at 10:00 be?

Harry: That would be great.

Ron: See you then.

Counselor's Comment.   This session has some typical elements of an initial career counseling session, along with some typical person-centered responses. Harry states that he is experiencing discouragement, depression, shame, and anger towards himself. His behavior is starting to become that of the long-term unemployed: he avoids job-seeking, he makes excuses or lies to his family and friends, he doubts whether he will ever find professional work again, he blames himself for all his career traumas in a stern, unrelenting hindsight. His confusion about whether to leave or stay in his field is typical of people facing institutionalized unemployment—whether steelworkers or college professors. He has lost confidence in himself and feels that he must rely on another person to solve his problems, a shameful prospect. By providing accurate reflective responses, I let him know that I understand his situation, even if I don't share his harsh self-indictment. I propose that the ultimate source of wisdom lies within himself, not in my expertise or in tests, which many clients regard as an Oracle of Delphi. Some clients have trouble accepting this at first, insisting that if they were all that wise, they wouldn't need help. Harry seems to have figured this out by himself, having observed his friend Joe move from a workaholic career to a gratifying position with a smaller, more humanistic firm. At the time he teased Joe, but admits during this first session that he was secretly jealous of Joe at the time. He wanted to seek career assistance, but was afraid that his family would be upset with him if he seemed vocationally unstable. Finally, I have much information about Harry, but I'm not sure yet what it means to him. I do feel sure that Harry wants to make a change, that he is well motivated, and that he desires my collaboration in that change.

Harry's Second Session

The first part of the second session was spent going over Harry's work history. He expressed preference for those activities that involved direct contact with people, either clients or staff; he disliked administrative tasks, such as budget, planning, research, reports. He said, "I never realized how much of my job I disliked ever since I moved from case work into administration." The Fantasy Want Ads session began with about half the hour remaining

Harry: Mostly I've cut out managerial jobs, not just in helping agencies. And then I have a couple that you'll probably find loony.

Ron: Well, we'll just have to see. What do you want to look at first? [This gives Harry control over the choice of how to cover the exercise.]

Harry: Let's look at the management jobs. The first three are director positions with small nonprofit organizations. They're not what I would call helping organizations—they're like . . . well, take this first one. It's a professional organization for life insurance agents. They do testing and certification, education, things like that.

Ron: What is it that you find attractive about that position?

Harry: Well, really, it's the title "Director," being "back in the saddle." I don't feel like I have a lot in common with life insurance agents, but maybe I could help them with their problems, their issues, you know, make life easier for them.

Ron: So the part of the job that mainly interests you would be helping the employee members?

Harry: That's right.

Ron: That sounds less like being an administrator than a helping professional. What do you think?

Harry: [pause] I think you're right. It's like when we were looking at my work history and I was realizing how many duties I just put up with so that I can have client contact and contact with my staff. I see how over the years the administrative stuff has just kept encroaching on what I really want to do, which is help people. I just kept on . . . I gave that up as I rose up the ranks. You know, looking at these ads now, I don't see one of the administrative jobs that I'd really want to do. I guess I chose them really out of habit more than anything.

Ron: Yes, and maybe because you've been feeling so bad being unemployed that you'd rather be back in something familiar which you don't like than continue to feel worthless, right?

Harry: Exactly. I really don't want to go back into management, not even agency management. But I feel so lost I don't know what else to do.

Ron: You feel like you've lost your identity and it would be better to have that old identity back, even if you hate your job, than to have none at all.

Harry: [Animatedly] Exactly! I feel so much pressure to get something soon. [Drops head into palm of hands.] And I don't know where it's coming from. Mary and the boys are supportive of me. I told her what you said and she told me that if I needed to change fields that was fine with her. But I feel so worthless I guess, not using my education, not going to work every day—I feel like a bum!

Ron: Harry, I'm curious why you're so hard on yourself. You say that your wife and your sons are supportive of you, you say that frequent layoffs are the nature of your administrative work, yet you seem ashamed of your current situation. In fact, you seem to have shame about ever going into social work.

Harry: I just think it's my fault that I'm in my current situation. I stayed with work I don't really like and all it's brought me is insecurity. You know, I really betrayed my dream. [Gazes out the window, deep in thought.]

Ron: [I sit, waiting to see what he's thinking about. This seems like it might be a critical point in his self-exploration and I don't want to interfere. I *am* curious what he means by "I really betrayed my dream" but I don't want to pull him up from whatever deep place he is exploring. I wait for about a minute.]

Harry: Do you know why I went into social work?

Ron: No, but I'd be interested in knowing.

Harry: I wanted to make a difference. I had been working in a family business—I'd gotten a management degree because that's what my dad did and that's what he wanted for me. He wanted me to take over his store. I didn't know what else to do, I didn't have any particular goals, so I did it. But in 1960, maybe a little earlier, I was getting dissatisfied. I felt like what I was doing was unimportant—who cares if you cut shoplifting costs or tighten up on inventory? Then came Kennedy. I guess like everybody else I felt a surge of idealism. Do you remember what that was like?

Ron: I do. [He wants to know if I understand but he's physically agitated. Whatever he's going to tell me is very important and I want to interfere as little as possible. I'll keep my comments to a minimum, just enough to let him know I'm tracking with him.]

Harry: I'd gotten married by then. We didn't have any children but it was unrealistic to think that Mary and I could do something like VISTA or the Peace Corps. But she and I felt the same way. *We could make a difference!* I started looking at different jobs, different careers. And that's when I discovered social work. I was really excited! I had thought social workers were the people who did welfare, adoptions, that kind of thing.

But I found out that there were other areas—medical social work, abused children, that kind of stuff. And I was particularly interested in psychiatric social work . . . [pause, self-conscious reaction] . . . Tell me if I'm taking too much time.

Ron: I'm really interested in this, Harry. I'd like to hear more.

Harry: O.K. So Mary and I made a deal. We'd move to another city, wherever I could get into graduate school. She'd continue working full time and I would go to school full time. It would mean a lot of beans and hot dogs, but it would be for only 2 years. All she asked me to do was to talk to people, to be sure before I made the move. So I did.

Ron: And what did you find out?

Harry: I got really excited. Every person I talked to, I got more and more excited. So Mary helped me research different schools, I applied, and I got accepted. You know, at that time there weren't too many men going into social work. Most of them were interested in administration. But I wasn't. I wanted to work with *people* . . . [angry] . . . That's where I betrayed myself!

Ron: How do you mean?

Harry: I hated the coursework—it was required—on policy, administration, rules, regulations, grant-writing—all the stuff I ended up doing. What I really liked was the courses on the family, psychopathology, counseling, the stuff dealing with individual human beings. I *loved* my practica and the internship I went on just confirmed that this was what I was meant to do. And yet I got away from it . . . [gazes out window again, dejectedly.]

Ron: It's not too late to recover your dream.

Harry: What? [confused]

Ron: It's obvious that it's still an important dream to you or you wouldn't be so upset at yourself. If you feel that strongly, maybe we can find some way to get back your idealism.

Harry: But it's so impractical. [fumbling for newspaper ads] You know, I cut out three ads for counselors or social workers—that's what I thought you would find screwball. Can I read them to you?

Ron: Sure, I'd be interested.

Harry: Well, the first two are for counselors in institutions, one is for a psychiatric hospital and the other one is for a children's home. I guess those aren't so far-fetched, except I'd take a pay cut. But the one that really interested me was this one. [holding up ad for me to read.]

Ron: Why don't you read it to me?

Harry: O.K. It says, "Private counseling center seeks psychiatric social worker, degreed, for adult caseload. Psychotherapy, individual and group. Addiction experience a plus. Possible partnership opportunities." And then it gives a phone number.

Ron: How does it make you feel, reading that ad?

Harry: Oh, I'm really excited! What I'd like to do—of course, this is impossible—would be to work at a place like that, develop my own caseload, get back my counseling skills, you know—then open my own little practice, like, a small clinic, just two or three of us working together. I'm so sick of working for other people—I've always wanted to be my own boss, but I just couldn't see how to do it. But, of course, I'm too old to do that.

Ron: [supportively] Says who?

Harry: [animated] You mean it doesn't seem silly to you?

Ron: I'm just watching your reaction. You're so excited—this is the first time in our two sessions that I've seen you this excited about work.

Harry: I wanted to tell Mary, but I thought she would think it was silly.

Ron: Did she think it was silly 25 years ago?

Harry: No, that's right—but we wouldn't have as much money, at least at first.

Ron: So there might be some practical problems. But that's not the same as her thinking it's "silly."

Harry: Would you talk to her for me?

Ron: You're afraid of her reaction?

Harry: I don't want her to say that I've wasted the last 15 years or so, when I could have done this earlier.

Ron: It sounds like those are *your* feelings about this change—you *should* have known 15 years ago that you might like private practice and you *should* have been able to predict that administration would be insecure and that you wouldn't like it? [asked as a question]

Harry: You know, I never really wanted to go into administration. I kept getting administrative jobs because of my undergraduate degree, people kept seeing me as a manager. It was hard to turn down the promotions because it meant more money for our family.

Ron: [I feel that his shame about perfectly reasonable career choices is keeping him from experiencing his excitement about this discovery of private practice.] Harry, when your boys make a mistake—let's say, they pick a wrong course in school, or they mismanage their money one semester, what's your reaction when they feel guilty?

Harry: I tell them not to beat themselves, that's how we learn, by making mistakes.

Ron: It sounds like you're a better parent to your boys than you are to yourself.

Harry: Jeez . . . I don't know. Sometimes I sound like my old man.

Ron: Was your father hard on you?

Harry: Very hard. Hard on himself, too. He was always unhappy.

That's probably why he drank so much. And he died young. So you think I'm doing the same thing to myself as he did to me?

Ron: What do you think?

Harry: It sure seems like it. [long pause while he seems to think about a variety of matters, occasionally looking at the Fantasy Want Ads in his lap] You know, I think I'm really interested in this area of a private practice. I think it would give me much more security than I've experienced with agencies. That's real surprising, isn't it? More security working for myself. But, *I* certainly wouldn't lay myself off now, would I? [laughing] This really is what I want to do, but I thought you would think it was crackpot, starting a private practice at my age. [posed as a question]

Ron: [teasing] So you were afraid I would tell you to stop with the fantasies and get back to business, get your feet on the ground?

Harry: That's right. You know, I told Mary that I was interested in starting a clinic and she thought it was a great idea. She said that it was a way I could use all my years of administrative experience without becoming an administrator. It was really you that I was afraid of—well, not "afraid of," not like you were my father or something. [pause] Hmm, that's interesting—that I would bring up my father in reference to you. I don't think that I've been seeking your approval like I used to seek his. I wonder what that means.

Ron: Something in our discussing your career dreams makes you think of me as your father. Like I was an authority figure?

Harry: Yeah, like I needed your permission to leave this administrative B. S. and go into something I like. My father hated his job for many years, but he never admitted it. I guess he just considered that as the nature of work—you *do* it, you don't have to *like* it.

Ron: So, I wonder if this has to do with "permission" as you say, like you need your father's permission to be happy, even if he's dead? Or maybe it has to do with something else?

Harry: I don't know how you figure these things out, but there is something else. You know, I'd thought about "Do I need my father's permission to be happy" and I felt pretty certain that that was a minor issue. I'm not saying that it's not there at all, but I think my going to Al-Anon, particularly to Adult Children of Alcoholic groups, I've pretty well gotten past that "internalized critical parent." [laughing] Now, don't correct me—I know it's showed up here a little bit. But, I mean, in general, I think I do what I want to do, which often is something my father wouldn't approve of. But I was thinking about this whole issue of happiness—about having a job I enjoy, look forward to going to each day. It's been so long since that happened.

Ron: So that would be a different experience for you. [teasing] Do you think you could handle the strain of being happy?

Harry: [laughing] You laugh, but actually I think you've said what I was feeling. I think that if I had work which *really* interested and excited me, then I might kick myself for all the years I was unhappy. But it's more than that. Because, you see, I think I *can* achieve really meaningful, gratifying work. That's where my dad comes in. I feel kind of guilty if I can have a really exciting career and he never had anything except shit. He pretended that he liked it, he told us all the great things about the store, but, you know, underneath, I think he really felt trapped. He felt responsible for us, he was responsible for his employees, he had to keep things going for his customers . . . [pauses in remembrance]

Ron: You know who he forgot to be responsible for? Himself.

Harry: [excited] You're right! He never could break away. I'm sure there were things he wanted to do . . . I don't know what they were, because that would have been bad form to talk about them. But as much complaining as he did, he must have had other things which interested him.

Ron: Maybe.

Harry: You mean maybe he just thought that he *had* to keep working at the store, like [hits himself on the forehead with the palm of his right hand] Jesus Christ! like *I* thought I had to keep working in social work administration because . . . because for no reason! Because I was responsible for my staff, my programs, my clients, my wife, my son, Hell! responsible for the whole world except Harry!

Ron: So, maybe it's time to change.

Harry: Let's do it! What do I do next?

Ron: What do you think you need to do?

Harry: Well, I'm going to apply for this job in the paper, but I don't want to limit myself to just advertised jobs. You said that 80% of jobs are not advertised, so I need to figure out some way to find those unadvertised jobs.

Ron: How do you think you could do that? You've worked in [city] how many years?

Harry: Over 15 years.

Ron: And do you think you know a lot of therapists, psychiatrists, psychologists?

Harry: More than anyone I can imagine. And I know a lot of them socially, because I was an administrator—I had to go to a lot of parties at hospitals, clinics, stuff like that.

Ron: How do you think these other therapists would react to news that you were starting a private practice?

Harry: Oh, they'd think it was great! They'd probably tease me about my age, about the pie not being big enough for one more serving, you know, that kind of thing. But, really, I think they would be happy to help me get started. Certainly, I've done a lot of favors for many people in this town, and this would give them a chance to help me back.

Ron: Why don't you do this for next session—tell me what you think about it? Make a list of *all* the people you know in [city], grouping them by category: people from your job—co-workers, referral sources, therapists, vendors; people from church; people from Al-Anon; friends . . . and so forth.

Harry: *Everybody* I know?

Ron: Everybody, because you never know how someone might be able to help you. A person might not directly be able to help but they might know someone who could. There's another reason for doing this—it will make you aware of just how many people you've impacted in [city] in the last 15 years.

Harry: You know, this makes my head rush. I thought you were going to give me a hard time, but you're already starting to help me create a strategy. Do you *really* think I can do it?

Ron: Do *you* think you can do it?

Harry: I sure do!

Ron: Then, that's good enough for me. You have the credentials to be a private-practice therapist?

Harry: Sure.

Ron: And you know a lot of people who can help you get started?

Harry: Right.

Ron: And you have the support of Mary and your boys?

Harry: I know they'll back me all the way.

Ron: So, the last question is, do *you* support yourself? Can you be responsible for Harry first, instead of last?

Harry: That's going to be the toughest part. But, you know, that's a problem—coping with happiness—that's a problem I wouldn't mind having.

Ron: So, next time, bring in that list of people you know, and we can begin problem solving the task of building a practice.

Harry: Is this something you can help me with?

Ron: Yes, I have a lot of experience helping people start their own business, particularly consulting practices. I have helped any number of therapists get started, so I'm sure we can figure out what you need to do together. 'Course, the hard part will be your—contacting people for referrals. But I can help you with tips that have worked for others. And you'll find things that work out best for you.

Harry: This is really exciting! You know, when I started with you last week, I thought we were going to do job-seeking—sort of, you would show me a more effective way to get the same kind of job I've been hating for about 18 years. I never would have imagined we'd end up here.

Ron: Well, this must be what you want, because all I've done is clarify and expand on your ideas, your feelings. This wasn't an idea *I* had, this came from your Fantasy Want Ad exercise.

Harry: Yeah, and an hour ago I thought you might feel it was "loony."

Ron: What do you think now?

Harry: I think it's a great idea and I think you believe it's possible.

Ron: More important, *you* think it's possible.

Harry: That's right, I really believe I can do it.

Ron: See you next week.

Counselor's Comment.   During this session, Harry's excitement has been building as the dream of a private practice takes shape and forms in his mind as a practicable alternative to continuing his unsatisfying career in social work administration. It's important to note that the freedom and acceptance he experienced in the first session transferred to his home, in the completion of the Fantasy Want Ad exercise. Had the counselor been more directive, focused on "transferable skills, job leads," and other external matters, then Harry most likely would not have come up with a goal that deviates from his career track of the previous 18 years. Other interesting features of this session are the psychotherapeutic elements having to do with identity, introjected critical parent, guilt toward his father for being happy, and some genuine grieving for his father's unhappiness. I might expect that this experience would result in further processing of his relationship with his father and increased compassion for his father and for himself. If Harry had continued to find guilt toward his father hampering his progress toward his goal, I would have suggested a personal-growth group, because this is a common issue clients struggle with. My plans at the end of the second session are to help Harry with whatever he would like assistance with. He expressed the need for practical practice-building help, but I don't assume at this time that he will require extensive additional counseling. He might need some support, he might need help with items like advertising, renting space, and so forth. If he does, I will continue to push self-reliance, helping him only in those areas where he lacks the skills or information. Frequently, requests for help are not a sign of the client's deficiency in skill or information, but are an expression of low self-confidence and fear. Instead of quickly jumping in and providing the answer, my preference, as illustrated several times in this second session, is to question the client as to his or her resources. This solves the problem they were asking help for, but has the

additional benefit of increasing self-confidence. Because career counseling is more information laden than psychotherapy, the counselor
must resist the temptation to quickly provide answers to requests for
expertise or information. While such doling out of information may be
enhancing to the counselor's professional ego, it falsely demonstrates to
the client that he or she lacks the ability to problem solve and increases
reliance on the counselor.

Harry's Third Session

The third session was a problem-solving session. Harry had become
increasingly enthused about the practicability of the private practice
option as the week between Session 2 and 3 progressed. Each person he
called supported the idea. He negotiated a contract with his wife and sons
as to some lifestyle changes that would lower their cost-of-living expenses, so that he would have the time necessary to "grow" his practice. He
made several calls about subleasing space, so that his overhead would be
low. He found out about answering services and looked into the costs of
printing business cards. He renewed his memberships in clinical associations that he had dropped during his years of administrative work. He
got a copy of the local United Way directory of agencies, which he
thought would be a fertile ground for referrals.

Looking at Harry's behavior provided me with a "litmus test" for his
expressed enthusiasm. He had carried out my assignment of listing his
friends and business associates; but he had done much more, by a factor
of 10. His initiative reflected the kind of risk-taking that is essential for
private practice or self-employment of any type. Whether it would
continue or not I had no way of knowing. I didn't feel like it was just a
honeymoon reaction. However, I knew that self-employment was risky
and lonely, so I referred Harry to an entrepreneur's club, which offers
monthly luncheon meetings for mutual support and problem solving. I
wanted Harry to understand that many of the problems he would
encounter, practical and emotional, were normal components of entre-
preneurship, rather than pathologies. I would continue to be available to
him and would not deny him sessions. However, if he could get support
from fellow entrepreneurs or, if necessary, psychotherapeutic support
in a growth group, these I see as "more respectful" ways of assisting him
in this major life change.

Harry's career counseling was really finished after the second session.
Subsequent sessions were "follow through," helping him to implement
his goal. He *did* establish a private practice and today, 3 years later, has
two social workers and a psychiatrist affiliated with him, in his own
clinic. He considers himself much more secure than he ever was

working for nonprofit agencies. He makes more money than he ever made as a director. And he is happier than he has been since he graduated from social work school.

* * *

The counselor occasionally veered from a pure person-centered stance when he opened up certain areas that he thought important; such as, wondering about the influence of Harry's father. Overall, these variations from the approach did not interfere with the strong attention to Harry's world, and often seemed to be well received by Harry. Ron may have been more pure in the approach in a therapy session.

Beth

Beth is a 32-year-old who came to me requesting that I help her to "get back into teaching." In her first several sessions she gave me considerable information about herself. She had been unemployed professionally for about 1 year at the time she sought counseling, working part time as an office clerical worker. She had originally trained in college as a teacher but had not liked teaching the 1 year she tried it. She returned to school at age 24 and secured a degree in commercial art. She had moved from [city] to Manhattan at the end of her training, seeking employment as a commercial artist for an advertising agency. She unsuccessfully sought work for 3 months, then secured a position with a large, national advertising firm. She worked for that firm for 5 years, progressing to art director. Then, with several friends, she started a restaurant business. Like most undercapitalized ventures, it failed after 15 months. Her advertising firm happily took her back at her old job, where she remained for another year. At that point, the agency lost the account on which she was creative director and she was laid off, not an unusual occurrence in the field. Because her self-confidence was already damaged by the experience in the restaurant (which she considered a demonstration of her "bad judgment"), she became very frightened when she was laid off. Rather than look for other positions in New York City, she made plans to return to [city], where her aged parents live alone. She sought work as a creative director or art director in [city] but was unsuccessful.

During the second session I suggested doing the Fantasy Want Ad exercise as a way of clarifying her goals for herself. I was skeptical about her desire to return to teaching and I felt that there were significant issues of low self-esteem and loss of self-confidence that were causing her to espouse a goal she had found dissatisfying 10 years earlier.

While doing the Fantasy Want Ads together, Beth discovered that she did not want to switch from her field, but that she had given up after unsuccessfully looking for 6 or 7 months. She expressed absolutely no interest in teaching. So, after the third session, I began teaching her more productive job-seeking skills. She had, the previous year, mailed resumes and cover letters to all the advertising agencies in town. I suggested to her that this was an unproductive way to seek employment, but it *was* a safe way to avoid face-to-face rejection. She admitted that she was scared of rejection and began crying. She spoke of her despair at finding something in her field, her loss of confidence. She also disclosed for the first time that, after she had made the decision to leave New York and return to [city] to live with her parents, her old firm had offered her a new position, actually a promotion. However, she felt obligated to fulfill her plans because her parents were so excited about her returning to her home town. I wondered at that point if there were not issues other than job-seeking and career involved, but it was premature to comment.

Following the acquisition of job-seeking skills and much supportive counseling, both individual and group, Beth began job-seeking. She made appointments, showed her portfolio, got second and third interviews, and was generally very productive. However, the job offers that she received did not seem to interest her, even though they were comparable to her job in New York City. She found fault with each of the jobs, even though they seemed attractive to me, based on her criteria for gratifying employment.

This interview took place after 3 months of individual and group counseling, following a 3-day trial work period at an advertising agency.

Beth's 15th Session

Beth: You know, I thought I would like it at [agency], but for some reason it just didn't feel right.

Ron: Are you able to think about what that reason is?

Beth: I am. The second day I was there I had some very strong feelings that I was in the wrong place.

Ron: Do you mean the wrong agency or that you shouldn't be in an agency at all?

Beth: [cautiously] Neither. You know what I decided? I don't think I want to work in [city] at all. You keep pointing out that I'm turning down jobs that fit my description of the kind of job I'd like. So I was wondering—that second day I was at [agency]—what's wrong? Last year, I thought this was what I wanted, to return to [city] and work in advertising. But, all of a sudden I've become very picky. I think I know what it is.

Ron: What?

Beth: I don't want to live here at all! I realized that I want to return to New York and work there. I moved here—well, let me tell you what I did last week. You'll be proud of me. I drew up a list of pros and cons, New York and [city]. I had a whole list of pros under New York and only one pro under [city].

Ron: And what was that?

Beth: My parents live here. And I realized [reaches for tissue, begins weeping]—I realized that I moved here to run away from a relationship that was ending and because I thought it would please my parents for me to be closer. I think I felt guilty that they were getting older and that I should be nearer. But it hasn't worked. I don't want to live here. I *love* New York! Everybody says to me, down here, they say "Oh, I know why you left New York. It's so dirty, so crowded, so much crime, so much this or that. But they're wrong. I *love* the hustle and bustle, I love taking the subway. I love not needing a car, going to plays, going to foreign movies. What I hated was being laid off and my boyfriend and I breaking up at the same time.

Ron: So New York was a place of great pain at the time you left?

Beth: Right.

Ron: But, before that, you had been happy there for 7 years?

Beth: Right. But when I got laid off, all those fears about myself that came from my restaurant experience—I wondered if I could find a job, I thought about how long it had taken me when I first got there, I remembered how lonely I had been . . . it all seemed overwhelming. And [city] seemed to be a place of refuge.

Ron: Because your parents were here?

Beth: Right. And it's not like my friends are here. Sure, I know people from when I grew up. But my *real* friends are in New York. I'm on the phone every single day, talking to somebody. I make myself go out here, but I'd really like to see my friends in New York.

Ron: So what does all this mean?

Beth: I think it means that I was depressed and discouraged and I needed a vacation. [laughs] I got that confused with moving back here.

Ron: And do you *really* think that it would be the same as starting all over again?

Beth: No, of course not! That's ridiculous! But that's how I felt. I thought I had made a big mistake leaving to start the restaurant.

Ron: You thought that at the time? Or did you think that after the restaurant closed?

Beth: Afterwards. It was great while it lasted.

Ron: And you got your job back—in fact, a promotion, right?

Beth: That's right.

Ron: So, explain to me how leaving to start a restaurant was a mistake, since you had fun, you got a better job afterward . . . ?

Beth: I don't know, it just all seems to merge together. Breaking up with Bob, the agency losing my account, getting laid off, it all just came down at once.

Ron: So it was stressful time for you?

Beth: That's right. I felt like I was failing at everything.

Ron: But it doesn't sound like you really believe you were failing. Instead, it seems like you got overwhelmed by a lot of changes that occurred at once.

Beth: Right. I just felt totally stressed out. And I wanted to come home to get taken care of.

Ron: Listen to that, "to get taken care of." You've been thinking that you came home "to take care of your parents," but maybe you came home for them to take care of you.

Beth: That's right! Then I don't have to feel guilty if I leave. It just means that I'm better, I've got things together, and they've helped me. So, instead of them feeling bad that I'm leaving—I mean, they'll miss me and everything—but maybe they'll see it as they helped me and now I can resume me career—in New York. I thought they would take it personally, my moving back to New York.

Ron: It sounds like it was *you* who felt that they would take it personally. How would *they* feel about it?

Beth: Well, I started sounding them out about it this weekend. They said they'd miss me, but they want me happy. They said that they hated to see me so miserable here. I had been telling them about the job offers which I turned down and when I told them that I thought it was because I wanted to live back in New York, they said that made a lot of sense to them. They joked about it—they said that, what I save in phone bills, I could fly home every couple of months to visit them.

Ron: So it sound like they're supportive of the idea of you moving back.

Beth: I didn't know what you would say about it, so I wanted to wait until we talked. But I already contacted my old firm. And I called some other firms which had made me offers over the years. If I'm going to go back, I might as well look at making a change, getting the best job I can.

Ron: How do you feel about this outcome?

Beth: Well, it sure is surprising to me! But, you know, if I hadn't come to see you, I probably would have gone back into teaching and hated it. Then, I might have looked for an art job here in town, and it would have looked so good, in comparison to teaching, that I would have taken it and never realized that I wanted to go back to New York. I think this has really helped me to see what I want, and my job is just part of what I want. And I can't get here what I have in New York— friends from the last seven or eight years. I don't want to start over.

Ron: So, it sounds like you're surprised and pleased at the outcome?

Beth: That's right. You did help me find out that I wanted to stay in advertising, stay in art. But *I* found out that I wanted to go back to New York.

Ron: [laughing] I guess that makes you my co counselor in this relationship.

Beth: I think I must be finished. Thank you very much for your help. I'd like to write to you when I get to New York, if that would be okay?

Ron: I'd like that. I'm interested in how things turn out for you, what changes you make.

Beth: Goodbye. And thanks.

Counselor's Comment. This client took much longer than Harry to make her discovery about moving back to New York, although her initial discovery about return to teaching versus staying in art came relatively rapidly. The importance of this case is the illustration of the benefits of nondirective career counseling. Given a free playing field, Beth experimented with job-seeking in her field in [city], but something was not right. Because I did not know the meaning of her refusal of job offers, I merely pointed out the phenomenon, without interpretation. Having called her attention to it, I assumed Beth could make the best meaning of her behavior. And she did.

Beth has returned to New York City and is happily employed as creative director for a smaller, more creative agency than her former agency. She reports that she is happier than before. She does not regret moving back to [city], for it clarified how important residing in New York was to her happiness.

* * *

Ron's way of seeking understanding is sometimes from an external frame of reference. He sometimes pointed out things to Beth and was perceived as doing so by her. These suggestions, however, were not from an authoritarian stance. Rather, they were from a perspective of better understanding what Beth's internal world was like. It is an interesting example of how one can offer many forms of responses, and even responses that could be viewed as authority based when one maintains the experiencing of empathic understanding and unconditional positive regard toward the client.

SUMMARY

Our review of Ron's work with these two clients illustrates a couple of the facets of person-centered career counseling that appear different from person-centered therapy.

First, Ron does express some of his thoughts from an external frame of reference. Some of these thoughts seem more idiosyncratic to Ron's knowledge about other theories; however, some of these external thoughts relate to external aspects of career work. Ron even introduces possibilities for vocational exploration to his clients. The most notable in the example being that of the want-ad fantasy. These insertions and thoughts that are external to the client's expressed experiencing are quite tentative and Ron's attitude is one of readily searching for the client's way and direction. He continues in spite of these external perceptions and introductions to maintain the attitude of trusting the client's direction, pace, and own way.

Ron's enthusiasm for success of Harry comes through in one of the sessions where he attempts to encourage Harry to take a chance rather than following Harry's immediate experience. This is a more spontaneous response than one that was deliberate and designed for any particular purpose. It, perhaps, demonstrates the person to person interaction of the two individuals. From the person-centered perspective, it is important to note the complexity of such responses, and that it is important for the counselor to be confident in his dedication and intent to trust the authority of the client's experience for his own life.

Second, Ron uses some of the resources available to him and communicates his understandings of the client's interest in career change while staying open to any other direction. He asserts some directions that they might go as ways to gain more understanding of the client's career directions. Ron offers ideas that are sometimes ways of testing the self concepts that these two individuals seem to be developing in the world of work.

This chapter offers a model for person-centered career counseling that is based on the principles of person-centered therapy. Super's definition of vocational adjustment is used as a context for this definition. Our definition is the following:

Person-centered career counseling is a relationship between a counselor and client, arising from the client's career concerns, which creates a psychological climate in which the client can evolve a personal identity, decide the vocational goal that is fulfillment of that identity, determine a planned route to that goal, and implement that plan. The person-centered career counselor relates with genuineness, unconditional positive regard, and empathy; the locus of control for decisions remains with the client out of the counselor's trust in the self-actualizing tendency of the individual. The focus in person-centered career counseling is that of attitudes and beliefs that foster the natural actualizing process rather than on techniques and goals.

The axioms that are integral to this definition are:

Axiom 1: The person-centered career counselor has attitudes and behaviors that focus on promoting the inherent process of client self-actualization.

Axiom 2: There is an initial emphasis on a certain area of client concern, that of work.

Axiom 3: There are opportunities for the client to test his or her emerging concept of personal identity and vocational choice with real or simulated work activities.

Axiom 4: The person-centered career counselor has certain information and skills available to the client through which a career goal can be implemented.

Examples were taken from transcribed tapes of a private career counselor in an effort to illustrate the counselor's dedication to the person-centered principles while working within a clearly career-oriented context.

The person-centered career counseling model present in this chapter is intended to integrate the person-centered approach with the specific needs of the career counseling relationship. The focus in the model, as exemplified in the two transcribed examples, is the person-to-person interaction that promotes self-discovery by the client. Various counseling responses occur, but the locus of control remains with the client. There is a lack of "treatment planning." The relationship is collaborative and emergent. The counselor facilitates exploration of self-identity, assists in the formulation of vocational expression of that identity, and participates in the planning and execution of methods to implement that expression. Although various "techniques" may be used in this testing and implementation of a self-concept (such as testing or the rewriting of a resume) the underlying counselor trust in the client's actualizing tendency keeps the emphasis on the dynamic, spontaneous person-to-person relationship.

The authors encourage theoretical response and applied research to this model. We are particularly interested in fostering person-centered attitudes with career practitioners in school and industry, who have both employer and client pressures on them for technique laden "quick solutions." As illustrated, a person-centered career counselor can use testing exercises, vocational literature, and other techniques, however, he or she is not to provide the client with a ready-made identity, but to clarify and illuminate the client's own view of self. "Techniques" can be a useful but minor assistance to creating "a psychological climate in which the client can evolve a personal identity, decide the vocational goal which is fulfillment of that identity, determine a planned route to that goal, and implement that plan."

REFERENCES

Arbuckle, D.S. (1961). *Counseling: An introduction.* Boston: Allyn & Bacon.

Bixler, R.H., & Bixler, V.H. (1946). Test interpretation in vocational counseling. *Educational and Psychological Measurement, 6,* 145–156.

Bordin, E.S., & Bixler, R.H. (1946). Test selection: A process of counseling. *Educational and Psychological Measurement, 6,* 361–373.

Bown, O.H. (1947). The client-centered approach to educational and vocational guidance. *The Personal Counselor, 2,* 1–5.

Bozarth, J.D. (in press). The essence of client-centered, person-centered therapy. In G. Lietaer, J. Rombauts, & R. Van Balen (Eds.), *Client centered and experiential psychotherapy toward the nineties.* Leuven: Katholieke Universiteit te Leuven.

Bozarth, J.D., & Shanks, A. (1989). Person-centered couples therapy. *Person-Centered Review, 4*(3), 280–294.

Brodley, B.T., & Bozarth, J.D. (1986, September). *The core values and theory of the person-centered approach.* Paper presented at the meeting of the Association for the Development of the Person-Centered Approach, Chicago, IL.

Combs, A. (1947). Nondirective techniques and vocational counseling. *Occupations, 25,* 261–267.

Corey, G. (1988). *Theory and practice of counseling and psychotherapy* (3rd ed.). Monterey, CA: Brooks/Cole.

Covner, B.J. (1947). Non-directive interviewing techniques in vocational counseling. *Journal of Consulting Psychology, 11,* 70–73.

Crites, J.O. (1974). Career counseling: A review of major approaches. *The Counseling Psychologist, 4,*(3), 3–23.

Doleys, E.J. (1961). Are there "kinds" of counselors? *Counseling News and Views, 13,* 5–9.

Grummon, D.L. (1972). Client-centered theory. In B. Stefflre & W.H. Grant (Eds.), *Theories of counseling* (2nd ed., pp. 73–135). New York: McGraw-Hill.

Hart, J.T., & Tomlinson, T.M. (Eds.). (1970). *New directions in client-centered therapy.* Boston: Houghton Mifflin.

Kirschenbaum, H. (1979). *On becoming Carl Rogers.* New York: Delacorte.

Miller, M.J. (1988). A client-centered career counseling assessment method. *Person-Centered Review, 3,*(2), 195–212.

Patterson, C.H. (1964). Counseling: Self clarification and the helping relationship. In H. Borow (Ed.), *Man in a world of work* (pp. 434–459). Boston: Houghton Mifflin.

Patterson, C.H. (1973). *Theories of counseling and psychotherapy* (2nd ed.). New York: Harper & Row.

Raskin, N.J. & Rogers, C.R. (1989). Person-centered therapy. In R.J. Corsini & G. Wedding (Eds.), *Current psychotherapies* (pp. 155–194). Itasca: F.E. Peacock.

Rogers, C.R. (1940). The Process of Therapy. *Journal of Counseling Psychology, 4,* 161–164.

Rogers, C.R. (1942). *Counseling and psychotherapy.* Boston: Houghton Mifflin.

Rogers, C.R. (1951). *Client-centered therapy.* Boston: Houghton Mifflin.

Rogers, C.R. (1957). The necessary and sufficient conditions of therapeutic personality change. *Journal of Consulting Psychology, 21,* 95–103.

Rogers, C.R. (1959). A theory of therapy, personality, and interpersonal relationships, as developed in the client-centered framework. In S. Koch (Ed.), *A study of a science. Study 1: Conceptual and systematic. Vol. 3 Formulations of the person and the social context* (pp. 184–256). New York: McGraw Hill.

Rogers, C.R. (1977). *Carl Rogers on personal power: Inner strength and its revolutionary impact.* New York: Delacorte.

Rogers, C.R. (1980). *A way of being.* Boston: Houghton Mifflin.

Rogers, C.R. (1986). Client-centered approach to therapy. In I.L. Kutash & A. Wolf (Eds.), *Psychotherapist's casebook: Theory and technique in practice* (pp. 2–15). San Francisco, CA: Jossey-Bass.

Rogers, C.R. (1987). Person-centered or client-centered? *Person-Centered Review, 2*(1), 11–13.

Rusalum, H. (1954). New insights on the role of occupational information in counseling. *Journal of Counseling Psychology, 1,* 84–88.

Samler, J. (1964). Occupational exploration in counseling: A proposed reorientation. In H. Borow (Ed.), *Man in a world at work* (pp. 411–433). Boston: Houghton Mifflin.

Seeman, J. (1948). A study of client self-delection of tests? in vocational counseling. *Educational and Psychological Measurement, 8,* 327–346.

Super, D.E. (1950). Testing and using test results in counseling. *Occupations, 29,* 95–97.

Super, D.E. (1951). Vocational adjustment: Implementing a self-concept. *Occupations, 30,* 88–92.

Super, D.E. (1957). The preliminary appraisal in vocational counseling. *Personal and Guidance Journal, 36,* 154–161.

Super, D.E. (1988). Vocational adjustment: Implementing a self-concept. *Career Development Quarterly, 36,* 188–194.

3

Psychodynamic Career Counseling

C. Edward Watkins, Jr.
University of North Texas

Mark L. Savickas
Northeastern Ohio Universities College of Medicine

The term *psychodynamic* refers to psychological systems that use motives, drives, and related covert variables to explain behavior (English & English, 1958). *Psychodynamic career counseling* refers to counseling approaches that are guided by attempts to understand, make meaning of, and utilize individual motives, purposes, and drives to facilitate career exploration. Psychodynamic theories include both Freudian and neo-Freudian theories (e.g., approaches developed by Adler and Sullivan). In various forms, Freudian and neo-Freudian thought have been applied to career development theory, research, and practice.

In this chapter, we examine some of the different psychodynamic theories that have applications for career counseling. The first portion of the chapter considers three psychodynamic theories and the career theory and research derived from these theories. The second portion focuses specifically on the practical application of certain psychodynamic techniques or concepts to career counseling. The three theories we examine include psychoanalytic, Eriksonian, and Adlerian. Although other attempts have been made to apply different psychodynamic theories to vocational behavior (McSherry, 1963), the three we focus on have been of historical importance or, in our opinion, have the most to offer from a theoretical/practical perspective.

PSYCHOANALYTIC, ERIKSONIAN, AND ADLERIAN THEORIES AS THEY RELATE TO CAREER COUNSELING

Psychoanalytic Theory

Early Theorizing About Work, Career, and Vocational Behavior. Freud, the creator of psychoanalysis, is said to have regarded the ability to love and work as being critical to psychological health and well-being. Interestingly, however, if Freud's works are reviewed, he gave minimal attention to work and its importance to humankind. The early analytic theorists who did make major statements about work included the following: Brill (1949), Hendrick (1943), Lantos (1943, 1952), Menninger (1942), and Obendorf (1951). Osipow (1983) stated that "Brill, of all the analysts, devoted the most attention to career choice" (p. 37). We see reflected in Brill's writings two basic ideas that seem to have permeated early psychoanalytic theorizing on work: (a) work is a result of sublimation; and (b) work allows the pleasure and reality principles to be combined. As a product of sublimation, work was a means by which unacceptable impulses and wishes could be channeled into socially acceptable behaviors that contributed to society (e.g., transforming of aggressive, murderous impulses into a surgical occupation). In combining the pleasure and reality principles, work was a means by which the individual could satisfy both id and ego demands.

Like Brill, Menninger (1942) and Obendorf (1951) viewed work as a sublimation. Menninger considered work to be closely aligned with the destructive instinct and the primary method for transforming aggressive energy into something useful. Obendorf (1951) was interested in the investment of libidinal energies in work behaviors. In particular, Obendorf was concerned with how libidinal investment of energy affected excesses (over-industry) or deficiencies (indifference or laziness) in work behavior.

Lantos (1943, 1952) examined the effect of the instincts on work behavior. Critical to one or both of her papers is the concept of self-preservation and the distinction to be drawn between work and play. For her, the *purpose* of an activity was what distinguished work (to preserve oneself or others) from play (to solely gratify instincts). Departing somewhat from the previous papers, Hendrick (1943) proposed the existence of a work principle to complement the pleasure and reality principles. He contended that work is motivated by the need to efficiently use one's intellectual and muscular abilities. The instinct to master was considered to be reflected in work pleasure. For proposing an alternative principle to explain work behavior, Hendrick was criticized (Lantos, 1952; Menninger, 1942; Obendorf, 1951).

Evaluation. In early analytic theorizing about work, the key watchwords seem to have been *sublimation*, the pleasure and reality principles, and *instinctual gratification*. Unfortunately, much of this writing is quite abstract and seems vary far afield from career counseling. The concepts are hard to translate into career work in any meaningful way. Also, as Neff (1965) pointed out, three potential limitations of these papers include: (a) a heavy preoccupation with the instincts; (b) the idea that adult work behavior is determined largely by parent–child interactions in the first 6 years of life; and (c) minimal attention to social and cultural influences on behavior.

Later Theorizing About Work, Career, and Vocational Behavior. If later theorizing is to be examined, then the work of Bordin and his colleagues must be considered. In 1963, Bordin, Nachmann, and Segal presented a psychoanalytically based framework for understanding vocational development. Their model attempted to explain the effects that needs, impulses, and motivations have on vocational behavior. Bordin et al. identified 10 dimensions that can be of value in gaining an understanding of vocational behavior. Some of these were as follows: nurturing (feeding, fostering), oral (aggressive, biting), manipulative (physical, interpersonal), sensual (sight, sound, touch), and anal (acquiring, timing-order, hoarding, smearing). In addition to the 10 dimensions, Bordin et al. also identified other aspects of the dimensions that needed to be considered. Some of these included the degree to which a dimension was important in an occupation, the means by which an impulse was expressed, and whether the occupational activity is directed toward people or things.

To help lend their framework a more concrete feel, Bordin et al. applied their conceptual dimensions to three occupations: social work, plumbing, and accounting. For example, they saw social work as being a very *nurturant* occupation that involved the feeding and fostering (i.e., helping) of clients. Plumbing involved (physical) *manipulation* of pipes and valves and required the use of the *exploratory* (detecting leaks) and *flowing-quenching* (arranging pipes and valves) dimensions. Accounting primarily involved the (interpersonal) *manipulation* through giving advice and recommendations and *anal* dimensions (e.g., acquiring investments, timing-ordering systems and audits). Thus, the idea for Bordin et al. was to consider individual needs and impulses and align these with the occupation that best gratified these needs and impulses.

Bordin et al.'s framework was the first and only serious attempt to apply Freudian theory to building a model of vocations. The model now is more a matter of historical interest than otherwise. It did produce some interesting research but informed practice minimally, and seemed to suffer from some of the same limitations characteristic of early psychoanalytic theorizing about work (e.g., instinctual base). Bordin et al.'s original model did not really consider some of the later developments in Freud's thinking (which gave way to ego psychology and object relations theory).

Although Bordin sees value in his original model, he has attempted to update it (Bordin, 1984). In his revision, Bordin set forth seven propositions that in some respects involve a softening of aspects of his original model. Bordin talked about people striving to get a sense of wholeness through work, the mapping of occupations, and building a unique identity that incorporates aspects of one's mother and father. Bordin continues to be concerned with key motives, intrinsic satisfactions, and the mapping of occupations. However, the more recent key motives and satisfactions Bordin mentioned include curiosity, precision, and power. (Bordin, 1980, 1984, 1987).

Evaluation. Bordin's original model is primarily consistent with classical, id-based, Freudian theory, whereas his revision is more consistent with an ego-analytic or ego-psychology viewpoint. Bordin's original model and early psychoanalytic writings seemingly sensitized counselors to the importance of intrinsic needs, motives, and satisfactions and the way in which these affect vocational behavior. Since the 1960s, however, attention to Bordin's model and psychoanalytic conceptualizations of vocational behavior have been minimal. Analytic theory as it relates to careers seemed to stop some two decades ago. The only real statement since Bordin et al.'s 1963 article has been Bordin's 1984 chapter. Perhaps the harshest but seemingly most realistic statement we could make about a psychoanalytic career theory is that it is now dead or, at best, moribund.

Psychoanalytic Research

Because most relevant psychoanalytic career literature has been summarized elsewhere (Bordin, 1984; Osipow, 1983; Roe, 1964), we only briefly mention it here. Whenever psychoanalytic career studies are considered, several early studies are typically identified (Galinsky, 1962; Nachmann, 1960; Segal, 1961; Segal & Szabo, 1964). Galinsky compared clinical psychology and physics graduate students on their early life experiences and found the two groups indeed did manifest some differences. Nachmann compared lawyers, dentists, and social workers on their perceptions about their early life experiences. Similar to Galinsky, Nachmann found some anticipated differences between the three groups (e.g., mother more dominant in recollections of social workers, parents of dentists most concerned with cleanliness and hygiene). Segal compared writers and accountants, finding that accountants were more controlled emotionally but writers were more hostile and better able to tolerate ambiguous emotional situations. Segal and Szabo again compared groups of writers and accountants and found that accountants had more positive feelings toward their parents and a more firm identification with their fathers. Each of these studies is considered to provide some support for a psychoanalytic model of vocational development.

Other studies, which tested such psychoanalytic concepts as identification and ego strength, have been reviewed by Osipow (1983). Osipow said that "ego strength seems to have been studied most carefully and with the greatest success, [whereas] identification [has been studied] least carefully and with results of a contradictory nature" (p. 54). Bordin (1984) reviewed various studies that he considered to bear upon his revised model. Bordin considered current data to be supportive basically of the psychoanalytic or revised ego psychological model of vocational behavior.

Evaluation. Like psychoanalytic theorizing about careers, research on careers conducted from a psychoanalytic perspective seems at a standstill. In Osipow's (1983) review, most all of the reference material is pre-1970. Bordin's (1984) review, although more supportive in tone, largely consists of pre-1970 research material. Much of the recent material referenced by Bordin is not really vocational in nature and does not seem to be conducted with vocational behavior in mind. More traditional analytic theory and research seems dead in terms of what it has offered career counselors over the past couple of decades.

Eriksonian Theory

Erik Erikson's (1963, 1968) contributions to our understanding about personality are many. Since the early to mid-1960s, some attempts have been made to apply Erikson's theoretical contributions to vocational behavior. However, to place these efforts in perspective, it is first necessary to understand Erikson's theory of psychosocial development.

The primary appeal of Erikson's theory lies in its developmental nature and its inclusion of the entire life span. From Erikson's perspective, individuals pass through eight stages of growth and development. Within each stage, the person is confronted with different psychosocial tasks or crises that require adaptation and resolution. A resolution of the tasks occurring in one stage fortifies the individual and enables him or her to better deal with the developmental tasks of the successive stage. A failure to resolve the tasks of one stage renders the individual less able to deal with the developmental tasks of the successive stage.

The eight stages that are described by Erikson include the following:

1. trust versus mistrust;
2. autonomy versus shame and doubt;

3. initiative versus guilt;
4. industry versus inferiority;
5. identity versus identity confusion;
6. intimacy versus isolation;
7. generativity versus stagnation; and
8. ego integrity versus despair.

Ideally, for each of the eight stages, individuals develop a greater proportion of the first-mentioned (e.g., initiative) instead of the second-mentioned (e.g., guilt) variables. Each of Erikson's eight stages has potential implications for career development. However, the fifth stage—identity versus identity confusion—has received the most attention in the career literature. The identity versus identity confusion stage occurs primarily during the adolescent years when such questions as the following are being asked: Who am I? What are my values? Where am I going with my life? What do I have to offer as an individual?

But what does forging an identity have to do with career development? From an Eriksonian viewpoint, individuals make statements of identity through the occupations they choose. An occupation, then, is a means by which an individual's identity can be implemented. It is a means by which individuals express who they are, how they see themselves in relation to others, and how they see themselves as contributing to the world about them.

Erikson's theory easily lends itself to the formulation of hypotheses about identity and its effects on career development. Some fundamental hypotheses that derive from Erikson's theory are presented subsequently. These hypotheses have been alluded to in the works of Erikson (1968) himself, by researchers extrapolating the work of Erikson to the career domain (cf. Galinsky & Fast, 1966; Hershenson, 1967; Munley, 1977; Tiedeman & O'Hara, 1963), or can be readily inferred from readings of and speculating about Erikson's work and its relevance to career development.

1. *Individuals with highly crystallized identities, in contrast to people who have poorly crystallized identities, will be more apt to have successfully negotiated previous developmental stages.* This is a means of recognizing the importance of having successfully negotiated the tasks and stages that lead up to confronting the identity versus identity confusion stage. Provided these tasks and stages have been dealt with successfully, the likelihood of the individual developing a crystallized sense of identity is enhanced considerably.

2. *Individuals with highly crystallized identities, in contrast to those with poorly crystallized identities, tend to have more useful information at their*

disposal with which to make career decisions. Because of having a well-crystallized identity, these individuals seemingly would be more knowledgeable about themselves, their interests, and abilities. Such knowledge of self would also result in culling career materials for information that would be of the most use personally. A person with a poorly crystallized identity may peruse career materials, but his or her search in theory would not possess the needed direction and foresight. Moreover, this person also would not possess the amount of self-knowledge characteristic of individuals with a well-crystallized identity.

3. *Individuals with highly crystallized identities, in contrast to individuals with poorly crystallized identities, are better able to choose a career that is most suitable to them.* If one has a well-crystallized identity, is able to most effectively use career materials, and has a broad knowledge of information about oneself, then in theory the individual would be able to better make a good career decision. Conversely, the person with a poorly crystallized identity would be more apt to make an inappropriate career decision.

4. *The more crystallized the sense of identity, the more decisive the individual will be in choosing a career.* The more crystallized the sense of identity, the more favorable is the expected outcome. The less crystallized the sense of identity, the less favorable the outcome will be in terms of choosing a career. A solid crystallization of identity, then, is seen as critical to deciding on a career.

5. *Individuals with highly crystallized identities, in contrast to people with poorly crystallized identities, are more career mature.* The person with a highly crystallized identity is more apt to have mature attitudes about careers, the place of careers in people's lives, and the positive and negative features associated with careers and the world of work. In a sense, career maturity is reflective of personal maturity. Individuals with poorly crystallized identities can be considered both personally immature and career immature.

6. *Individuals with well-crystallized identities, when being seen by a counselor for career issues, may benefit most from self-directed activities, career information, and related interventions that capitalize upon their identity development.* If clients have good information about themselves and the career directions in which they want to move, then they may be able to profit most from learning about informational sources of potential value to them (e.g., the *Occupational Outlook Handbook*) or engaging in activities that take into account their self-knowledge. Conversely, for clients with poorly crystallized identities, a counseling process that assists them to better define themselves, learn about who they are, and identify their values and needs would probably be most beneficial.

7. *Individuals with highly crystallized identities, in contrast to individuals*

with poorly crystallized identities, tend to be more satisfied with and adjusted to their careers. The person with a highly crystallized identity seemingly is more satisfied with oneself personally and vocationally. Individuals with highly crystallized identities are more apt to like what they do and feel good about it.

8. *Individuals with highly crystallized identities, in contrast to individuals with poorly crystallized identities, tend to manifest more efficient work behavior, to be more productive, and to manifest less problematic work behavior.* In theory, individuals with highly crystallized identities would know themselves better, make the most appropriate career choices, and be more satisfied with their careers and work. It follows then that this would be reflected in actual work behavior. There may be less depression, absenteeism, and other workrelated problems from employees with well-crystallized identities. There may be more of these problems from employees who possess poorly crystallized identities.

These are but a few examples of the implications Erikson's work can have for career psychology. We have largely focused our discussion here on identity and its effects on vocational behavior. However, all of the eight stages have possible implications for career development (Munley, 1977).

Evaluation.   Erikson's theory seems to have much to offer to career development. The framework is comprehensive and covers the entire life span. The potential importance of each stage for career behavior can easily be seen. But, career theorists need to turn their attention more directly to the implications of the different stages. By examining the stages inclusively, we may be able to develop an all-encompassing picture of how they contribute to the career development process across the life span. So far, this sort of integrative work has been lacking in the career literature.

In terms of theory, the identity stage seems to have been examined most thoroughly. The identity stage has much to offer career counselors from a conceptual standpoint; it provides a means of thinking about identity formation, how identity affects the implementation of self vocationally, and how identity affects other variables that bear upon the career choice process. Thus, the identity stage as conceived by Erikson is a highly useful and usable theoretical construct that can be applied to the career counseling situation.

If there is one criticism to put forth about Erikson's theory, we must acknowledge that little work has been done to translate it into career counseling technique. Erikson's work has focused almost exclusively on the implications of his theory for general personal functioning and addressing personal concerns through therapeutic intervention. It seems equally important to develop more concrete means by which his work can be applied to the career counseling process.

Eriksonian Research

Most of the Eriksonian career research focuses on the identity stage and is summarized here. Munley (1975) found that students who manifested mature career attitudes and made adjusted vocational choices were more successful comparatively in negotiating the first six stages in Erikson's theory. His study supported the idea that career development occurs within the broader context of psychosocial development. Holland, Gottfredson, and Power (1980) attempted to operationalize the vocational identity construct by developing a vocational identity scale. They defined *vocational identity* as "the possession of a clear and stable picture of one's goals, interests, and talents" (p. 1191). Holland et al. reported the evidence to support their vocational identity measure was strong. Based on this study and previous research (Holland, Gottfredson, & Nafziger, 1975; Holland & Holland, 1977), Holland and his associates indicated that individuals high in vocational identity tend to be more confident, mature, and decided than individuals low in vocational identity.

Since Holland et al.'s (1980) study, several investigations examining the usefulness of the vocational identity construct have been performed. In studying a group of medical students, Savickas (1985) found vocational identity to be related to progress in ego-identity achievement and degree of vocational development. Other studies have found the vocational identity construct to be useful for nontraditional students and homemakers (Haviland & Mahaffy, 1985; Olson, Johnston, & Kunce, 1985). Grotevant and Thorbecke (1982) found vocational identity to be related to masculinity for both men and women, but found vocational identity to relate differently to patterns of achievement motivation in men and women.

Earlier research, although not drawing on Holland et al.'s work, still tended to find support for Erikson's theory as it applies to career development. Davis (1965) reported that ego identity was related to career choice commitment. Bell (1968) found the degree of certainty about career choice to be related to ego identity. Rosenfeld (1972) found level of ego identity to affect the degree of similarity between self and probable occupational concepts. Hershenson (1967) reported that a relationship existed between occupational fit and ego identity.

Evaluation. The research has been supportive of Erikson's theory as it relates to career development, suggesting that identity development significantly affects various career variables (e.g., career decisiveness and career adjustment). As Munley (1977) pointed out, "the theory does not lead to predictions in terms of what kind of person chooses a certain kind of job, but rather helps identify personality factors associated with success in handling career development tasks" (p. 266). This statement is also true for the research. The research seems most useful in giving us a base to understand the relationship between personality and vocational development.

The identity research seems to offer some implications for practice. For example, clients low in identity may need special assistance in better establishing a cohesive identity before a career choice can be most viably made. Clients with a good sense of identity may not require such special assistance and may best benefit from informational sources and self-directed activities. Although these implications for career counseling can be drawn, we again are given very little to use in terms of career counseling techniques.

Adlerian Theory

Although Adler considered the importance of work in his writings, only in recent years has more direct attention to Adlerian theory and vocational behavior emerged (McKelvie, 1979; McKelvie & Friedland, 1978, 1981; Savickas, 1988; Watkins, 1984b). Watkins (1984b) developed what is perhaps the most formal attempt to translate Adlerian theory into vocational theory. He examined four variables integral to Adler's theory: lifestyle, life tasks, family atmosphere and family relationships, and early recollections. Some of his theorizing, as well as the theorizing of other Adlerian practitioners, as it relates to these four variables is summarized below.

Lifestyle. Lifestyle has been defined as being synonymous with the concept of "personality" (Dinkmeyer, Pew, & Dinkmeyer, 1979). Mosak (1971) has defined lifestyle as being each person's unique style of perceiving, thinking, and acting. Lifestyle, then, is the overall schema (or apperceptive schema to use Adler's phrasing) by which individuals understand and make sense of the world about them. Numerous lifestyle types (e.g., useful, driving, controlling) have been identified (Adler, 1956; Mosak, 1971).

The lifestyle of the person can often be summarized in one word. This one-word description captures the basic manner in which individuals think about and approach the world. This basic manner is manifested in all spheres of life, including social relationships, love relationships, and work. From a career standpoint, individuals implement their lifestyle through the vocation or occupation they choose.

The three components of the lifestyle have potential vocational implications. The attitude held toward oneself affects the way in which individuals function, present, and think about themselves as workers. The attitude held toward others affects how people regard and work with their co-workers. The attitude held toward the world in general affects the perceived significance of and purpose of work in individuals' lives. Lifestyle is an all encompassing organizational framework that impinges on work, career, and vocational behavior.

Work As Life Task. Adler identified three tasks that individuals confront as they move through life: love, social relations, and work. Because work often occupies people 40 hours each week or more, is the primary means of earning wages and fostering subsistence, and is a primary means by which society is maintained and perpetuated, its identification as a major life task by Adler seems fitting. Within Adlerian theory, the manner in which individuals approach work is considered to influence the type of work and work environment in which they can function. Similarly, the way in which individuals approach work relationships is considered to affect the type and range of people with whom they can work. These ideas reflect a fundamental hypothesis in Adler's theory: That the individual's *lifestyle* will be brought to bear on one's orientation to tasks and relationships. In this regard, work and work behavior are no exceptions.

Social interest—a basic concern for others and desire to contribute—is another important variable to consider in relation to work. Work can be seen as a primary means by which individuals implement social interest (i.e., a means by which they contribute to society). Social interest in theory influences the general output and productivity of the worker. Thus, with ability and related variables being equal, the highly socially interested person in contrast to the person low on social interest should be more productive at work.

Family Atmosphere and Relationships. Family atmosphere refers to the basic environment that characterizes family interactions. What is the predominant mood or atmosphere that exists within the family? From an Adlerian view, children first learn about work and working within the family context. It is thought that perceptions of and relationships with parents (or parental figures) affect the values and expectations individuals hold about work. Through observing the father, the child acquires information about men as workers and the place of men in the world of work. Through observing the mother, similar information is obtained about women. In terms of siblings, they provide an opportunity to learn about working together or with someone else—with a co-worker of sorts. Children are given some of their first lessons in collaboration with their siblings or sibling substitutes (e.g., friends with whom one can create a sibling-like relationship).

Birth order also deserves mention here. Adler identified several birth-order positions, with each being aligned with certain behavioral and personality characteristics. For example, first-born children are often considered to be responsible, dependable, conscientious individuals who feel comfortable with taking charge; the last-born child is sometimes referred to as pampered. Birth order creates a set of interactional–environmental events that potentially affect work identity and work behaviors. By virtue of being a first-born, children can be placed into a family situation that affects their ultimate work style and work behaviors.

Early Recollections. Early recollections (ERs) are memories that occur before the age of 8, are visualizable, and single, specific incidents. ERs are purposeful. People remember certain childhood events or situations because they are meaningful. ERs are reflections of the present (Verger & Camp, 1970).

Just as ERs are important to personality makeup, they also are important to work behavior and vocational functioning. ERs contain information about the manner in which the individual will think about and operate in the world of work. Moreover, ERs are integral in sustaining, supporting, and guiding individuals' work behavior.

Evaluation. Adler's personality theory and approach to personal counseling are regarded as highly practical and useful. Adler's contributions also are useful because they are common sense in nature (i.e., they are easily understood). Many practical concepts of Adler's approach, which have been translated into personal counseling, seem equally usable in career counseling. For example, the concept of a lifestyle type is quite similar in some ways to a trait–factor conceptualization. That family atmosphere and family relationships would affect one's schema about work and work behavior seems tenable. That early recollections would contain information pertinent to work and career seems tenable as well.

Although we believe Adlerian theory has much to offer, two criticisms or observations about Adler's approach as it relates to vocational behavior merit comment: (a) the need to translate therapeutic applications into vocational counseling applications; and (b) the need for more attention to theorizing about vocational behavior from an Adlerian perspective. The major problem, from our perspective, in implementing an Adlerian vocational approach lies in translating a theory of psychotherapy into a theory of vocational counseling. The concepts of lifestyle, social interest, and related variables have been directly applied in psychotherapy and well-illustrated practically (Manaster & Corsini, 1982). But for vocational counseling, the techniques of practice require modification. Recently, creative attempts have been made to render Adlerian concepts more useful to vocational counseling practice (e.g., Savickas, 1988, 1989). For example, rather than using a lifestyle inter view, the vocational counselor can obtain lifestyle information via examination of role models, favorite books, and favorite sayings. Such efforts are more "experience-near" and not as far afield for career exploration purposes as some traditional Adlerian methods. This type of creative work is requisite if Adlerian theory is to prove useful in vocational counseling.

In terms of our second point, there clearly is a need for more direct attention to theorizing about vocational behavior from an Adlerian perspective. As stated earlier, most theorizing about vocational behavior from an Adlerian viewpoint has appeared within the past decade. If the theoretical implications of Adlerian theory for the vocational realm are to be realized, then more specific and direct attention will be needed in this area. We hope further, more microscopic attention will be given to how the variables of lifestyle, social interest, family atmosphere and family relationships, early recollections, and related variables affect individuals' vocational lives.

Adlerian Research

Birth Order. Birth order has received the most attention overall. Basically, research has attempted to examine the relationship between birth order and occupational choice. Higher than expected numbers of first-born children have been found to be represented among physicians, attorneys, members of Congress, teachers, and nurses (Angers, 1974; Layman & Saveracker, 1978; Muhlenkamp & Parsons, 1972; Very & Prull, 1970; Zweigenhaft, 1974). First-born women have been described as being more comfortable, oriented toward, and more likely to be successful in academics (Bryant, 1987; cf. Lynch & Lynch, 1980). Similarly, first-born females have been found to be more highly represented among doctorate recipients (Melillo, 1983). Birth order has also been found to affect patterns of achievement motivation (Snell, Hargrove, & Falbo, 1986).

Although a number of other studies could be cited, the basic conclusion to be drawn from these research efforts is as follows: Birth-order position can have an effect on achievement patterns and the occupation toward which individuals gravitate. With this point acknowledged, however, it is important to bear in mind that in Adler's theory birth order is a psychological position. The perception of the birth position by the child, his or her parents, and siblings is what is most important (see Shulman & Mosak, 1977). Just because someone is born first, this does not automatically have cookbook-type personality implications.

Lifestyle. A few empirical studies have examined the effects of lifestyle on careers and the usefulness of lifestyle analysis in career assessment. For example, Cline, Riordan, and Kern (1978) found that an Adlerian lifestyle analysis could be as effective as the Self-Directed Search (Holland, 1985, Appendix B) in predicting vocational choice. Gentry, Winer, Sigelman, and Phillips (1980) found that some of the Adlerian lifestyle types (as defined by Thorne, 1975) were related to some of the vocational personality types put forth in Holland's (1985) theory. Bichekas and Newlon (1983) studied a group of hospice home-care nurses in an effort to better understand their lifestyle dynamics; they reported that the nurses' lifestyles were characterized by a desire for control and predictability. In performing a similar study, Emerson and Watson (1986) also found a desire for control and predictability to characterize the lifestyles of hospice home-care nurses. Last, Newlon and Mansager (1986) reported that 66% of their sample of Catholic priests were identified as being of the "right, superior, or good lifestyle." These five studies form the bulk of what has been done empirically in relation to lifestyles and vocational behavior.

Early Recollections. In recent years, the most research attention examining the relationship between Adlerian concepts and vocational behavior has focused on early recollections (ERs). Holmes and Watson (1965), in studying the ERs of education and medical science subjects, concluded that the content of early memories was related to an individual's vocational choice. Manaster and Perryman (1974) studied students representing five different professional groups and found that the ERs of the respective groups contained some distinguishing characteristics (e.g., nurses' memories mentioned mother figures more). Attarian (1978) studied students majoring in one of six majors (e.g., drama, astronomy). Based on ERs, he reported that judges generally could categorize students correctly into their respective major areas.

In three investigations, Hafner and Fakouri (1984a, 1984b; Hafner, Fakouri, & Etzler, 1986) studied the ERs of different student groups. In their first study, they found the ERs of students majoring in accounting, secondary education, and psychology to possess distinguishing features. They next found the memories of graduate students in clinical psychology, dentistry, and law to also be distinctive. Last, they found the memories of students in chemical, electrical, and mechanical engineering to differ. As Hafner et al. stated, the "manifest content of ERs has some value for distinguishing among occupational groups, no matter how similar the occupations, and should be seriously considered for use in vocational guidance" (p. 365). Other similar studies have also found support for the vocational relevance of ERs (Elliot, Amerikaner, & Swank, 1987; McFarland, 1988).

Social Interest. Although social interest is one of the most important concepts of Adler's theory, it is the least researched in regard to vocational behavior. Watkins (1984a), as one aspect of a research study, found social interest to positively relate to self-management effectiveness in students' work behaviors. Amerikaner, Elliot, and Swank (in press) examined the social interest, vocational preferences, and job satisfaction of individuals working and majoring in six areas (e.g., mechanical technology, biology). Interestingly, they found that social interest was positively related to job satisfaction and recommended that counselors incorporate discussion of it into career counseling.

Evaluation. Adlerian-oriented research on vocational variables suggests that birth order, lifestyle, early recollections, and social interest have implications for understanding vocational behavior. However, the best we can now say is that we have a tentative base supporting the relevancy of Adlerian variables to the career counseling process. In most areas reviewed here, the number of research studies has been all too few. Admittedly, a basic problem with Adlerian research has been a lack of viable instrumentation to use in studying Adler's concepts. However, attempts have been made to develop more valid and reliable tools to measure Adler's concepts (Watkins, 1982, 1983). As these efforts continue, the sophistication and credibility of Adlerian studies on vocational variables will be enhanced substantially.

Although it is encouraging to see more empirical attention given to Adlerian theory, it is not always clear what some of the research means for career counseling. For example, although the early recollections research is interesting and potentially useful, it remains for memory differences between groups to be translated concretely into meaningful counseling information. This type of research will need replication to see if memory differences found for a certain group stand up when an identical occupational group of different individuals is studied. Moreover, if differences in ERs exist in subgroups of a particular occupation, as Hafner et al. (1986) suggest, then the possible configurations of memory differences within and across occupations could be so large as to defy comprehension. Last, if the concept of lifestyle is to be effectively studied, it seems important to devise an "experience-near" lifestyle typology that translates lifestyle types into meaningful vocational behaviors. These are but a few of the questions or issues that present themselves. With some of these questions, problems, and issues recognized, there still appears to be a promising beginning to testing the relevancy of Adlerian theory to vocational behavior and career counseling. As referred to earlier, however, the need to render the theory and research "experience-near" to career counseling and vocational behavior is critical. We hope future efforts will better address this concern.

PSYCHODYNAMIC CAREER COUNSELING

The first half of this chapter contained a review of psychodynamic contributions to vocational development theory and the psychology of occupations. Few of these contributions explicitly dealt with career counseling. Thus, little of this knowledge has been presented to counselors in a readily useable way. Unfortunately, most practitioners have little inclination or time to translate research findings on the psychodynamics of vocational development and occupations into career counseling methods. Moreover, many of those who have tried to translate these contributions into practice became discouraged because they could not blend psychodynamic constructs with contemporary vocational guidance methods. This failure was not their fault; rather, as we argue here, it is a major flaw of psychodynamic vocational research. The few practitioners who found effective ways to translate psychodynamic constructs into practice have done so by shifting their perspective from objective vocational guidance to subjective career counseling.

The remainder of this chapter consists of two parts. In the first part, we analyze the relevance of psychodynamic theory to career counseling. This analysis is based on a comparison of the objective and subjective perspectives on vocational behavior and the use of these perspectives in vocational guidance and career counseling. In the second part, we describe the predominant psychodynamic model for career counseling along with pertinent assessment techniques and counseling methods.

Perspective

Counselors may take two perspectives on their clients' vocational behavior—the objective and the subjective. The objective view consists of conceptions of the client formed by observers, whereas the subjective view consists of apprehending the client's conception of his or her personal experience. Although the English language does not explicitly recognize this distinction, other languages do. For example, in German *Personlichkeit* denotes the actor's interpersonal style and the impression that one makes on others. *Personalitat* denotes the actor's understanding of the reasons for his or her behavior (MacKinnon, 1944). In this chapter, the word "vocational" denotes the objective perspective, so vocational behavior, development, and guidance all deal with *Personlichkeit*. When we deal with *Personalitat* we use the word "career" to mean "subjective career" or an individual's thoughts about his or her past, present, and future vocational life.

The Objective Perspective

Vocational guidance operates from the objective perspective. Guidance counselors help clients become more objective, realistic, and rational in making vocational choices. The guidance paradigm as first proposed by Parsons (1909), and still practiced by many counselors today, consists of three steps. First, counselors help clients increase their self-knowledge through objective appraisal and discussion of their abilities and interests. Together, a client and counselor articulate the client's strengths and weaknesses and how they differ from those of other people. Second, counselors help clients gather realistic occupational information and learn how differences in abilities and interests structure the world of work. Third, counselors help clients rationally identify and explore occupations at the levels and in the fields that correspond to a client's abilities and interests. Guidance concludes when clients use "true reasoning" to match themselves to fitting occupations and then make viable occupational choices that should eventuate in job success and satisfaction.

Vocational guidance always has been based on a community's consensually valid attempts to objectively explain individual differences in behavioral dispositions. Objective explanations use the common sense of the group, not the private sense of individuals. Thus, objective explanations are not metaphysical realities, they are merely intersubjective agreements (Berger & Luckman, 1966) or social facts. The common sense of some ancient cultures looked to the stars and astrology to explain individual differences. The Greeks of antiquity relied on Galen's humoral formulation of temperament (i.e., melancholic, choleric, phlegmatic, and sanguine) to explain individual differences. The explanations offered by palmistry and phrenology were widely popular in U. S. society at the turn of the century. In fact, Lysander Richards' (1881) textbook, *Vocophy*, relied on phrenology to explain vocational behavior.

Parsons' (1909), in his seminal formulation of the vocational guidance model, shifted counselors' thinking from phrenology to character traits. While Parsons wrote *Choosing a Vocation*, psychologists were already developing trait theory to explain individual differences. Traits quickly replaced astrology, palmistry, phrenology, and constitutional types as common sense and scientific explanations of behavior.

Trait theory of individual differences sustains the contemporary practice of vocational guidance. Trait theory attributes recurring uniformities in a person's social behavior to personality structure. Thus, behavioral continuity reflects personality and behavioral discontinuity reflects the environmental demands. The underlying dimensions that structure behavioral clusters are called *traits*. Scientific and lay observers of an actor encode their impressions of the actor's social conduct in trait vocabularies. For example, an observer might attribute a person's behavior to the trait of honesty. Note that this trait is value laden. According to Hogan (1983), "the primary function of trait ascription is to evaluate other people, specifically, to evaluate their potential as resources for the group" (p. 60). Thus, in a group that divides labor among its members, traits can be used to assign work roles. The honest person would make a better banker than would a dishonest person. Today, trait theory offers several different approaches that counselors may use to appraise individuals and describe occupational groups.

Contemporary practitioners of vocational guidance operationalize the trait-theory approach to objective vocational guidance with actuarial methods. The counselor as actuary estimates the probabilities of a client succeeding in various occupations. Counselors base these estimates on data gathered through assessment of the client with psychometric instruments that objectively measure individual aptitudes and interests. After matching a client's aptitude test and interest inventory results to aptitude and interest patterns that characterize various occupations, counselors can recommend fitting occupational levels and fields to the client. The enormous popularity of instruments like the Strong Campbell Interest Inventory, Kuder inventories, Differential Aptitude Test, and General Aptitude Test Battery testify to the widespread use of trait theory and actuarial methods. Readers who are unfamiliar with the actuarial approach to objective vocational guidance in its most highly developed form can find its epitome in an article by Goodyear and Healy (1988).

The objective perspective of trait theory and the common sense of the actuarial method permits counselors to offer vocational guidance to groups of clients at the same time. For example, school counselors can test a whole 10th-grade class of students as a group and later interpret the results to individuals in a group by explaining trait theory of individual and occupational differences, how to interpret one's test results, the steps in the matching model, and how to gather occupational information. In fact, the objective perspective even allows individuals or groups to get vocational guidance without meeting a counselor. Holland's Self-Directed Search (1985, Appendix B) and Paper Guidance System (1974) lets students, on their own, assess themselves, learn about occupational differences and the structure of the world-of-work, and match themselves to fitting occupations. Computerized programs for vocational guidance can assess clients, give customized test interpretations, and vocational guidance without counselors being present.

The Subjective Perspective

The objective perspective of vocational guidance supported by trait theory, actuarial methods, and psychometric instruments has dominated counseling practice during this century. The objective perspective does not recognize the significance of subjective experience (*Personalitat*) nor seek to understand it in the subject's own terms. Thus, the possible contributions to counseling practice that may be envisioned from the subjective perspective on vocational choice have remained relatively unexplored.

Career counseling operates from the subjective perspective. It helps clients understand their behavior from their own point of view. When operating from the objective perspective, the counselor acts authoritatively as a representative of the community and its common sense. When operating from the subjective perspective, the counselor elicits clients' subjective conceptions of themselves and their world and acts as interpreter to help clients understand their selves and the meaning they give to their lives. The counselor elicits occupational possibilities, not through traits, but through facilitating self-exploration and interpreting meaning. These procedures help clients acknowledge and discuss unexamined (or unconscious) ideas and feelings they have about making vocational choices. These personal ideas and feelings compose the client's private-sense conceptions of self, work, and life.

Private sense cannot comprehend traits as an explanation of vocational behavior. Individuals do not use differences between themselves and others to explain their behavior to themselves. In fact, individual difference variables do not exist for individuals. Without objective feedback from teachers or counselors, people do not ordinarily sense their position relative to other people across a taxonomy of traits. What they do sense is their own needs and goals. Individuals comprehend these needs and goals as the reason for their behavior. Purpose, not traits, structure actors' causal explanations. The behavioral clusters, which from the objective perspective are explained by traits, are explained by actors as intentional action. People use subjective purpose and resultant life patterns, not objective traits, to explain behavioral continuity, sustain identity coherence, and foresee future behavior.

Life pattern theory sustains contemporary career counseling. At mid-century, Super (1954) elaborated the subjective perspective on career counseling by developing "career pattern counseling." Super devised career pattern theory as an extension of life pattern theory. Essentially, the theory of life patterns states that analysis of an individual's life history reveals tendencies and patterns that can characterize that life story. The life history approach to career pattern counseling seeks to aid the individual by identifying past and probable future patterns of development.

> The assumption underlying this approach is that one way to understand what an individual will do in the future is to understand what he did in the past. It postulates that one way to understand what he did in the past is to analyze the sequence of events and the development of characteristics in order to ascertain the recurring themes and underlying trends. This type of analysis differs from the actuarial method in which each specific factor is evaluated and weighted and a prediction of behavior is made on the basis of observed correlations with similar behaviors of other people. In the life pattern approach an attempt is made to project trends into the future, to extrapolate, modifying each "thema" in the light of others in order to predict future development and behavior. (Super, 1954, pp. 13–14)

Super developed a version of life history method that he called "extrapolation based on thematic analysis." Essentially, this method enables counselors to identify life themes by analyzing a case history. When using the thematic-extrapolation method to clinically study clients and their development, counselors act more like biographers than actuaries (Savickas, 1988).

Psychodynamics of Object and Subject

The dichotomy between objective and subjective perspectives may be used to analyze the failure of psychodynamic theory to significantly influence research and practice in vocational psychology. Psychodynamic theory is a tool to understand the subjective outlook of a client not the objective characteristics of that client. Counselors examine the psychodynamics of subjects not objects. Psychodynamic theory falters when counselors try to use it from an objective perspective. It just does not blend well with the study of objects, trait theory, or actuarial methods; consequently, the published attempts to use psychodynamic theory as a basis for vocational guidance impress many readers as awkward or forced. The next three paragraphs discuss the three major ways in which scholars have tried to use psychodynamic theory from the objective perspective.

The first way in which psychologists tried to link psychodynamic theory to vocational guidance was to replace interests and abilities with psychodynamic constructs. The most comprehensive attempt was offered by Bordin et al. (1963). As described earlier, they used 10 psychoanalytic dimensions to differentiate occupations. "Assuming then, that a counselor should wish to base vocational counseling on this framework, a trait–factor approach would be used, but client modes of impulse gratification, psychosexual development, and anxiety level would take the place of interests and abilities" (Osipow, 1983, p. 42). Berg's (1954) presentient comment captures the reaction many counselors have had to this approach: "both trait and psychoanalytic theory were organizations of knowledge concerning human behavior. At a time when words of Freudian flavor such as *libido* or *anal eroticism* would cause many people to blush or bristle, the same people received findings about aptitudes or abilities with a quiet acceptance usually reserved for gospels" (p. 19). Another example of attempts to replace interests and aptitudes with psychodynamic constructs is the effort to classify occupational differences using Adlerian constructs and the early recollection technique. Because Adlerians emphasize the social rather than the sexual, their attempts have fared better. However, to date, attempts to replace interests and aptitudes with psychodynamic constructs, whether pursued by Freudians or Adlerians, have played only a minor role in vocational psychology and guidance.

The second approach to linking psychodynamic theory to vocational guidance has fared slightly better than attempts to devise a psychodynamic trait taxonomy of people and occupations. In this approach, interests and aptitudes are not replaced. Instead they are interpreted as expressions of more fundamental psychodynamic constructs. Counselors use psychodynamic theory as a framework to interpret interest inventories and ability tests. A classic example of this approach is Goldberg and Gechman's framework for making psychodynamic inferences from Strong Vocational Interest Blank profiles. In order to go beyond objective trait interpretation of the scores, they offer a "systematic process for organizing SVIB results within a psychodynamic framework and for using this framework for making inferences about personality" (Goldberg & Gechman, 1976, p. 286). They noted that clients need help to realize the importance of overall patterns and long-term developmental issues. Although Gobetz (1964) did not focus exclusively on psychodynamics, he provided counselors with many psychodynamic inferences in his interpretive syllabus for the Kuder Preference Record.

The third approach to using psychodynamic theory in objective vocational guidance has been the most successful, yet, at best, its success in influencing practice has been slight. The slight success it enjoys comes from its recognition that making psychodynamic inferences from interest inventory results may be circuitous. To be more direct, some counselors add to their assessment battery a measure of a psychodynamic construct. Typically, they do this by including a measure of psychological needs in their vocational test battery. Although a few counselors measure needs with projective techniques such as the Thematic Apperception Technique and the Rotter Sentence Completion Blank, most counselors who measure clients' psychological needs do so with structured personality inventories such as the Edwards Personal Preference Schedule and the Personality Research Form. In practice, counselors who administer needs inventories often use the results to explain the origin of interests. For example, they might tell clients that their social service interests arise from their psychological needs for nurturance, dominance, and affiliation. For clients with undifferentiated interests, counselors may use clients' most pressing needs to predict which interests might emerge and to prescribe exploration activities that can stimulate interest crystallization. The limited success of needs assessment in improving vocational guidance and characterizing occupations has been thoroughly analyzed by Osipow (1983, chapters 3 and 7).

Most practicing counselors have never embraced these three approaches to using psychodynamic theory in objective vocational guidance. We think that three reasons explain this lack of acceptance by counselors. First, psychodynamic theory has not been elaborated with work in mind. Its focus is psychosexual and psychosocial not psychoeconomic. Recent contributions have addressed this gap in psychodynamic theory (e.g., LaBier, 1986; Rohrlich, 1980), but for career counselors these efforts may be too little and too late. Second, the language of psychodynamic theory is vague, provocative, artistic, and psychopathologically oriented. As such, it cannot easily compete with the commonsense language of trait theory in holding the attention of career counselors who are more pragmatic, empiric, and health-oriented. And third, psychodynamic constructs have not been shown by rhetoric or research to be an improvement over the traditional guidance constructs of interests and abilities. We expect that occasional attempts to use psychodynamic constructs in an actuarial way will continue to occur in the future. However, we do not anticipate that they will ever be persuasive or particularly useful to most career counselors. This is not to say that psychodynamic theory cannot be useful to career counselors. On the contrary, psychodynamic theory and methods offer a way to operationalize the subjective perspective on career decision making. In fact, if psychodynamic methods ever become popular among career counselors, then it probably will be due to increased interest in the subjective perspective on career development.

The great potential value of psychodynamic theory for vocational counselors lies in its model and methods for understanding subjects' views of their vocational choices and how they make and implement their choices. Psychodynamic theory assists the counselor as biographer to understand a client's private sense by attending to life patterns. Psychodynamic theory offers an apposite method for identifying life patterns and extrapolating them to career pattern counseling, the life history (case study) method. Career counselors may do well to follow the lead of Henry Murray, who in synthesizing the psychodynamic theories of Freud, Adler, and Jung, made the life history method central in his thinking about assessment. Although not the only way, it may be the most developed way of implementing Super's thematic-extrapolative approach to career pattern counseling. While counselors wait for other methods to emerge from life-cycle, ecological, biographical, and hermeneutical theories (Collin & Young, 1986; Sonnenfeld & Kotter, 1982), they already have available well-developed psychodynamic methods.

Blending Objective and Subjective Perspectives

The real value of psychodynamic career counseling is to complement the objective perspective with the subjective perspective. Viewing clients from both the objective and subjective perspectives offers counselors two vantage points on a client. From the first position the counselor attempts to "see how the client is like others" and from the second position the counselor attempts "to understand the rhythm, the themes, and the cycles of that life" (Frey, 1973, p. 38). From these two positions, counselors can consider aptitudes and interests in a matrix of life experience as recommended by Berg (1954). By integrating the objective and subjective pictures of a client, career counselors may be more useful in helping clients mesh their "inner reality" with "outer reality." Taking two perspectives also enriches counselors' trait-theory conception of "congruence" as the fit between the objective person and objective environment. Adding the subjective person and the subjective environment to definitions of congruence enables counselors to deal with the psychodynamics of fit. A model of fit that comprehends both objective and subjective fit (such as the one depicted in Fig. 3.1) allows counselors to address psychodynamic variables such as reality contact, accuracy of self-knowledge, defense mechanisms, and coping strategies.

Counselors who understand clients from both perspectives have a better picture of clients' vocational development and career decision making. With this picture, counselors can do more than objectively describe how a client compares to the group and translate the client's interests and abilities into fitting occupations. Counselors can also subjectively explain clients' interests and abilities, not as possessions, but as solutions to problems of growing up (Carter, 1940). By combining trait descriptions and life-theme explanations of interests (as Uncle Remus might say to Briar Rabbit, "what you got and how you use it") counselors can more effectively clarify clients' choices and enhance their ability to decide. The purpose of combining the objective and subjective perspectives in career counseling is to help clients find socially viable (objective) and personally suitable (subjective) vocational opportunities to develop their life themes and grow through work. Such work will feel essential, not external, because it is an integral part of the life theme.

Psychodynamic career counseling is not a replacement for objective vocational guidance, it is a supplement. As Super (1954) commented counselors "must use both methods, sometimes emphasizing the one, and sometimes the other" (p. 16). Despite the advantages of combining

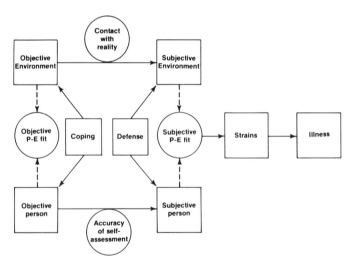

FIG. 3.1. A model describing the effects of psychosocial stress in terms of fit between the person and the environment. Concepts within circles are discrepancies between the two adjoining concepts. Solid lines indicate causal effects. Broken lines indicate contributions to interaction effects (from Harrison, 1978, copyright © 1978 by Wiley. Reprinted by permission).

objective and subjective perspectives in career counseling, it requires more time than most counselors can afford to allot to every career client. Thus, it is not for everyone (Holland, 1973). In particular, it is not for those clients who can be served effectively by group guidance, computer-assisted counseling, or paper guidance systems.

Four types of clients seem to benefit greatly from adding the subjective perspective. The first type are those clients who seem indecisive as opposed to undecided or who seem particularly unrealistic in self-appraisal and naive about life. Interest inventories assume a certain degree of maturity in the respondent. Indecisive and unrealistic clients often need help to become more complete before taking these inventories in a meaningful way. The second type are those clients referred by other counselors as "difficult cases" and those who have already finished vocational guidance with a different counselor. We find that the subjective perspective often reveals the private-sense misconceptions that made them difficult clients and frees them to develop their careers. The third type are adult clients such as mid-career changers, displaced homemakers, and discharged employees who already have an objective view of their interests and abilities. And the fourth type includes culturally different clients who may not be adequately served by an "objective" view that draws on a common sense different from their own.

Model, Techniques, and Methods

In this section, we briefly discuss the psychodynamic life-theme model along with associated assessment techniques and counseling methods. In doing this, we identify resources for further study and suggest how counselors may begin to add psychodynamic career counseling to their repertoires.

Life-Theme Model

A common model for psychodynamic career counseling emerges from all psychodynamic theories because each of these theories deals explicitly with life themes. All psychodynamic theories conceptualize people as somewhat neurotic and consider overcoming neurosis to be the most important life problem that faces each person (Hogan, 1983). A person's neurosis has a theme that various psychodynamic theorists have called a *life line, lifestyle, life plan, life drama, life plot,* and *life project.* Psychodynamic theorists vary in how they conceptualize life-theme content (e.g., Freud's oedipal complex, Erikson's identity confusion, or Adler's inferiority feelings). Yet, the theorists share the view that life-theme process involves adaptation to overcome adversity, that is, "improvements in the organism's pattern of interactions with its environment which increase its chance for survival, cultural self-realization, and perpetuation of its type" (Rado, 1969, pp. 7–8). Adaptation develops the unfinished individual toward more completeness, wholeness, and integration.

Freud succinctly described this process of moving through life when he wrote, "Where id was, there ego shall be." He asserted that "I" develops from mastering "it." Adler's phrase to describe this same process was "from a felt minus to a fictional plus." They both meant that the life process consists of actively mastering what you passively suffer. As Milton wrote in *Paradise Lost*, "our torments also may in length of time become our elements." Less poetically, MacArthur said that victims must become victors. In short, people develop by turning symptoms into strengths and strengths into social contributions. Subjective career counseling deals with turning neurotic symptoms into strengths and objective vocational guidance deals with turning personal strengths into social contributions. The substance of vocational decision making can be viewed both ways. For example, interests may be viewed as both solutions to problems in growing-up and salient personal traits that connect an individual to the community.

To us, an article by Csikszentmihalyi and Beattie (1979) serves as the best introduction to the study of life-theme theory and its applicability to career development. After comparing the concepts of life theme presented in different theories, they succinctly defined a *life theme* as "a problem or set of problems which a person wishes to resolve above everything else and the means the person finds to achieve solution" (p. 50). They asserted that individuals' career choices correspond to their chosen method for solving their central problem. Based on their study of 30 male adults, Csikszentmihalyi and Beattie concluded that life themes develop in four steps as people (a) recognize an existential stress, (b) label the main problem, (c) state the cause of the problem in a form that allows solution, and (d) adopt a method of solving the problem. They go on to discuss this conclusion and illustrate it with several case reports. While reading these case reports, counselors may begin to think about assessment techniques and counseling methods with which they could implement the life-theme model of career development.

Counselors who apply the life-theme model in their psychodynamic career counseling typically use clinical assessment techniques to identify life themes, interpretation methods to increase clients' understanding of their life themes, and counseling methods to examine the current meaning and extrapolate future implications of the themes. Clinical assessment techniques provide methods for intensive study of the meaning that an individual attributes to self, other people, and life. Simply asking clients to report the meaning that structures their lives rarely elicits a usable answer because most people do not realize that their life has a theme. They are so embedded in the webs of meaning that they have created that they do not imagine the absence of this meaning nor conceive the presence of a pattern. After they discern the pattern, counselors use interpretation methods to reveal these tacit, unexamined, or unconscious life themes to clients. Counselors select interpretation methods that help clients recognize who they are and accept themselves not interpretation methods that label or diagnose clients. When clients can articulate their life themes and view their careers as biographies, counselors use thematic-extrapolative counseling methods to ease clients' self-exploration of their life themes in relation to future goals and present decision making as well as methods that encourage clients to act based on how things look to them.

Assessment Techniques

Counselors who wish to add psychodynamic career counseling to their repertoires usually need to develop skill in assessing life themes to augment their existing skill in interpretation and counseling methods. Counselors who can sense patterns are better prepared to develop skill in clinical assessment than counselors who have difficulty with pattern recognition. Those counselors who want to develop a sense for patterns usually need coaching and encouragement from colleagues while they learn psychodynamic assessment techniques. Without this support, they may too quickly conclude that clinical assessment requires a gift that they lack and then continue to rely exclusively on objective psychometric instruments and actuarial methods. Our experience has taught us that if these counselors persevere, then they can develop skill at clinical assessment. Neophytes often benefit from experimenting with several different psychodynamic assessment techniques until they find one that suits them. Fortunately, they have many alternative techniques to choose among because counselors have adapted numerous psy-chodynamic assessment techniques for use in career assessment (Klopfer, 1965). Four of these are particularly worthy of consideration: structured interviews, projective techniques, autobiographies, and card sorts.

Structured Interviews. A structured interview is useful for assessing life themes. During a structured interview, a counselor asks the client a predetermined set of questions that have been designed to elicit life-theme material. Counselors who prefer Adler's version of psychodynamic theory, Individual Psychology (IP), have developed a structured interview to investigate life themes revealed by clients' descriptions of family life during their formative years. Two recent versions of the traditional IP lifestyle interview provide counselors with excellent self-instructional materials (Powers & Griffith, 1987; Shulman & Mosak, 1988). McKelvie and Friedland (1978, 1981) adapted the IP lifestyle interview "for pinpointing the life question" during career counseling. In their "career goal counseling" model, McKelvie and Friedland recommend that counselors formulate a life question that expresses a client's life goal and the obstacles that block movement toward it. Then counselors may help clients recognize their answers to the life question by articulating clients' strategies for moving toward their goals. McKelvie and Friedland gave case illustrations to show how counselors may use their "goals/obstacles/strategies" paradigm to help career clients clarify what they wish to do with their lives, articulate obstacles that stand in their way, and develop effective strategies to move toward their goals and cope with obstacles.

Two other structured interviews merit consideration. Holloway (1973) devised the Life Script Questionnaire to implement the Transactional Analysis approach to assessing life themes. The questionnaire consists of 56 questions selected to reveal a client's life plan. Although certainly not psychodynamic in origin, the genogram assessment technique developed by family therapists has been used by career counselors to clinically study clients' individuality. Okiishi (1987) described a model for using a three-generational graphic model of a family of origin to assess career clients' self-observation and world-view generalizations as they relate to career development. Okiishi demonstrated this assessment technique by presenting and discussing one client's genogram. An in-service instructional videotape produced by the Menninger Foundation (1985) teaches counselors how a genogram can be used to ease self-exploration of life themes expressed through love and work.

Projective Techniques.   Like structured interviews, projective techniques for psychodynamic assessment have been adapted for career counseling. In particular, the Adlerian early recollection technique has been used by career counselors. McKelvie (1979) discussed how to use the early recollection technique with the goals/obstacles/strategies counseling paradigm. Forer (1957) and Dole (1958) devised vocational sentence completion blanks and Ammons, Butler, and Herzig (1950) devised a vocational adaptation of the Thematic Apperception Test. Although the Forer Vocational Survey and Ammons' Vocational Apperception Test have been commercially published, neither technique has been highly developed or widely used.

Autobiographies. In addition to the adaptations of these classic projective techniques, career counselors have used another projective technique that also relies on verbal production. The future autobiography technique uses an open-ended statement to elicit personal scenarios of the future. Statements that have been used include: "Write your obituary as it will appear in the New York Times 50 years from now" and "Imagine life goes great for you, then write in detail about the events that occur during a typical day in your life 10 years from now." From clients' "self-drawn cognitive maps of how their future lives will be purposive" (Maw, 1982), counselors extract life themes. Other counselors use autobiography stimulus questions that include the past and present. For example, Danielson and Rothney (1954) asked clients to respond to three questions: "What kind of person am I?," "How did I get that way?," and "What do I hope to become?" Hahn (1963) used three similar topics: "What I think I am like," "How other people see me," and "What I would like to be like." To learn more about the autobiography technique, counselors should read Annis' (1967) discussion of the uses of autobiographies in counseling psychology.

Card Sorts. Some clinical assessment techniques combine interview and projective techniques. In these approaches counselors use projective stimulus materials to evoke clients' opinions about themselves and work. Then counselors use interview techniques to elaborate and explore the meaning of clients' initial responses. During this dialogue, counselors listen for themes to evolve and then help clients to recognize these themes. Vocational card sorts exemplify this approach. Card sorts present stimulus material, one per card, such as occupational titles and leisure activities. Clients sort a set of cards into three piles indicating "would choose," "no opinion," or "would not choose." During the sorting, the counselor asks clients to think aloud so that the counselor can hear clients' interpretations of the stimuli and reasons for each sorting decision. After completing the sorting task, the counselor interviews the client. Dolliver (1967) considered vocational card sorts to be "a structured interview technique that deals mainly with a client's reasons for making the choices" (p. 920). Moreover, Goldman (1983) considered vocational card sorts to be "similar to a work sample or a projective test, the card sort thus permits observation of the person's approach to the task fast or slow, decisive or hesitant, specific or vague, clear or cloudy, simple or complex, informed or uninformed about the world of work" (p. 108). Tyler (1961) implicitly addressed the use of vocational card sorts to assess life themes when she wrote that "the core of individuality consists of a person's choices and the way he organizes them" (p. 195). Counselors who want to use card sorts should read a chapter on this technique by Slaney and McKinnon-Slaney (1990) that discusses its history, current versions, variety of uses as well as a case report that shows how life theme emerges from the sorting task.

Counseling Methods

Several career counseling theorists have elaborated methods that blend the objective and subjective perspectives on career counseling. The most widely known are probably Super's (1957) scheme for the cyclical use of directive and nondirective methods and Crites' (1976) model for comprehensive career counseling. Whether or not many career counseling practitioners systematically blend the objective and subjective in their practices is unknown. The camps may be so divided that most practitioners of objective vocational guidance may ignore psychodynamic methods and most practitioners of subjective career counseling may eschew actuarial methods. However, there are several published accounts of career counseling practice that explicitly integrate objective and subjective methods for interpretation, individual counseling, and group counseling.

Interpretation Methods. Structured interviews, projective techniques, autobiographies, and card sorts have been presented here as assessment techniques. These clinical techniques deal with the person directly as opposed to actuarial assessment techniques that deal with the person via social comparisons. Maybe this is why Goldman (1983) noted that clinical assessment techniques are as much counseling methods as they are assessment techniques. The boundary between their use for assessment or counseling is permeable, thus leaving counselors great leeway in how they present the assessment results to clients. Counselors may use test-interpretation methods to make the presentation a discrete activity or microintervention within counseling or integrate the presentation of assessment results into the ongoing counseling dialogue by using answers to assessment questions as counseling leads. Discussions of methods for and research on test interpretation (Biggs & Keller, 1982; Goodyear, 1988) indicate that both microintervention and integration can be effective yet we prefer the integrative method proposed by Crites (1981) because it blends the objective and subjective perspectives on test interpretation.

Regardless of the approach to presenting assessment results to clients, the counselor operating from the psychodynamic life-theme model seeks to explain the client to the client by making intelligible interconnections among the episodes of the client's life. To do this, counselors may summarize their understanding of the client's life theme to answer the subjective assessment question, "What is this person trying to do?" (Dailey, 1971) and the objective assessment question, "Which abilities and interests can the client use to continue to do this in the world of work?" (p. 45). In formulating integrative interpretations, counselors should use their knowledge of psychodynamic theory, the client, and one's own self. Counselors may then present their "summation of understanding" (Powers & Griffith, 1987) in the form of hypotheses about the client's uniqueness and similarity to other people. Effective interpretations move clients to see themselves and their choices more clearly, prepare clients to examine the issues and make the decisions that prompted them to seek career counseling, and help clients to organize their diffuse career tensions into specific vocational intentions.

Career-Style Methods. To blend the objective and subjective perspectives on individual career counseling, Savickas (1989) devised a method that integrates the psychodynamic life-theme model with Holland's (1985) actuarial model. Rather than adapting existing materials, Savickas developed a structured interview for life-theme assessment that uses the typical subject matter of vocational counseling. A sequence of eight stimulus questions organizes the career-style interview. The questions deal with role models, favorite books, magazines, leisure activities, school subjects, mottos, ambitions, and decisions. He explained the rationale for each question, discussed how to present them, and specified how to assess client responses. Assessment of responses leads to identification of life theme and determination of a Holland RIASEC code. The assessment produces ideas about a client's private sense, career style, career path, interests, and occupational prospects. Career-style counseling then uses this assessment information along with the results of Holland's Self-Directed Search as it progresses along five structured phases: (a) summation of understanding of life theme and career path, (b) examination of private sense as it affects career decision making, (c) discussion of how clients' interests extend their life stories and point to certain occupations as useful, (d) preparation of a list of occupations to explore and instruction on how to explore them, and (e) coping with choice barriers.

Transactional Analysis Methods. An even more complete blending of the objective and subjective perspectives occurs in Kurtz' (1974) Transactional Analysis (T.A.) program for career counseling in groups. After explaining the rationale, Kurtz described a structured program for using T. A. methods. The group experience has five components. It begins with an ice-breaker exercise and a lecture on T.A. The second part consists of three Parent Ego-State exercises to help clients understand the influences on their vocational development and explore their values. One of these exercises has participants select five occupations from Holland's Vocational Preference Inventory that their parents would select for them and five that would disappoint their parents if the clients were to choose them. The third part uses two Child Ego-State exercises to help clients understand their fantasies and needs as these influence their career decision making. The fourth part engages the Adult Ego-State by taking the objective perspective and using aptitude test scores and Strong Campbell Interest Inventory results. In the fifth part, clients use script analysis to understand their own life as an unfolding drama. The group concludes after helping each member integrate all phases of the experience and formulate specific vocational plans. Counselors can easily adapt the methods in Kurtz' group counseling program to individual career counseling.

We conclude this section by recalling a prediction concerning the future of the subjective perspective in career counseling practice. Berg (1954), in commenting on Super's career pattern theory, predicted

> that in a decade or two we shall routinely be using the research results of career pattern theory with the same facility that we use the findings which stemmed from trait theory . . . trait and career pattern theory will probably be bundled into some inclusive bin labeled "vocational counseling practice" and we shall talk of aptitudes in a matrix of life experience. (p. 20)

Now, more than 35 years after Berg's prediction, we find that most counselors who offer vocational assistance still limit their practice to trait theory, psychometric techniques, and actuarial methods. Ironically, we now call this objective vocational guidance, career counseling.

SUMMARY

In this chapter, we reviewed psychodynamic theories as they are used by vocational psychologists and career counselors. In the first half of the chapter, we considered vocational theory and research derived from the psychodynamic theories of Freud, Erikson, and Adler. In the second half of the chapter, we considered the use of the psychodynamic model and associated methods for career counseling. Without question, psychodynamic theories typically have not been well applied to career counseling practice. But, as we have attempted to explain here, some psychodynamic theories and concepts can be used to inform one's thinking about vocational behavior. In similar fashion, some psychodynamic techniques and methods can be effectively integrated in one's career counseling efforts. In summary, psychodynamic theory has a distinct contribution to make to the practice of career counseling. We hope that counselors continue to use psychodynamic theory to study vocational behavior and develop new methods and techniques for career counseling.

REFERENCES

Adler, A. (1956). *The Individual Psychology of Alfred Adler* (H. L. Ansbacher & R. R. Ansbacher, Eds.). New York: Basic Books.

Amerikaner, M., Elliot, D., & Swank, P. (in press). Social interest as a predictor of vocational satisfaction. *Individual Psychology.*

Angers, W. P. (1974). Position in the family in relation to teaching as a career choice. *The Individual Psychologist, 11,* 15–21.

Ammons, R. B., Butler, M. N., & Herzig, S. A. (1950). A projective test for vocational research and guidance at the college level. *Journal of Applied Psychology, 34,* 198–205.

Annis, A. (1967). The autobiography: Its uses and value in professional psychology. *Journal of Counseling Psychology, 14,* 9–17.

Attarian, P. J. (1978). Early recollections: Predictors of vocational choice. *Journal of Individual Psychology, 34,* 56–62.

Bell, N. (1968). *The relationship of occupational choice to ego identity and self-concepts.* Unpublished doctoral dissertation, Utah State University, Logan, UT.

Berg, I. A. (1954). Comment on career patterns as a basis for vocational counseling. *Journal of Counseling Psychology, 1,* 19–20.

Berger, P. L., & Luckman, T. (1966). *The social construction of reality.* New York: Doubleday.

Bichekas, G., & Newlon, B. (1983). Life-style analysis of hospice home care nurses. *Individual Psychology, 39,* 66–70.

Biggs, D. A., & Keller, K. E. (1982). A cognitive approach to using tests in counseling. *Personnel and Guidance Journal, 60,* 528–531.

Bordin, E. S. (1980). A psychodynamic view of counseling psychology. *The Counseling Psychologist, 9*(1), 62–70.

Bordin, E. S. (1984). Psychodynamic model of career choice satisfaction. In D. Brown & L. Brooks (Eds.), *Career choice and development* (pp. 94–136). San Francisco, CA: Jossey-Bass.

Bordin, E. S. (1987). Aim and trajectory. *The Counseling Psychologist, 15,* 358–367.

Bordin, E. S., Nachmann, B., & Segal, S. J. (1963). An articulated framework for vocational development. *Journal of Counseling Psychology, 10,* 107–116.

Brill, A. A. (1949). *Basic principles of psychoanalysis.* Garden City, NY: Doubleday.

Bryant, B. L. (1987). Birth order as a factor in the development of vocational preference. *Individual Psychology, 43,* 36–41.

Carter, H. D. (1940). The development of vocational attitudes. *Journal of Consulting Psychology, 4,* 185–191.

Cline, J. M., Riordan, R. J., & Kern, R. M. (1978). An investigation of the interjudge agreement on a subject's vocational choice and life style type. In L. Baruth & D. Ekstein (Eds.), *Lifestyle: Theory, research and practice* (pp. 70–77). Dubuque, IA: Kendall/Hunt.

Collin, A., & Young, R. A. (1986). New directions for theories of career. *Human Relations, 9,* 837–853.

Crites, J. O. (1976). Career counseling: A comprehensive approach. *Counseling Psychologist, 6*, 2–12.

Crites, J. O. (1981). Integrative test interpretation. In D. H. Montross & C. J. Shinkman (Eds.), *Career development in the 1980s: Theory and practice* (pp. 161–168). Springfield, IL: Charles C. Thomas.

Csikszentmihalyi, M., & Beattie, O. V. (1979). Life themes: A theoretical and empirical exploration of their origins and effects. *Journal of Humanistic Psychology, 19*, 45–63.

Dailey, C. (1971). *Assessment of lives.* San Francisco, CA: Jossey-Bass.

Danielson, P., & Rothney, J. (1954). The student autobiography: Structured or unstructured. *Personnel and Guidance Journal, 33*, 30–33.

Davis, M. (1965). *Vocational choice and self-others expectations congruence vs. function of ego identity.* Unpublished doctoral dissertation, Catholic University, Washington, DC.

Dinkmeyer, D., Pew, W. L., & Dinkmeyer, D., Jr. (1979). *Adlerian counseling and psychotherapy.* Monterey, CA: Brooks/Cole.

Dole, A. A. (1958). The Vocational Sentence Completion Blank in counseling. *Journal of Counseling Psychology, 5*, 200–205.

Dolliver, R. H. (1967). An adaptation of the Tyler Vocational Card Sort. *Personnel and Guidance Journal, 45*, 916–920.

Elliot, D., Amerikaner, M., & Swank, P. (1987). Early recollections and the Vocational Preference Inventory vs. predictors of vocational choice. *Individual Psychology, 43*, 353–359.

Emerson, S., & Watson, M. J. (1986). Adlerian life-styles among Catholic priests. *Individual Psychology, 42*, 367–374.

English, H. B., & English, A. C. (1958). *A comprehensive dictionary of psychological and psychoanalytic terms.* New York: Longmanns, Green.

Erikson, E. H. (1963). *Childhood and society* (2nd ed.). New York: Norton.

Erikson, E. H. (1968). *Identity: Youth and crisis.* New York: Norton.

Ernest, C., & Angst, J. (1983). *Birth order: Its influence on personality.* New York: Springer-Verlag.

Forer, B. R. (1957). *Forer Vocational Survey Manual.* Los Angeles, CA: Western Psychological Services.

Frey, D. H. (1973). Being systematic when you have but one subject: Ideographic method, $N=1$, and all that. *Measurement and Evaluation in Guidance, 6*, 35–43.

Galinsky, M. D. (1962). Personality development and vocational choice of clinical psychologists and physicists. *Journal of Counseling Psychology, 13*, 89–92.

Galinsky, M. D., & Fast, I. (1966). Vocational choice as a focus of the identity search. *Journal of Counseling Psychology, 13*, 89–92.

Gentry, J. M., Winer, J. L., Sigelman, C. K., & Phillips, F. L. (1980). Adlerian life style and vocational preference. *Journal of Individual Psychology, 36*, 80–86.

Gobetz, W. (1964). Suggested personality implications of Kuder Preference Record (Vocational) scores. *Personnel and Guidance Journal, 43*, 159–166.

Goldberg, R., & Gechman, A. (1976). Psychodynamic inferences from the Strong Vocational Interest Blank. *Journal of Personality Assessment, 40*, 285–301.

Goldman, L. (1983). The vocational card sort technique: A different view. *Measurement and Evaluation in Guidance, 16*, 107–109.

Goodyear, R. K. (1988, August). Test interpretation: A review. In C. E. Watkins, Jr. & V. L. Campbell (Co-Chairs), *Testing and assessment in counseling psychology.* Symposium conducted at the annual meeting of the American Psychological Association, Atlanta, GA.

Goodyear, R., & Healy, C. (1988). UCLA's Career Counseling Center: A dialogue about a unique service. *Journal of Counseling and Development, 67*, 49–53.

Grotevant, H. D., & Thorbecke, W. L. (1982). Sex difference in styles of occupational identity formation in late adolescence. *Developmental Psychology, 18,* 396–405.

Hafner, J. L., & Fakouri, M. E. (1984a). Early recollections and vocational choice. *Individual Psychology, 40,* 54–60.

Hafner, J. L., & Fakouri, M. E. (1984b). Early recollections of individuals preparing for careers in clinical psychology, dentistry, and law. *Journal of Vocational Behavior, 24,* 236–241.

Hafner, J. L., Fakouri, M. E., & Etzler, D. R. (1986). Early recollections of individuals preparing for careers in chemical, electrical, and mechanical engineering. *Individual Psychology, 42,* 360–366.

Hahn, M. (1963). *Psychoevaluation: Adaptation-distribution-adjustment.* New York: McGraw-Hill.

Harrison, R. (1978). Person-environment fit and job stress. In C. L. Cooper & R. Payne (Eds.), *Stress at work* (pp. 175–205). New York: Wiley.

Haviland, M. G., & Mahaffy, J. E. (1985). The use of *My Vocational Situation* with nontraditional college students. *Journal of College Student Personnel, 26,* 169–170.

Hendrick, I. (1943). Work and pleasure principle. *The Psychoanalytic Quarterly, 12,* 311–329.

Hershenson, D. (1967). Sense of identity, occupational fit, and enculturation in adolescence. *Journal of Counseling Psychology, 14,* 319–324.

Hogan, R. (1983). A socioanalytic theory of personality. In M. Page (Ed.), *Nebraska symposium on motivation 1982: Personality—current theory and research* (pp. 55–89). Lincoln, NE: University of Nebraska Press.

Holland, J. (1973). *Some practical remedies for providing vocational guidance for everyone* (Rep. No. 160). Baltimore, MD: The Johns Hopkins University, Center for Social Organization of Schools.

Holland, J. (1974). *The paper guidance system.* Baltimore, MD: The Johns Hopkins University, Center for Social Organization of Schools.

Holland, J. L. (1985). *Making vocational choices: A theory of vocational personalities and work environments.* Englewood Cliffs, NJ: Prentice-Hall.

Holland, J. L., Gottfredson, D. C., & Power, P. G. (1980). Some diagnostic scales for research in decision-making and personality: Identity, information, and barriers. *Journal of Personality and Social Psychology, 39,* 1191–1200.

Holland, J. L., Gottfredson, G. D., & Nafziger, D. H. (1975). Testing the validity of some theoretical signs of vocational decision-making ability. *Journal of Counseling Psychology, 22,* 411–422.

Holland, J. L., & Holland, J. E. (1977). Vocational indecision: More evidence and speculation. *Journal of Counseling Psychology, 24,* 404–414.

Holloway, W. H. (1973). *Clinical transactional analysis with use of The Life Script Questionnaire.* Aptos, CA: Holloway Books.

Holmes, D. S., & Watson, R. I. (1965). Early recollections and vocational choice. *Journal of Consulting Psychology, 29,* 486–488.

Klopfer, W. G. (1965). A symposium on clinical appraisal in vocational counseling. *Personnel and Guidance Journal, 43,* 867–885.

Kurtz, R. R. (1974). Using a Transactional Analysis format in vocational group counseling. *Journal of College Student Personnel, 15,* 447–451.

LaBier, D. (1986). *Modern madness: The emotional fallout of success.* Reading, MA: Addison-Wesley.

Lantos, B. (1943). Work and the instincts. *International Journal of Psychoanalysis, 24,* 114–119.

Lantos, B. (1952). Metapsychological considerations on the meaning of work. *International Journal of Psychoanalysis, 33,* 439–443.

Layman, W. A., & Saveraker, A. (1978). Birth order and sibship size of medical school applicants. *School Psychiatry, 13,* 117–123.

Lynch, R. M., & Lynch, J. (1980). Birth order and vocational choice. *Journal of Experimental*

Education, 49, 15–18.

MacKinnon, D. W. (1944). The structure of personality. In J. McV. Hunt (Ed.), *Personality and the behavior disorders* (Vol. 1, pp. 3–48). New York: Ronald Press.

Manaster, G. L., & Corsini, R. J. (1982). *Individual psychology: Theory and practice*. Itasca, IL: Peacock.

Manaster, G. J., & Perryman, T. B. (1974). Early recollections and occupational choice. *Journal of Individual Psychology, 30*, 232–237.

Maw, I. L. (1982). The future autobiography: A longitudinal analysis. *Journal of College Student Personnel, 23*, 3–6.

McFarland, M. (1988). Early recollections discriminate persons in two occupations: Medical technology and nursing. *Individual Psychology, 44*, 77–84.

McKelvie, W. (1979). Career counseling with early recollections. In H. A. Olson (Ed.), *Early recollections: Their use in diagnosis and psychotherapy* (pp. 234–255). Springfield, IL: Charles C. Thomas.

McKelvie, W., & Friedland, B. V. (1978). *Career goals counseling: A holistic approach*. Baltimore, MD: F. M. S. Associates.

McKelvie, W., & Friedland, B. V. (1981). The life style and career counseling. In L. Baruth & D. Eckstein (Eds.), *Lifestyle: Theory, practice and research* (2nd ed., pp. 57–62). Dubuque, IA: Kendall/Hunt.

McSherry, J. P. (1963). *The interpersonal theory of Harry Stack Sullivan related to certain aspects of vocational development*. Unpublished manuscript, Graduate School of Education, Harvard University, Boston, MA.

Melillo, D. (1983). Birth order, perceived birth order, and family position of academic women. *Individual Psychology, 39*, 57–62.

Menninger Foundation (1985). *Love and work: One woman's study of her family of origin*. Topeka, KS: Educational Video Productions.

Menninger, K. A. (1942). Work as a sublimation. *Bulletin of the Menninger Clinic, 6*, 170–182.

Mosak, H. H. (1971). Lifestyle. In A. G. Nikelly (Ed.), *Techniques for behavior change* (pp. 7–81). Springfield, IL: Charles C. Thomas.

Muhlenkamp, A. F., & Parsons, J. L. (1972). Characteristics of nurses: An Overview of recent research published in a nursing research periodical. *Journal of Vocational Behavior, 2*, 261–273.

Munley, P. H. (1975). Erik Erikson's theory of psychosocial development and vocational behavior. *Journal of Counseling Psychology, 22*, 314–319.

Munley, P. H. (1977). Erikson's theory of psychosocial development and career development. *Journal of Vocational Behavior, 10*, 261–269.

Nachmann, B. (1960). Childhood experiences and vocational choice in law, dentistry, and social work. *Journal of Counseling Psychology, 7*, 243–250.

Neff, W. S. (1965). Psychoanalytic conceptions of the meaning of work. *Psychiatry, 28*, 324–333.

Newlon, B. J., & Mansager, E. (1986). Adlerian lifestyles among Catholic priests. *Individual Psychology, 42*, 367–374.

Obendorf, C. P. (1951). Psychopathology of work. *Bulletin of the Menninger Clinic, 15*, 77–84.

Okiishi, R. W. (1987). The genogram as a tool in career counseling. *Journal of Counseling and Development, 66*, 139–143.

Olson, S. K., Johnston, J. A., & Kunce, J. (1985). Validity of My Vocational Situation for homemakers and displaced homemakers. *Measurement and Evaluation in Counseling and Development, 18*, 17–25.

Osipow, S. H. (1983). *Theories of career development* (3rd ed.). Englewood Cliffs, NJ: Prentice-Hall.

Parsons, F. (1909). *Choosing a vocation*. Boston: Houghton-Mifflin.

Powers, R. L., & Griffith, J. (1987). *Understanding life-style: The psychoclarity process*. Chicago: The Americas Institute of Adlerian Studies.

Rado, S. (1969). *Adaptational psychodynamics: Motivation and control*. New York: Science House.

Richards, L.S. (1881). *Vocophy*. Malboro, MA: Pratt Brothers.

Roe, A. (1964). Personality structure and occupational behavior. In H. Borow (Ed.), *Man in a world at work* (pp. 196–214). Boston: Houghton Mifflin.

Rohrlich, J. B. (1980). *Work and love: The crucial balance*. New York: Summit Books.

Rosenfeld, R. (1972). *The relationship of ego identity to similarity among self, ideal self, and probable occupational concepts among college males*. Unpublished doctoral dissertation, University of Maryland, College Park, MD.

Savickas, M. L. (1985). Identity in vocational development. *Journal of Vocational Behavior, 27*, 329–377.

Savickas, M. L. (1988). An Adlerian view of the publican's pilgrimage. *Career Development Quarterly, 36*, 211–217.

Savickas, M. L. (1989). Career-style assessment and counseling. In T. Sweeney (Ed.), *Adlerian counseling: A practical approach for a new decade*. (3rd ed., pp. 289–320). Muncie, IN: Accelerated Development.

Segal, S. (1961). A psychoanalytic analysis of personality factors in vocational choice. *Journal of Counseling Psychology, 8*, 202–210.

Segal, S., & Szabo, R. (1964). Identification in two vocations: Accountants and creative writers. *Personnel and Guidance Journal, 43*, 252–255.

Shulman, B. H., & Mosak, H. H. (1977). Birth order and ordinal position: Two Adlerian views. *Journal of Individual Psychology, 33*, 114–121.

Shulman, B. H., & Mosak, H. H. (1988). *Manual for life-style assessment*. Muncie IN: Accelerated Development.

Slaney, R., & McKinnon-Slaney, F. (1990). The vocational card sorts. In C. E. Watkins, Jr. & V. Campbell (Eds.), *Testing in counseling practice* (pp. 317–371). Hillsdale, NJ: Lawrence Erlbaum Associates.

Snell, W. E., Jr., Hargrove, L., & Falbo, T. (1986). Birth order and achievement motivation configuration in women and men. *Individual Psychology, 42*, 428–438.

Sonnenfeld, J., & Kotter, J.P. (1982). The maturation of career theory. *Human Relations, 35*, 19–46.

Super, D. (1954). Career patterns as a basis for vocational counseling. *Journal of Counseling Psychology, 1*, 12–19.

Super, D. (1957). *The psychology of careers*. New York: Harper & Row.

Thorne, F.C. (1975). The life style analysis. *Journal of Clinical Psychology, 31*, 236–240.

Tiedeman, D. V., & O'Hara, R. P. (1963). *Career development: Choice and adjustment*. New York: College Entrance Examination Board.

Tyler, L. E. (1961). Research explorations in the realm of choice. *Journal of Counseling Psychology, 8*, 195–202.

Verger, D. M., & Camp, W. L. (1970). Early recollections: Reflections of the present. *Journal of Counseling Psychology, 17*, 510–515.

Very, P. S., & Prull, R. W. (1970). Birth order, personality development and the choice of law as a profession. *Journal of Genetic Psychology, 116*, 219–221.

Watkins, C. E., Jr. (1982). A decade of research in support of Adlerian psychological theory. *Individual Psychology, 38*, 90–99.

Watkins, C. E., Jr. (1983). Some characteristics of research on Adlerian psychological theory, 1970–1981. *Individual Psychology, 39*, 99–110.

Watkins, C. E., Jr. (1984a). *An examination of the relationship between social interest and self-management effectiveness.* Unpublished doctoral dissertation, University of Tennessee, Knoxville, TN.

Watkins, C. E., Jr. (1984b). The Individual Psychology of Alfred Adler: Toward an Adlerian vocational theory. *Journal of Vocational Behavior, 24,* 28–47.

Zweigenhaft, R. L. (1974). Birth order, approval seeking and membership in Congress. *Journal of Individual Psychology, 30,* 205–210.

4

Developmental Career Counseling

David A. Jepsen
The University of Iowa

Over a decade ago, John Crites (1974a) reviewed five major approaches to career counseling: trait-and-factor, client-centered, psychodynamic, behavioral, and developmental. A career counseling approach was defined by both theoretical *models* and practical *methods*. Models connotes the ideas used by counselors in construing diagnosis, process, and outcomes. *Methods* are the specific procedures used to implement the model such as choice of appraisal procedures or structuring the initial interview. As the contents of this volume attest, the number of approaches has increased since the 1970s. The models and methods within each of the five "major" approaches have also expanded. This expansion is especially noticeable for the developmental approach.

Developmental career counseling models have increased in complexity since the 1970s as more ideas from developmental theory have been applied to career behavior across the life span. The works of well-known developmental psychologists such as Piaget, Erikson, Kohlberg, Perry, and Loevinger have suggested new career developmental models in the 1980s, for examples, (e.g., Astin, 1984; Blocher & Siegal, 1981; Gottfredson, 1981; Neff, 1985; Vondracek, Lerner, & Schulenberg, 1986). Career counseling models have been enriched by psychological theories focusing on recurring life events within the career such as decision making (Janis & Mann, 1977) and coping with stress (Lazarus & Folkman, 1984). Whereas Crites' (1974a) review relied almost exclusively on the work of Donald Super to represent developmental career counseling, a thorough contemporary review must also include the contributions of many others.

The list of practical methods available for developmental career counselors has grown in the 1980s. Recent writings by counselors working with adults (e.g., Carlsen, 1988; Liebowitz & Lea, 1985; Schlossberg, 1984; Yost & Corbishley, 1987) and by counselors working within organizations (e.g., Hall et al., 1986) have elaborated on the everyday counseling application of developmental methods. Popular self-help books and workbooks have suggested activities that were derived from methods advocated by developmental career counselors. For example, Bolles (1988) urged some job-changers to use the autobiography in much the same way as Crites (1981a) proposed in his summary of developmental career counseling.

This chapter builds on Crites' earlier work by summarizing and integrating recent published work about the broadened notion of developmental career counseling. It is divided into three sections, each built around a problem arising from the recent expansions to developmental career counseling. Material in the first section addresses the problem of what distinguishes the developmental approach from other approaches to career counseling. The second section covers the expansion in theoretical models, specifically ideas derived from developmental psychology that are useful to developmental career counselors. The third section covers the counseling methods commonly identified with the developmental approach. The purposes are threefold: (a) to clarify the distinctions between developmental career counseling and other types of career counseling; (b) to discuss developmental models, assumptions, and concepts used as cognitive tools by developmental career counselors; and (c) to describe selected developmental career counseling intervention strategies and techniques.

DEVELOPMENTAL CAREER COUNSELING AS A DISTINCT APPROACH

Development is a very fashionable word in counseling circles. Confusion among career counselors about what a developmental approach is seems likely because the term *development* has been applied to many aspects of human services work and consequently has lost some of its particular meaning. It has been applied to counseling interventions, to placement and out-placement functions, to employee assistance programs in organizations, and to training and educational programs. This section addresses the issue of what distinguishes "developmental" career counseling models and methods from other approaches.

There is no one official developmental career counseling approach, rather there are many approaches called *developmental*. Developmental career counselors are distinguished more by their orientations and common beliefs than by adherence to single theoretical models. These orientations and beliefs are derived from a *tradition* in the counseling movement that, in turn, is based on knowledge from developmental psychology. Developmental counselors' common orientation is expressed in a particular *language* used to describe careers and problems and similar expectations for counselor *role*.

Developmental Traditions in Counseling. Developmental career counseling emerged in the 1950s as a distinct approach to helping people find success and satisfaction in their work. Two scholars from Columbia University, Eli Ginzberg and Donald E. Super, are generally credited with generating the major ideas that gave rise to a developmental approach in career counseling. Ginzberg, an economist with Freudian persuasions, and a group of co-workers at Columbia University, authored the landmark book titled, *Occupational Choice* (Ginzberg, Ginsburg, Axelrad, & Herma, 1951), which changed the face of vocational psychology and, subsequently, career counseling.

Super, a psychologist, responded to Ginzberg's work with important statements of his own about the developmental nature of vocational choice and adjustment. His views were set forth in an influential series of journal articles published in *Occupations* (1951), *American Psychologist* (1953), and *Journal of Counseling Psychology* (1954) and were extended and integrated into his book, titled *The Psychology of Careers* (1957b).

The work of Ginzberg and Super, with their respective collaborators, symbolizes a watershed point for career counseling. Indeed, Super (1951) proposed a redefinition of vocational guidance as "the process of helping a person to develop and accept an integrated and adequate picture of [self] and of [one's] role in the world of work, to test that concept against reality, and to convert it into a reality, with satisfaction to [self] and benefit to society" (p. 92). The changes had important implications for how counselors *thought* about clients' careers and, consequently how they chose to *act* in terms of the strategies and interventions initiated with clients. They laid the groundwork for what has become known as developmental counseling.

Beilin (1955) thought that both Ginzberg and Super had proposed special cases of general developmental theory. He contended that the pattern of a person's vocational choices evolving over time qualifies as one aspect of the individual's total development. Therefore, such patterns are subject to the same general developmental principles reflecting certain fundamental processes common to diverse aspects of development such as physical, intellectual, emotional, and social. These principles were identified by Beilin and are summarized here:

1. Development is a continuous process.
2. The developmental process is irreversible.
3. Developmental processes are differentiable into patterns.
4. Aspects of the developmental processes are pre-eminent at various periods, called stages, in the life span.
5. The outcome of normal development is increasing maturity.
6. Developmental phenomena show increasing differentiation and integration of new parts.
7. Development progresses from dependence to independence, from egocentric to socially relevant behavior.

Beilin identified the *potential* that the developmental principles had for constructing new career models, but practical methods for career counselors were not widely available until recently. Borow (1961) underscored the promise of developmental ideas for practice. He cautioned that it would be difficult to translate the ideas into counseling applications, probably more difficult to translate developmental principles than learning principles. A casual review of the emphases in career counseling literature over the intervening quarter century would support Borow's prediction. Nevertheless, Borow contended, developmental principles are essential to a career counseling approach that helps people lead more effective vocational lives.

Prevailing beliefs among counselors about choosing and adjusting to work were challenged in the 1950s in at least three important ways. The first challenge was the assertion that choosing and adjusting to work is a continuous, largely irreversible process spanning a large portion of the life history. Second, the processes were construed as "growth patterns" explained by principles derived from developmental psychology rather than the psychology of individual differences. Third, the processes were believed to be sufficiently complex and abstract so that multiple intellectual perspectives are required, hence the disciplines of economics, sociology, anthropology, and psychiatry were consulted for new ideas.

Developmental Language. A distinguishing feature of any career counseling approach is the particular meaning intended by the important terms. Both the modifying terms *career* and *developmental* connote particular meanings; definitions are probably held in common by developmental counselors but not by advocates for other approaches.

Career is more or less synonymous with individual *work life history*. This overarching concept connotes a broad *target* for career counseling methods (Super, 1957b; Tiedeman, 1961). In its broadest sense, career usually designates the full sequence of work positions held by one person across the life span including the positions held in preparation for work such as chores, part-time jobs, education, and training. In contrast, the term *career* sometimes has a much narrower focus in other career counseling approaches; for example, the organizational career refers to the sequence of positions within a single work organization and the occupational career refers to the sequence of positions held in those jobs grouped under a particular occupation. Developmental career counselors seldom use *career* to refer to anything less than a major segment of the life span, nor anything more than the experiences of one person.

Work career is embedded within life history as one strand is entwined in a rope. Super (1980) has drawn this part–whole relationship by using the term *lifestyle* to designate the full array of life roles enacted simultaneously in fulfilling the life functions of work, love, and play. Examples of these roles are child, student, worker, leisurite, spouse, and parent. These roles are played within the context of family, neighborhood, and community as well as the workplace. The continuous flow of one person's life constitutes the full life history. Thus, the work career is interrelated with the family cycle and the pattern of leisure to form the full life history.

A career is examined and understood from several perspectives. A career has meaning both from the perspective of the person experiencing it as well as from the perspective of an external observer. Raynor (1982) emphasized this distinction: "A career is both a phenomenological concept and a behavioral concept. It is the link between what a person does and how that person sees himself or herself. A career consists of time-length senses of self that are defined by action and its outcomes" (p. 262).

Work has multiple dimensions of meaning regardless of the perspective. Among the several meanings are those described as economic, social, cultural, and, in the broadest sense, health, as well as psychological. Work represents a way of earning a living, a position in a social system, a common bond with cultural traditions, the expression of one's physical well-being, and the personal satisfactions derived from work activity itself. Recent discussions of work (e.g., Super, 1984a) use phrases like "quality of life" to capture the broad range of meanings associated with a work career.

In summary, the work career is an individual's life-long, sequence of work positions observed from both phenomenological and behavioral perspectives and subject to multiple meanings. The developmental career counselor uses career in a very broad sense and resists more restricted meanings such as synonyms for occupation or job. Consequently, developmentalists prefer to talk about constructing, shaping, or creating a career rather than choosing a career. People choose among acts that evolve into a career.

Development refers to the *intra*-individual variability in behavior patterns as people "grow up" in their work. The dimension along which individual characteristics are compared is that of qualitative differences across time rather than quantitative differences among persons. Differences within an individual life history appear between two different *forms* or patterns of the same functional *system* of behavior rather than between two different systems. *Development* refers to qualitative differences in the pattern of behaviors serving the same broad function or purpose. When these differences are observed as changes *within* a single life history, they are usually referred to as *developmental change.*

Clear examples of empirically supported developmental changes within careers are difficult to find. Jepsen (1984a) identified 10 major developmental themes in recent research literature and examined the evidence for developmental change. One theme that did show promise was called *vocational choice rationale,* the aggregate of reasons expressed in support of vocational choices. The complexity of rationale seems to increase over the adolescent years (Gribbons & Lohnes, 1968, 1982; Jepsen, 1975; Jordaan & Heyde, 1979).

Development is not construed as change in a single behavior pattern but rather as multidimensional changes; many functional systems of behavior arise side by side. The pattern of behaviors called *vocational exploratory behavior,* the instrumental and cognitive behavior intended to obtain information about vocational options, develops alongside vocational choice rationale. Increased frequency and improved quality of exploratory behavior and the increased complexity of reasons for choices are simultaneous challenges for people during most of their early work histories.

Development usually connotes changes that are normative and age-graded, typical rather than deviant for the age groups. Change is reflected in the *organization* of behavior as well as in the content alone and, in many cases, the transformation of its mode or structure. There are relatively few specific discussions of these transformations in developmental career counseling although some may qualify, on close examination. For example, we can imagine that a person's reasons for position choices go through qualitative changes from egocentric fantasies as reasons given during childhood to social principles as the reasons given in early adulthood.

The general language of developmental career counseling implies a distinct view about the *problems* clients experience in their careers. Developmental career counselors seem to consider three types of problems that significantly impede successful development. First, current behavior is problematic because it is *dysfunctional*, that is, the behavior is not organized effectively to serve the life functions or master the tasks expected of a person at a particular age or period in the life span. Another way to frame this type of problem is to focus on the barriers preventing clients from achieving immediate goals appropriate for their age group and social surroundings. Examples of dysfunctional behavior within a career include clients experiencing acute indecisiveness about choosing future positions, stress in present work positions, competing demands from work and family roles or strong dissatisfaction with work tasks and settings. Obviously these problems may be experienced at several age periods depending on the particular positions, tasks, and roles involved.

A second type of problem is *anticipated dysfunction*, that is, current behavior is functional but is likely to become dysfunctional unless it is changed to meet changing environmental demands. Development is impeded by barriers to achieving future goals. Discomfort derives more from responses to anticipated unpleasant experiences than from responses to contemporary situations. The anticipated experiences are usually communicated to the client by primary social groups such as family, teachers, or friends and thus the messages are a part of contemporary experience. Examples are clients who are undecided or conflicted in the face of clear choices or who are poorly informed and ill-prepared for a change in work positions.

A third type of career-related problem is presented by the client whose current behavior is functional and socially appropriate but somewhat *less than optimal*. Development is blocked in the sense that clients are blocked from a goal of fulfilling a conception of their potential. Examples are people who are employed and are generally meeting social expectations but feel a nagging pressure for greater success or satisfaction. Perspective is especially important to understanding this problem type. Observers such as teachers or parents may hold particular conceptions of the optimal career position or level of performance, but it is not shared by the person performing in the position. The behavior is not a problem appropriate for career counseling unless the client feels his or her present behavior is less than optimal.

The developmental approach is different from others in terms of everyday career counseling practices. Morrill and Forrest (1970) distinguished four types of career counseling practices on the basis of the *purposes* for helping the client. Type 1 is designed to aid the client with a specific decision at hand. The purpose of Type 2 is to help clients with both a specific decision and with later decisions by teaching decision-making skills. Type 3 has the purpose of assisting clients with the processes of making continual series of choices by teaching adaptive responses to environmental demands. Type 4 is designed to aid the client to utilize personal attributes to achieve self-determined objectives and to exercise influence on the nature of future choices. Developmental career counselors attempt to achieve all these purposes but are more likely than others to pursue the last type.

The four types were construed as falling on a continuum with three apparent dimensions: (a) the range of behaviors influenced, (b) the durability of the projected outcomes, and (c) the extent to which the client was expected to initiate activity. Developmental career counselors intend to influence a wide range of interrelated clients behaviors rather than simply helping clients collect and process information for a single decision. Counselors often expect clients to "transfer" the processes learned in counseling to other problems the client experiences rather than simply solving an isolated problem. Finally, developmental career counseling clients are expected to be active participants in their own career development rather than passive recipients of information or placement assignments. Thus, developmental career counselors have expectations for client changes that sometimes differ from colleagues loyal to other approaches.

Counselor Role. Developmental counselors prefer to play a particular kind of role in their clients' careers and that is a role analogous to the family physician or lawyer. Because developmentalists construe career as covering a long period of time, they prefer relationships that span a long period of time. These relationships are not necessarily continuous, weekly contacts, but are usually intermittent; they involve activities analogous to the annual physical exam or periodic review of financial plans as well as responding to immediate complaints about present work roles. The counselor functions as consultant, teacher, and therapist with regard to career problems depending, among other things, on the type and severity of problem the client is experiencing.

This role places considerable intellectual demands on developmental counselors. They are required to have broad, comprehensive knowledge about career development based in developmental psychology, vocational psychology, and counseling psychology as well as salient areas in sociology, economics, anthropology, social, learning, and organizational psychology. This professional knowledge should be buttressed by frequent consultation with specialists who have expertise in understanding aspects of work life relevant to career. For example, because work has economic implications, developmental counselors benefit from consultation with experts in the field of economics. Likewise, work has social meanings and sociologists can provide valuable insights on issues about power, status, and community or family structure.

Developmental counselors need both a strong knowledge base and the ability to process large amounts of information. For example, they must be able to integrate complex life history data and environmental data into a comprehensive whole and make some intuitive sense of it all. The ability to apply logical systems to data and make sound clinical inferences (Sarbin, Taft, & Bailey, 1960) and to avoid common errors in judgment (Nisbett & Ross, 1980) is fundamental to helping clients with problems related to their careers.

In summary, developmental career counseling covers a broad range of activity, but appears to be distinguished from other approaches by a common set of traditions, language, and roles. Developmentalists think differently. They are identified with different beliefs and principles first advanced by economists and psychologists in the early 1950s and which have become generally accepted since then. Developmentalists attach particular and distinct meanings to "career" and "development." They utilize concepts from theories about careers based on ideas from developmental psychology. As we see in the next section, they also make special assumptions and employ special concepts with particular meanings.

DEVELOPMENTAL THEORIES AND CAREER COUNSELING

Developmental theories are set apart from other theories in the behavioral sciences because they attempt to explain systematic and successive changes over time in the organization of mental phenomena. The subject of inquiry is the functional *systems of action* that undergo systematic and successive *changes* over time (Langer, 1969; Reese & Overton, 1970). With regard to the career aspects of development, the central adaptive function served by "career" systems of action is *work productivity*, producing goods and services to preserve and maintain life and to find personal meaning in doing so (Neff, 1985).

Developmental career counselors seem to have selected from developmental theories a common cluster of ideas for conducting their work and, consequently, have rejected competing ideas. Three devices are used in this section to clarify the ideas from developmental theory as they apply to career counseling: (a) philosophical *models* of human development explained by using metaphors, (b) *assumptions* about human development and their implications for career counseling, and (c) a set of *concepts* about careers derived from developmental theories.

Philosophical Models. Developmental theory is not monolithic; there are differences among theories labeled *developmental* in terms of philosophical models symbolizing different world views. Philosophical differences are illustrated by examining three models represented by vivid metaphors. The metaphors and descriptions are derived from the work of Reese and Overton (1970) and Vondracek et al. (1986). They do not cover all "world views" about human development, because the psychoanalytic view is absent. Nevertheless, they provide contrasts useful in clarifying the general nature of contemporary developmental career counseling.

The first model is the familiar analogy of the person operating as a complex *machine* such as a telecommunication satellite. The person interacts with the environment much as a satellite receives and sends signals. The person assumes a reactive position relying on the signals received for the substance of the signals to be sent. The exchange of signals leaves a trace or "connection" within the machine. The connections or associations are the elements of the behavior repertoire. Development is characterized as the continuous, quantitative accumulation of connections between signals received and signals sent.

The second model represents the person functioning as a sophisticated example of a *growing organism.* The person is an active agent initiating interactions with the environment as does an animal seeking food or a plant searching for light. Development is a self-constructive process. The person gives psychological meaning to experience much as the feeding organism changes the nature of the food or light in order to use it for sustenance. Activity is functional; it serves a purpose. The observer of this activity may discern an eventual end-point called maturity. The functional meanings of the interactions with the environment are the substance of psychological development.

A third model is built on the metaphor of the *transaction.* Psychologists who identify with dialectics favor this world view. The person is conceptualized as a changing system conducting transactions, analogous to business deals, with other changing systems within the environment (such systems as the community, the family, etc.). Some systems are embedded in others as a family is embedded within a community. The "gives and takes" during the transactions result in changes in the way the person-as-system is organized. This systemic change constitutes the person's psychological development.

Differences among the models are illustrated by the implications each world view has for how a counselor understands "vocational interests." Mechanistic models represent interests as a repertoire of stimulus–response connections that are learned and re-learned through encounters with the environment (Krumboltz & Baker, 1973; Osipow, 1979). The mechanistic theory implies counselors would interpret interest in an occupation as the product of repeated connections between a signal received about the occupation and a signal sent, an active and affective response such as showing a liking or preference for the occupation. An interest in a particular occupation is explained as a repeated positive affective response to occupational stimuli such as pictures, stories, observations, or descriptive information.

Organismic models of development, on the other hand, would represent interests as expressions of directional tendencies or dispositions inherent to the organism that become increasingly differentiated and integrated with experience (Roe & Seigelman, 1964). Interests demonstrate three qualities assumed by organismic views of development: (a) inherent potential organization, (b) the assimilatory function, and (c) constructivist power. An interest in an occupation is the result of an inherent affective tendency influenced by the assimilation over time of experiences that parallel those in the occupation and which the person has constructed or shaped into an expression, usually verbal, of preference or liking for the occupation.

Curiously, few contemporary psychologists have used the transaction model to represent vocational interests although John Dewey began to lay the theoretical groundwork almost a century ago (Fryer, 1931). Perhaps Carter's (1940) view of vocational attitudes (interests) as modes of adjustment follows the model approximately. Interest in an occupation represents the person's practical adjustment to a complex culture.

Developmental career counselors seem to favor the assumptions about development from the *organismic* world view. Many early career development theorists such as Super (1957b); Ginzberg, Ginsberg, Axelrad, and Herma (1951; Ginzberg, 1972, 1984); and Tiedeman (1961; Tiedeman & O'Hara, 1963) appear to have subscribed to the organismic assumptions in their models. The *transactional* viewpoint has influenced recent developmental theorists such as Blocher and Seigel (1981), Gottfredson (1981), and Neff (1985). Super's recent theoretical statements (Super, 1980, 1984b) show increased reliance on the transactional views. Vondracek et al. (1986) thought that a combination of the organismic view and the transactional view with special emphasis on the role of environmental context would serve as the best model for the integration of developmental psychology with vocational psychology.

Assumptions. The organismic world view contains certain assumptions about human development that are probably held in common by developmental career counselors but not by advocates for other approaches especially behavioral, psychodynamic, and trait-and-factor. Such an attribution is, of course, highly speculative because developmental theories are both varied and complex and writers about career counseling practices do not always make explicit reference to ideas from particular developmental theories. Nevertheless, a few major assumptions from the organismic world view are explicated to demonstrate their implications for developmental career counseling activities. These assumptions are stated in over-simplified form to isolate and emphasize the source of beliefs important to developmental career counseling.

1. *Development is a self-constructive process.* This assumption implies that people, especially children and adolescents, are active agents involved in creating a reality of their own. People actively construct an internal reality by *selecting* and *organizing* perceptions of external reality (Tyler, 1978). They shape their own choices within their career by selecting and organizing environmental reinforcers; they shape their own career roles by selecting and organizing social expectations. Developmental change in the person's work history occurs because of changes within the person's reality as well as changes external to the person.

Adherence to such a belief leads to several distinguishable counselor behaviors as, for example, in response to the recurring client problem called "unrealistic vocational aspirations" (Salomone & McKenna, 1982). Elkind (1980), a developmental psychologist, suggested counselors accept the person's view of reality (that is, their self-constructed aspirations) as valid for him or her but not necessarily for the counselor nor for others. The counselor helps the person to distinguish between personal reality and social reality. The developmentalist would probably aid the client to analyze the particular social realities of a job role from the perspective of whether the person could shape the job to fit his or her personal reality.

The counselor's focus is on the client as the principal actor rather than on the social environment comprised of supporting actors and stage settings. Thus, interventions emphasize actions initiated by the client rather than interventions effecting the environment but, of course, do not totally exclude the latter. The client is shown how to seek and interpret information about occupations rather than simply being placed in a career resource center or introduced to a person who knows about an occupation of interest to the client.

2. *The person's activity has both structure and function.* The human experience is understood for both the *structure* of the activity, the organization created by the person, and the *function* it serves, the purposes toward which the action is directed. The developmentalist assumes the person is not only an active agent but that the action is directed toward an end state. The person's sequential flow of experiences progress toward an end state called maturity. Analysis of a

person's growth may focus on the organization of present activity and direction inferred from comparisons to past organizations or comparisons to idealized end states (maturity).

This belief has led developmental counselors who are attempting to understand the structure of career development to adopt strategies of *description* and *interpretation*. The counselor collaborates with the client to gather and examine data *describing* the structure of person's experiences. Carlsen (1988) illustrated this collaborative strategy in the first phase of her "career therapy" for adults. For example, she asked the client to write out 10 descriptive titles in the form of answers to the "Who Am I?" question. Tyler's (1978) Listing Questionnaire asks the person to list all the present possibilities such as occupational possibilities. Both are examples of techniques designed to elicit client information useful in describing the structure of behavior.

Interpretation for developmental counselors is often in relation to function in the form of a model of maturity, usually construed in relation to the person's age group. Theoretical models of career maturity have been proposed for adolescents (Crites, 1974c; Jordaan, 1974; Super et al., 1957) and for adults (Levinson et al., 1978). (Both descriptive and interpretative techniques are elaborated later in this chapter.)

The broad function work serves in life is likely to be an important topic in developmental career counseling. Developmentalists may focus discussions on the instrumental purpose of work as much as the specific activities involved in particular jobs. Super (1983) suggested counselors attend to the relative *importance* of work to clients and their particular work *values*. Both focus on the functions work serves. For example, work values are expressed in terms such as material rewards (economic purposes) status, autonomy, authority (social purposes) and creativity, intellectual stimulation (psychological purposes).

3. *The person functions as a unified system.* The person is not structured as the sum of several separate attributes such as roles or traits. Although roles and traits are clearly distinguishable and useful tools in career counseling, understanding is enhanced by focusing on the whole rather than the parts, on the *synthesis* rather than the differentiated elements. The developmental counselor assumes the client is best understood as an individual person, admittedly a very abstract and difficult idea to grasp, rather than the sum of distinguishable characteristics. This allows the counselor to give attention to the more complicated, and perhaps more troubling, aspects of the client's career experiences. A client may play several life roles, for example, spouse, parent, worker, leisurite, and citizen, but he or she must act out the roles as *one* individual. Likewise the person has several distinguishable abilities but must apply one set of specific skills to work tasks. The *combination* of roles or the

combination of abilities is what the developmentalist helps the client comprehend.

Developmental career counselors find systemic assumptions useful in dealing with clients experiencing role conflict (Super, 1980) and the so-called "multipotentialed" client (Pask-McCartney & Salomone, 1988). The counselor is likely to emphasize the *combination* of roles or the *combination* of traits and, perhaps, derive new possibilities for action or new interpretations of the meaning of present actions.

4. *New systems of action emerge from old systems of action but in different forms.* Growth involves *trans*formations resulting in later forms of action that are not reducible to earlier forms. These distinguishable forms of action are arranged in an orderly developmental progression segmented into stages. Stages represent continuities and discontinuities in development; the hypothetical growth curve has intermittent surges and plateaus. Furthermore, segments of the curve represent new systems of action that differ qualitatively rather than quantitatively. Each system builds on the previous one but shows a different organization or structure.

This belief in emerging systems of action leads to distinct strategies for developmental career counselors. A counselor's understanding of the client's level of development or stage in the developmental progression is important to conveying this understanding to clients and to selecting effective interventions.

Identifying the client's stage in cognitive development, for example, has led to the formulation of distinctly different counselor interventions for "dualistic" college students, those who see the world in black–white, right–wrong categories. Touchton, Wertheimer, Cornfeld, and Harrison (1977) demonstrated that a high degree of diversity, large amounts of experiential learning, a high degree of structure, and a personal atmosphere showed increased sensitivity to client needs and greater gains in complexity of thinking about careers. Schmidt and Davison (1983) have suggested specific guidelines for instructor responses to journals written by "dualistic" students. Such journals are commonly used in career counseling or career classes.

Developmental Concepts.   The value of developmental theory to counselors, in the opinion of Elkind (1980), is "to introduce concepts or constructs that help the counselor organize his or her experience in new ways. Such constructs do not add to the counselor's experience, they can add to his or her insights into, and appreciation of that experience" (p. 353). Developmental career counselors share a particular repertoire of concepts that help to capture the common qualities observed in clients' careers. These concepts serve the function of reducing complexity and confusion when organizing observations and of aiding in revealing connections among observed behaviors (Jepsen, 1984b). For example, two concepts that help counselors understand the evolution of work-related experiences over time are stage and developmental task. This section contains descriptions of several concepts from developmental theory that serve as cognitive tools for solving career counseling problems and communicating with other counselors.

Stage is a concept representing segments of the life history and is useful to counselors in grasping the nature, sequence, and significance of clients' work careers. Nevertheless, career development theorists differ in the specific meaning associated with the concept (Jepsen, 1974). Super (1957b), for example, used life stage to describe five major segments of the life span: growth, exploration, establishment, maintenance, and decline. Each life stage demarcates the major *functions* of work life—and indeed "all aspects of life and living" (Super, 1957b, p. 72)—which engaged the person for an extended time period. The descriptive value of life stages as "organizing modes of career development" was demonstrated by Jordaan (1974) when he gathered research evidence and clinical observations to write a portrait sketch for each life stage. Jordaan (1974) gave a thumbnail sketch of the Exploratory Stage as the period during which individuals are expected to translate their self-concepts first into general and then into more specific occupational terms. The ambiguity and uncertainty created by entering a new subculture (that of teenager and budding adult) are the basis for much adolescent exploration.

By contrast, Tiedeman (1961) used the stage construct to represent structurally distinct segments of the process of making a particular decision. Each stage represents the way psychological activity is organized prior to and following a change in work positions. The process is repeated several times over the life span such as before and after entering a training program or academic major, a new job, or retiring from a job. The four stages prior to position entry are Exploration, Crystallization, Choice, and Clarification and the three stages after entry are Induction, Transition, and Maintenance. Tiedeman's Exploration stage, as distinguished from Super's Exploration stage, is described in terms of the cognitive organization of goals and fields associated with a particular decision problem. During exploration, overt activity is largely acquisitive and often appears random to the observer.

Super (1980) incorporated into his life-stage theory the description of sequential decision-making processes and called it a mini-cycle through which the person progresses when moving from one life stage to another in the five-stage maxi-cycle. This incorporation helps distinguish the two forms in which the "stage" construct is used by counselors: (a) as a description of the major career development functions during large segments of the life span; and (b) as a description of the organized patterns of behaviors, especially cognitions, forming "steps" (i.e., segments) in the decision-making process before and after particular career position changes.

A corollary concept to stage is that of *developmental task,* the series of problems to be mastered by the growing, active person in relation to his or her social environment. The tasks are what individuals must learn if they are to be judged from any perspective as a reasonably happy and successful person. Developmental tasks arise at or about a certain period in the life span. Successful achievement of the task leads to happiness and to success with later tasks, failure leads to unhappiness, disapproval, and difficulty with later tasks. According to Havighurst (1980), developmental tasks may arise from physical maturation, from pressure of the surrounding society on the individual, and from the desires, aspirations, and values of the emerging personality. They represent the behaviors expected by principle agents of socialization (e.g., family, school, peer group) and are associated with age segments of the life span. Developmental task is a useful conceptual tool for the counselor (and client in collaboration) to analyze and evaluate progress through the life span (Havighurst, 1980).

Super (1963) utilized the concept of developmental tasks to elaborate on the activity typical to each life stage. For example, the developmental tasks associated with Super's Exploratory stage are those of crystallizing, specifying, and implementing a vocational preference. Developmental tasks are often used by counselors as assessment criteria for determining successful development. The client's manifest behavior is matched against the task requirements to reveal a judgment of success, at least one of several such judgments the client confronts during the course of development.

The concept of career development leads logically to that of *career maturity* within the organismic world view (Super, 1957b). Generally speaking, career maturity refers to the degree of development, the place reached on the hypothetical continuum of development across the life stages, and is important for assessing the client's career status. Savickas (1984) provided an insightful analysis of the construct and its measurement based on the work of Super and Crites. He clarified several important distinctions between two definitions, called Career Maturity I (CM I) and Career Maturity II (CM II). CM I is an unidimensional estimate of the person's actual degree of progress relative to expected degree of progress on particular developmental tasks. CM I aids in addressing the appraisal question "What is the client's degree of career development on a given developmental task?" Examples of measures include the *Career Development Inventory-Adult Form* (Super, 1977) and the *Assessment of Career Decision Making* (Harren, 1980).

CM II, on the other hand, refers to a multidimensional attribute comparing the person with others in the age cohort on the behaviors involved in coping with the same developmental tasks. CM II aids in addressing the appraisal question "How is the client dealing with the full array of career developmental tasks?" Examples of measures are those derived from social learning theory and applied to specific behaviors such as checklists of career exploratory behavior (e.g., The Vocational Exploration Behavior Checklist; Krumboltz & Thoresen, 1964). Obviously, the assessment would involve a representative sample of responses to the full range of developmental tasks. Savickas applied a Stimulus-Organism-Response analysis and partitioned measures of the person's career attitudes and career competencies (e.g., *The Career Maturity Inventory;* Crites, 1978) into motivational and structural characteristics of the Organism, rather than include them as measures of responses to stimulus tasks.

The concept of *transition* is important in the language of most developmental counselors. Schlossberg (1984) used transition, in a general sense, to refer to "an event or non-event resulting in change" (p. 43). She emphasized the specific meaning for developmental transitions derived from the work of Levinson et al. (1978): transition is "a bridge or a boundary zone, between two states of greater stability. It involves a process of change, a shift from one structure to another" (pp. 49–50). The most apparent conceptual contrast with transition is stage; the latter refers to qualities of a steady state of equilibrium, whereas the former refers to a state of flux and re-organization. Super (1984b) used transition to refer to the change occurring "within" the person rather than events external to the person. Schlossberg did not consider a life event to be a transition unless it was so defined by the person experiencing it. Thus, a transition may refer to either the stimulus properties of the surroundings, the response properties of the person's behavior or the interaction between the two. It seems more consistent with the organismic world view to consider transition as the person's behavior.

The concept of *life event* has been used in developmental career counseling (Schlossberg, 1984) to refer to the environmental events likely to effect development, the so-called triggering events. Life events can be perceived as either threats or promises but they are the occurrences that create discontinuity for the person. Some life events are *planned* or expected, such as the normal decision points preceding transitions into new positions. Career examples include graduation from high school or a training program, a scheduled promotion or raise and retirement at the usual time such as age 65 or 70. Other life events are *unplanned* or unexpected, such as those life events experienced as abnormal crises or serious threats to career progress. Illnesses, accidents, family crises, changes in the business cycle, and changes in the climatic conditions are examples of unplanned life events that effect careers. Finally, there are *delayed* life events, sometimes called nonevents, that are normatively anticipated but do not occur. Examples of delayed events in careers are staying in the same rank rather than being promoted within the usual time period or continuing in school rather than graduating from high school with an age-group class. No matter what type of life event is experienced, it is clear that the actual event is external and functions as a stimulus to the person. In that sense it is set apart from the other concepts in this section, the remainder of which refer to properties of the person rather than the person's surroundings.

The concept of *social role* conveys the social character of career development as the person interacts within a social environment. It connotes the reciprocal relationship between self and groups of people. Havighurst (1980) felt the concept was essential to performing a developmental task analysis and Super (1963) felt it was essential to understanding self-concept. Super (1980) used the social role concept to represent the major forms of activity *expected* by the social system and *performed* by the individual. He lists nine roles most people perform across a life span and suggests several others performed by some but not all people. The role of job-holder is, of course, central to career development.

Self-concept is an idea integral to many theories explaining career choice and development and is particularly popular in developmental approaches to career counseling. The idea generally lacks an agreed upon meaning to which most theorists subscribe. Gottfredson (1985) acknowledged that, although self-concept definitions are diverse and have problems, it is still a useful concept for explaining the paths people take to fulfill their most basic needs and goals. The term has somehow survived many arguments and controversies and remains a part of most developmentalists' vocabulary. Even a broad definition of self-concept appears to serve a useful function as a "catch-all" category for self-references of all sorts.

Super's (1963) attempt to operationalize self-concept theory for integration into developmental theory yielded definitions of general use to counselors:

> Self-concepts are self-percepts which have acquired meaning and which have been related to other self-percepts. A self-concept is the individual's picture of himself [sic], the perceived self with accrued meanings. Since the person cannot ascribe meanings to himself [sic] in a vacuum, the

concept of self is generally a picture of the self in some role, some situation, in a position, performing some set of functions, or in some web of relationships. (p. 18)

He went on to enumerate several dimensions and metadimensions of self-concepts and self-concept systems thus confirming the challenging complexity of the idea. Later, Super (1984b) revealed that he preferred the terminology of personal constructs (Kelly, 1955) to that of self-concepts because it provides for the personal perception and construction of the environment. Of course, this modification would bring the "self"-conceptions in line with the self-constructive assumption described earlier.

Gottfredson (1981) employed a comprehensive definition in her developmental theory of occupational aspirations:

Self-concept is actually the totality of different ways of seeing oneself, some more important and central to one's sense of self than others. . . . Self-concept includes a person's sense of social self as well as more psychological attributes. It refers to one's own view of oneself, and it may not coincide with an outsider's objective assessment of that person's personality. (p. 546)

Gottfredson (1985) pointed out that it is useful to think about self-concept in terms of two major dimensions, identities, and self-esteem. *Identities* refers to the content of one's perceptions and beliefs about oneself and *self-esteem* refers to how one evaluates or feels about oneself.

In a broader context than career, Hamachek (1985) described an overview of "the self's development" including lists of behaviors associated with functional ("healthy") and dysfunctional ("unhealthy") expressions of the self's development during each of several life stages. The admittedly simplified overview and brief list provides counselors with more detail about the conceptual tool of self-concept.

CONTEMPORARY DEVELOPMENTAL
CAREER COUNSELING METHODS

Developmental career counselors strive to achieve the overarching goal of enhancing client career development (Crites, 1981a; Super, 1983), but they may have diverse intermediate objectives depending on the individual client's situation. The two forms of career maturity described earlier (cf. Savickas, 1984) signify at least two ideas against which developmentalists can conceptualize goals for career counseling. For example, client progress is manifested as new or dramatically revised career *roles* indicating upward movement through life career *stages*. An intermediate degree of change is manifested as new behavior patterns indicating successful management of career developmental *tasks*. A smaller magnitude of change is exemplified by the expressed satisfaction indicating successful coping with a single, expected career *life event*.

Because developmental career counselors are prepared to work with diverse problems and goals, they approach their work with several distinctive *strategic principles* in mind rather than a separate repertoire of techniques. Indeed, developmentalists use techniques and methods from several other approaches and do not seem to agree on one particular set of preferred techniques. These strategic principles serve as guidelines for counselor initiatives as they address the diverse problems a *clientele* presents.

Two general strategic principles are explicated in this section. Selected counseling techniques and methods—tactics used to implement the general strategies—are described under each principle. The techniques are representative of the developmentalist philosophy but are selective and not intended to indicate the wide range of techniques used in developmental career counseling. The principles are:

1. Descriptions and interpretations of a client's career help them construct fresh meanings and prepare to take action.
2. Counseling techniques and methods are more effective when adapted to the client level of development

The principles are seldom stated explicitly by developmental counselors but may be inferred from the actions they recommend. The first is based on the assumptions and concepts from the world view represented earlier by the organismic model while the second strategy is also based on assumptions from the transactional model.

Describe-and-Interpret Strategy

The describe-and-interpret strategy is derived from both the developmental psychologist's approach to understanding the nature of human development and the therapist's usual "contract" with the client. The developmental psychologist Jonas Langer (1969) succinctly summarized the initial scientific concerns within the organismic view of development: "The first step in explaining development is both descriptive and interpretive" (p. 8). The description emphasizes the developmental *processes* as well as the content and thus qualifies as a dynamic description. Developmental career counselors have to some degree imitated the psychologists' "first step" by giving description and interpretation a primary emphasis in their work. The strategy is also consistent with general psychotherapeutic processes which usually include history taking and interpretation. Erik Erikson (1964), both a developmental theorist and a therapist, emphasized three basic elements of the therapy encounter: (a) complaint (i.e., describing the dysfunction); (b) anamnersis (i.e., basic etiological reconstruction of the dysfunction); and (c) interpretation of the complaint and anamnersis to the client.

The strategy is more implicit than explicit in the career counseling literature but appears to have several elements:

1. the counselor collaborates with the client;
2. a thorough appraisal of the client's situation is conducted using multiple methods and sources;
3. dynamic descriptions of the client's career development processes are constructed using the appraisal data; and
4. interpretations of the descriptions lead the client to discover new meanings and possibilities for actions.

Counselor-Client Collaboration. Because clients create their own meanings and their own careers, it follows that they will profit from *collaboration with* the counselor throughout the counseling process rather than by completely *accepting from* the counselor's scientific or moral authority. Clients are, after all, the only source of vital "internal information" and they are the major witness to their own career history. The subject matter of career cannot be understood completely from the outside, therefore, client involvement is necessary. On the other hand, if the internal perspective on career experiences was satisfying, the client would probably not be experiencing a problem. The blend of the external perspective with the internal perspective is necessary for a complete appraisal of the career. In turn, this thorough appraisal allows for a broadened understanding and a strong foundation for action.

There is a second compelling reason to include the client as collaborator: developmental descriptions and interpretations apply to the creator of the career as well as the career that has been created. The counselor attends to both the created career and the creater-client. As Tyler (1978) succinctly summarized: "Individuals create themselves. To understand a person completely, we would need to trace the road he or she has taken on one occasion after another. It is development we must study, but the development of the shaper rather than the shaped" (pp.

233–234). The counselor's strategy includes persuading the client to become both self-revealing and self-observant, to participate and to observe alternately and to become both a case and a clinician.

Counselor–client collaboration has been advocated by several developmental career counselors beginning with Super (1957b) who viewed appraisal as a joint activity among counselor, consultant, and client and observed that experience has shown the best appraisals are those made collectively. Crites' (1974b) reappraisal of vocational appraisal led to the reconceptualization of vocational appraisal as an organic, ongoing part of career counseling within a collaborative relationship.

Potential conflict between the counselor's roles as both a collaborator and an authoritative resource can be resolved. As Tyler (1969) suggested, counselors simply plan to conduct their major information-processing activity, that is, the clinical inference processes, *between* counseling interviews rather than *during* them. The interview time is approached by the counselor with the intent of getting a "feel" for the client's experiences through collaboration with him or her.

Thorough Appraisal.   Developmental career counselors usually undertake a very thorough appraisal utilizing many methods that tap many sources. *Appraisal* is the term used to describe both the information-gathering and the information-processing counselor functions. The purpose is to derive a comprehensive and accurate picture of the client's career development, a "working image" of the person's evolving career.

Developmental assessment, according to Super (1983), is achieved in two steps: first, a broad-band "saturation" assessment covering a wide range of dimensions and, second, assessment focused on particular topics and in greater depth. The developmental assessment philosophy seems similar to that followed by Henry Murray (1938) in his studies of individual personality: After gathering data from several sources, a synthetic conception of the whole can be formulated and then, having grasped the whole, each part can be re-interpreted and understood in relation to the whole. The "whole" in developmental career counseling is usually a conceptualization of the client's complete career and the "parts" are the details revealed by the appraisal data.

Examples of procedures for the "saturation" step were recommended for developmental counseling by Super (1957a) and summarized by Crites (1974a). Three aspects of the client's situation are appraised: person appraisal, problem appraisal, and prognostic appraisal.

Person appraisal is an effort to develop a psychological picture of the client, analogous to the clinical case study (Crites, 1974b), based on a variety of demographic, psychometric and social data. The "picture" develops as a description of the person's present status and functioning on psychological, social, and physical dimensions. The present status is placed in the context of a developmental history by describing generally how each dimension has evolved over the life history. Examples of demographic data used for appraising the social dimensions of socio-economic status is obtained from client self-reports (in interviews or on questionnaires) about family member's education, income, and occupational prestige. Psychometric assessment of psychological dimensions such as self-concept, interests, abilities, and values is useful to the extent that the tests and inventories are supported by evidence of concurrent and construct validity (Crites, 1974b).

Developmental history taking, usually achieved in an early interview or through structured questionnaires, covers physical illnesses, family background, early activities, skills, choices and plans, and school achievement and adjustment. The client or a close friend or family member can provide their perceptions of the client's early development, for example, the person's early activity preferences or reading tastes to fill in the detail about the evolution of interests. A structured approach to taking a family history during career counseling suggested by Okiishi (1987) is the *genogram,* a three-generational graphic representation of a client's family of origin.

A slightly different focus in person appraisal is used by Carlsen (1988). She introduced her career therapy work to adult clients: "The first and most important task is determining 'who and what you are' in terms of skills, interests, values, and needs" (p. 190). The types of techniques she uses are a history-taking interview, testing such as interest, value and personality/need inventories, and autobiographical exercises including fantasy exercises, "Who Am I?", naming the "chapters" of life.

Person appraisal for Tyler (1978) is designed, in part, to help the client and counselor to discover the client's *possibility-processing structures,* the characteristic way a client organizes the perceived possibilities for action. These structures serve a function for clients analogous to the function of computer programs in data processing by helping them deal with almost unlimited possibilities. She encouraged clinicians to consider techniques from personal construct theory (Kelly, 1955) and especially sorting procedures. An example of a specific technique is the Vocational Card Sort Tyler (1961) developed for assessing individual differences in the subjective structuring of the occupational world. Goldman (1983) has recently affirmed the value of using the card sort as a counseling tool as well as for assessment purposes.

Problem appraisal focuses on the client's experienced difficulty or complaint, the intent is to identify and perhaps classify the problem (Crites, 1974b). The counselor attempts to stimulate clients to elaborate their thoughts and feelings about the nature, severity, and generality of the problem, the conditions associated with it, successful and unsuccessful attempts to alleviate the problem and the clients' motivations to make changes. Also covered are external factors related to the career problem such as family, finances, academic achievement, and interpersonal relations. The outcome is usually a diagnostic statement covering a balance of the person's strengths/resources and weaknesses/strains in relation to the life events precipitating seeking counseling.

Several schemes have been developed for classifying career problems. Because problem appraisal serves a diagnostic function, it is important for developmental career counselors to acknowledge the strengths and limitations of these classification systems. Rounds and Tinsley (1984) have provided an excellent discussion of the diagnosis and treatment of career problems. They remind us that problem classification is essential to communication among professionals and to prediction, both implicit and explicit, of differential intervention effects. A useful classification system must have three qualities: (a) a distinguishable domain of phenomena to be classified, (b) specific categories with defined properties, and (c) established classification reliability and predictive validity.

Rounds and Tinsley (1984) reviewed several systems and found that all have shortcomings. The systems they discuss under the rubric "developmental classifications" use career maturity as a "covert diagnostic perspective." They observed that career maturity inventory scores are treated as "diagnostic signs" like the scale scores on individual intelligence test subtests have been used to formulate clinical hypotheses and leads for further diagnostic exploration. No single diagnostic system is considered as "truly developmental" (Super, 1983), but the data are interpreted in relation to the effective management of appropriate career developmental tasks.

Despite shortcomings, the taxonomy of adult career problems by Campbell and Cellini (1981) is an example of a classification system that seems to have promise for use in descriptive diagnosis. The taxonomy includes four categories of career problems each defined by several adult career developmental tasks and the deficits that must be made up in order to master the task. For example, the category named "Problems in career decision making" involves the task of "Getting started" by overcoming the "lack of awareness of the need for a decision." The other three problem categories are: problems in implementing career plans, problems in organization/institutional performance, and problems in organizational/institutional adaptation.

Prognostic appraisal arrives at a prediction about the client's future behavior both in counseling and in the next phase of his or her career. Because there are many factors, some unknown, that effect counseling and career outcomes, these "predictions" are highly speculative. Crites

(1974b) clearly de-emphasized this aspect of appraisal largely because empirical evidence about predictions is discouraging. Nevertheless, the data obtained from the person appraisal, especially trait measures with sound predictive validity, are useful for the "next phase" prediction. For example, predictions of likely success in several colleges or college programs are usually available from entrance testing programs.

The thematic-extrapolative method was adapted by Super (1954) as an alternative to actuarial methods for making career predictions. It is based on two assumptions about predictions from case study data. The first assumption is that one way to understand what a person will do in the future is to understand what he or she did in the past. The second is that one way to understand what he or she did in the past is to analyze the sequence of events and the development of characteristics in order to ascertain the recurring themes and underlying trends. The career trends are projected into the future using a nonmathematical form of extrapolation, analogous to making trajectories on graphs. Two-dimensional graphic schemes that may serve as counseling aids are Super's (1980) life-career rainbow, with the dimensions of age and life-role time/emotional involvement, and Smelser's (1980) life contour graphs, with the dimensions of age and degree of involvement. The images of the future derived from the projection of trends and the examination of thematic patterns also allow for the discovery of new career meanings.

Prediction about client behavior during counseling interventions are based on the counselor's intuitive knowledge gained through experience with both the intervention and the client and, if available, knowledge gained through empirical research about differential intervention effects.

Dynamic Descriptions and Interpretations. Dynamic descriptions, based on data from person, problem, and prognostic appraisal, are utilized simultaneously with interpretative counseling techniques by developmental counselors. The purpose is to increase the effectiveness of client insights into their own career so they are better prepared to address the particular developmental tasks, transitions, and life events that require attention. Although developmental counseling advocates rarely specify behavioral objectives, there seems to be agreement with Leona Tyler (1969) that the more people become aware of the structures they have built up through previous development, the more they are able to influence their own subsequent development by the choices they make. Promoting this kind of awareness and facilitating this kind of choice is the main purpose of counseling. The structures to which she referred were general traits but cognitive and interpersonal structures should be added in view of the recent "cognitive revolution." The choices are the existential choices as well as decisions among clearly marked options. The framing of a decision is a critical determinant of how the choice is handled, thus awareness of the developmental context of career choices is especially important. Both the awareness and the choice are enriched by insights.

Insights in developmental career counseling are achieved through fresh connections in the client's conscious awareness of career material rather than through the counselor's imparting hidden meanings in subconscious material as is the case in psychodynamic counseling. The interpretation process, simply defined, is essentially arranging and organizing the discovery of new cognitive and affective associations among the appraisal data or between the data and elements of clients' tacit knowledge based in their experience. Among several types of interpretation described by Brammer and Shostrom (1982), this would be called *content* or *construct interpretation*.

The information known about the client's career is arranged or transformed into a *dynamic description* to allow the counselor and the client to discover new career insights. Descriptions of the client's career take many forms: they may be verbal and symbolic, oral or written, literal or metaphoric. They are called *dynamic* because both change processes and static conditions are described.

The purpose of dynamic descriptions, then, is to aid in the construction of fresh ideas about the person's career. These career ideas can be differentiated into different levels of complexity, at least for purposes of discussing counselor interventions. Three hierarchically arranged levels of ideas are suggested based on basic ideas from cognitive psychology. The most accessible career ideas are the relatively straightforward derivation of a single *concept*, a category of career experience unique to the individual client. An example is the idea of a skill category, such as "planning" to denote an aspect of paid and unpaid work experiences. A second level of career ideas involves the elaboration of a new *system* of concepts, the organization of concepts according to some personal rules or principles. An example is the system for groupings of skill concepts. The "planning" concept may be part of a network contrasted with other skill concepts along the dimension of "ideas versus things."

The third, and by far the most abstract, level of career ideas is the idiosyncratic and personalized system of meanings, or *meaning-schemes*. Career meaning-schemes are supra-concepts—they encompass embedded career concept systems—that both convey conceptual meaning but also constitute the experiences important to continued development. They may be thought of as major life themes or, perhaps, like Adlerian life styles. The term *meaning-scheme*, borrowed from Fingarette's (1963) analysis of insight in psychoanalytic thought, "points to patterns for behavior and experience, never just patterns of words, although words and concepts are the distinctive marks and peculiarly essential elements of meaning-schemes" (p. 22). Although personalized systems of meanings associated with experience are communicated by verbal concepts, they are constitutive of experience as well. The very experience of achieving a new meaning-scheme is an event of considerable importance that may be crucial to developmental progress.

A complete dynamic description is derived collaboratively by client and counselor. The techniques suggested by developmental career counselors in the literature are grouped into three general tactics roughly corresponding to the three levels of insights emerging. The first group describes how the data about the person's career (gathered during the appraisal process) are partitioned into concept categories and each category is "named" according to its distinguishing features. This step has obvious implications for the client's derivation of personal concepts about career. The ideas may be similar to the career development concepts listed earlier or novel concepts based on the client's unique perceptions. Practically any form of content analysis applied to a sample of client oral or written expressions will likely yield new categories and personal constructs. For example, Carlsen (1988) requested that adult clients title the chapters of their own life stories thus creating new categories.

An example comes from the data gathering techniques in George Kelly's (1955) personal construct theory. Recent work with versions of the Role Repretory Grid (Cochran, 1983; Neimeyer, 1989) offer semi-structured, inductive methods for arriving at personal constructs. Statistical analyses can be performed on single-subject data to provide ideas derived from more precise induction. Cochran (1983) cited several advantages to the method that are compatible with developmental counseling: The process of completing a grid provides an organized format for framing career decisions, the results reflect the subject's implicit career theories and both are experienced as personally relevant.

A simple Role Rep technique the author has used is to ask clients to draw three occupational cards at random from a deck and tell (a) which two occupations are most alike and why, and (b) what is different about the third occupation. The similarities and differences so identified are often useful personal constructions of rules for categorizing occupations. The procedure is repeated several times to identify several personal constructs about occupations. The same technique could be followed with other common career events such as skills, tasks, school subjects, and activities.

The second group includes techniques designed to arrange the concepts into a system or framework according to some personal reasons or rules. In a sense, the client and counselor are searching for a "theory" to explain the client's career as it has unfolded, as it is today and, by extrapolation, as it has potential to become. A simple example of the counselor stimulus is taken from the instructions for sorting cards in the Tyler Vocational Card Sort: " 'Now I would like you to break up these big groups [of cards] into smaller groups of occupations that for some reason go together in your mind . . . There are no rules about the number of groups you should some out with or about the number of cards in each group' " (Tyler, 1961, p. 196). By breaking up big groups of concepts into smaller groups that "go together" according to personal rules, the client is re-arranging the material thus allowing for new insights.

The several procedures employed to collect and interpret data to subjects in two research projects (Chusid & Cochran, 1989; McGregor & Cochran, 1988) provide examples of this group of techniques. Although not applied strictly to counseling, these techniques have promise for new applications in developmental career counseling. Cochran and colleagues used an adjective Q-sort method to obtain subject's descriptions of self, family roles, and work roles. (It may not be coincidental that Super, 1969, expressed his preference for adjective lists among appraisal techniques.) Principal components statistical analyses were applied to the data from each separate case. The researchers constructed a case portrait, their version of a "dynamic description," for each subject and interpreted it, an event that stirred deep emotions for several subjects. The researchers, rather than the subjects, created the portraits, but the interpretation was a shared event and seemed to produce important insights, perhaps new meaning-schemes.

The third group of descriptive techniques involve studying the schematic arrangement of client concepts, re-arranging the scheme in search of new connections, and identifying the underlying principles for the new arrangements. The concept names, the rules for their schematic arrangement, and the principles for organizing the schemes are all potential sources of new, and perhaps more complex, insights. Partial examples come from puzzle metaphors where concepts serve as pieces of a puzzle. Brandel (1982) described such a "puzzling" technique but apparently suggested that the counselor supply the constructs to be "fit" into the final puzzle. Chadbourne, Rosenberg, and Mahoney (1982) described a tool they call the Puzzle Pieces of Your World in which clients are supplied with 13 life-sector pieces cut to different sizes depending on client scores from the authors' Assess Your World inventory. The clients are directed to "put the puzzle together while thinking out loud" and the facilitator takes descriptive notes. These two examples capture the flavor of client manipulation, whether verbal or physical, of their own career constructs in order to derive new insights. What they may miss is the search for themes to capture large portions of the career experience.

Still another approach suggested by Gunnison, Shapiro, and Bradley (1982) is an adaptation of Kagan, Krathwohl, and Griffin's (1966) Interpersonal Process Recall to encourage the client and the counselor to think out loud about the concepts and schemes of his or her career. The approach seems to combine Gestalt insight problem-solving methods with the guidance of the counselor as consultant.

The discovery of new career insights is achieved through both inductive and deductive reasoning processes. Both processes require a representative sample of material about the person's career obtained through a well-planned appraisal. Inductive reasoning is applied when appraisal data are arranged according to "rules" emanating from the client's own thoughts and feelings rather than externally imposed category systems. In a sense, developmental counselors ask clients to re-arrange experiential information in a way they have not done previously using the client's "common-sense" reasoning. Insights result from the process of categorizing and the resultant groups and rules.

Deductive methods for achieving insights involve applying *concepts* from career development theory as categories in the second step and applying *assumptions or principles* from theories to derive hypotheses in the third step. This follows closely the interpretation approach described by Levy (1963) and gives the counselor a much more active role in the process. The counselor relies on knowledge of developmental concepts to suggest categories for grouping career data. Counselors organize client's career data for interpretations by using the concept definition as the rules or criteria for collating the data. The concepts presented earlier in this chapter can be defined to the clients and then used to categorize the data about their career experiences. For example, the *life-events* concept may offer a category for differentiating among the environmental stimuli critical to client actions in the future. The *transition* concept may be used to discriminate turbulence experienced in the present from states of comfort and equilibrium experienced in the past or from anticipated future states.

The network of concepts in a developmental theory may be useful for forming schemes in the second step of interpretation. Straightforward uses of career development theory for organizing career material are becoming more obvious to counselors in recent years. Analogues and metaphors are often helpful for communicating about theories. For example, Super's (1980) life-career rainbow serves as a useful analogue for organizing career experience data longitudinally and, consequently, as an aid for interpreting those data. Crites' (1974c) model of career maturity for adolescents may be a framework for collecting and interpreting data for that age cohort. He has developed a set of career maturity inventories (Crites, 1978) to measure the elements in the model but Gottfredson and Holland (1976) have shown that data gathered from a trait–factor approach may also be used. Perosa and Perosa (1983) have demonstrated the usefulness of Janis and Mann's (1977) decision-making model for describing mid-career changes.

Cognitive categorization of the career experience material into conceptual patterns and "displaying" the patterns – orally or symbolically – before the client and counselor enables both to make new discoveries important to the client's career development. The patterns may suggest new insights for the client. At the same time, they may suggest hypotheses about the client's career that can be checked through gathering new data or retrieving other forms of available data. These data are incorporated into the "display" and the search for connections continues. The client looks for "meaning making," whereas the counselor searches for clinical hunches. The counselor may serve as a guide or consultant or a source of authoritative observations about the display.

Adaptive Strategy

Recent advances in the theoretical understanding about the nature of developmental levels have allowed counselors to consider specific applications of this principle to career counseling assessment and intervention. At the same time, the technology necessary for confident application seems to have lagged far behind the understanding. Advances in understanding are exemplified by Loevinger's (1976) comparison of the levels of client-centered therapy processes and levels of ego development and found that a whole system of counseling is roughly parallel to a dimension of psychological development. Kohlberg and Mayer (1972) invoked a philosophical and psychological justification for the aim of education as development toward the highest levels of reasoning about moral and factual choices and suggested that educational interventions be adapted to match the student's developmental level.

These elaborate arguments and those of Piagetian translators and interpreters (e.g., Elkind, 1974) have influenced career development theorists. For example, there are subtle differences between Super's early descriptive formulations about development (e.g., Super, 1957b) and his latest theoretical statements (e.g., 1980, 1984b) that include transition steps. There has been a distinguishable shift in thinking among career developmental theorists toward adopting more of the transactional world view and its assumptions (Vondracek, Lerner, & Schulenberg, 1986). Thus, the adaptation principle has emerged as a potential guideline for developmental career counselors.

This strategic principle has been emphasized in recent writings about developmental counseling (Ivey & Gonsalves, 1988), and career counseling (Blocher & Seigal, 1981; Super, 1983). The principle is fundamental to instructional applications of Kohlberg's developmental theory (Rest, 1974), theories of cognitive complexity (Hunt, 1975), and Perry's developmental scheme (Widick, 1977). Leona Tyler (1969, 1978) has long advocated for developmental counseling: "The psychological purpose of counseling is to facilitate development" (1969, p. 16). She also suggested initial appraisal of the client's situation, classification into one of several problem categories, and differential counseling strategies and techniques.

Among career counseling approaches, Blocher and Seigal (1981) clearly support applying the adaptation principle, but they do not propose specific counseling techniques. They postulate the following:

> Psychological intervention should involve, first, thorough understanding of the nature of present conceptual systems, and second, the presentation of optimally discrepant or novel information through a variety of media in order to facilitate development and the resulting experience of increased predictability, freedom, and control. (p. 41)

Super's (1983) *developmental task counseling* seems to provide the most specific techniques for applying this principle. He emphasized "the need to take people as they are, where they are in their career development, and help them move on to the next stage" (p. 561). Super's developmental assessment model (contrasted with the trait–factor models) proposed that the counselor determine clients' readiness for career transitions before assisting them with exploration, planning, and action. The appropriate aspects of experience to assess are developmental tasks because they are easier to grasp than stages and because they can be somewhat disassociated with age, that is, tasks can more readily be seen to reoccur in several stages and may even occur earlier than is typically expected.

As a part of what they called *developmental therapy*, Ivey and Gonsalves (1988) advocated for style-shift counseling strategies. The main counseling objective is to "introduce movement in the developmental sphere." Their version of the strategic principle is summarized in three "needs" or requirements that suggest specific tactics for counselors:

1. The need to take into consideration, as a point of departure of any counseling intervention, clients' developmental levels.

2. The need to design counseling and therapeutic interventions that match clients' developmental levels.
3. The need to promote horizontal and vertical development using different therapeutic strategies. (p. 410)

Each "need" is elaborated to show its promise for application to career counseling practice. The practical limitations of present "technology"—the collection of techniques and their strategic application—are also discussed.

The first requirement calls counselor's *attention to client's developmental level*, their ordinal position on a developmental continuum. Assessments of life stage, developmental task, and career maturity can be utilized to estimate client level. The comprehensive appraisal procedures described earlier provide the information for such an assessment. As an example, Super (1983) proposed three assessments prior to interventions: *work salience*, the importance of work roles relative to other life roles, the *work values* sought in the work role, and *career maturity*, the general readiness to address the next career decisions or career transitions.

Standardized, paper-and-pencil inventories have been constructed for the express purpose of assessing work salience (Super & Nevill, 1986a), work values (Super & Nevill, 1986b), and either career maturity (Super, Thompson, Lindeman, Jordaan, & Myers, 1981) or the adult equivalent called career adaptability (Super, 1977). Instruments for assessing career maturity/adaptability cover the dimensions of planfulness, exploration, information, decision making and reality orientation, and represent measures of Career Maturity I. Each inventory manual provides age norms and illustrative sample cases as aids to interpretation, but the results of these inventories are not easily translated to developmental "levels." Therefore, counselors may be required to apply their clinical intuition when using the scores to estimate "level" and readiness.

After work salience, work values and career maturity are assessed, the results are presented to the client for acceptance or revision. The client is helped to assimilate—transform the incoming information so it can fit into existing forms of client knowledge—an understanding of both his or her present stage and next stage of career development and understanding the meanings he or she assigns to work and other life roles. Decisions about the issues to be addressed in counseling are made conjointly. Super listed five such issues:

1. Exploration for maturing?
2. Exploration in breadth for crystallization?
3. Exploration in depth for specification?

4. Choice of preparation, training, or job objective?
5. Searches for job and other outlets for self-realization?

Precision in the diagnosis of client level is the most important practical problem to be solved before this first step is implemented successfully. Career maturity inventory scores provide a general estimate of overall career developmental level, not nearly so precise as the estimates of level of intellectual development but perhaps about as useful as estimates of level of social development. Developmental career counselors must await more evidence that these measures assess a level on the developmental continuum before they can be used with confidence. At present, it appears that only the Career Maturity Inventory-Attitude Scale (Crites, 1978) is supported by some evidence that it does assess something approaching a developmental dimension over the adolescent and young adult years (Jepsen, 1984a).

Assessments of client level may apply best to individual career development tasks such as the task of choosing an occupation during late adolescence. Counselors have several instruments to choose from as Slaney (1988) has indicated, and several are supported by evidence of their validity. The counselor and client can obtain a reasonably good estimate of progress toward mastering the task and calibrate interventions accordingly.

The second point requires counselors to focus attention on the matter of *matching the intervention to the client level*. This is a deceptively difficult step to take because it requires *accurate judgments* about critical dimensions of both client level and interventions. As Vondracek et al. (1986) have made clear, there are numerous levels of analysis for interventions including the *"target" level* (e.g., whether the "target" is the individual, the individual's primary groups, or the social system of which the individual is part) and the *timing* of interventions (e.g., whether to support or challenge the individual's present status). The judgment about dimensions of interventions often requires information the counselor may not have available.

A sophisticated attempt to make these judgments was demonstrated by Widick, Knefelkamp, and Parker's (1975) application of Perry's developmental scheme (Perry, 1970) to college classroom teaching. When preparing instructional procedures for students in the dualistic stage (as contrasted with procedures for students in other stages), they distinguished among approaches that *challenge* student assumptions and those that provide *support* for student efforts to learn. Examples of instructional approaches to provide support was the structure of the class and a personal atmosphere in the classroom. Challenge was provided through diversity of viewpoint in course content and instructional methods and through experiential learning models. The same distinctions between challenge and support were applied to approaches in career planning courses (Touchton, Wertheimer, Cornfeld, & Harrison, 1977) and instructor responses to student journals (Schmidt & Davison, 1983).

Super (1983) suggested the matching idea can be applied to test selection and interpretation. The counselor makes a simple, binary distinction between clients who are ready to utilize results of conventional ability tests and interest inventories and those who are not. People vary in their capacity to find meaning in test scores and to use the results as the basis for planning. Super felt that those who have this capacity are those who (a) demonstrate the attitudes of being autonomous, believing in personal control over one's career; (b) have adequate future time perspective, can conceptualize the past and anticipate the future—immediate, intermediate, and distant; and (c) has sufficient self-esteem or feelings of self-worth. People who do not have these capacities are not likely to benefit from test results or may experience setbacks in their development.

Crites (1981b) "integrative test interpretation" represents an application of the matching principle *within* the test-interpretation process. The strengths and limitations of two specific test-interpretations methods, the trait–factor and the client-centered, suggest differential use. The former is best suited for helping the client to understand the "outer reality" of the personal and environmental constraints on his or her possibilities, whereas a client-centered approach is best suited for focusing on the clients' "inner reality" of their idiosyncratic phenomenal field.

A more detailed example of client-intervention "matching" is from Schmidt and Davison's (1983) application of Perry's developmental scheme to derive specific guidelines for instructor's responses to student journals. The suggested responses employ the assumption of "plus one staging," that is to provide a challenge moderately discrepant from the student's present position on the developmental continuum. This is an example of Blocher and Seigal's (1981) "optimally discrepant or novel information." Although the guidelines have not been applied to career material, the use of career autobiographies and decision journals as adjuncts to career counseling as suggested by Crites (1981a) may be enhanced by attention to matching the quality of counselor response to client developmental level.

The barrier to successful implementation of the second "need" is the lack of information about interventions in the form necessary to make judgments about the match. Only a few interventions are presented to counselors with alternative approaches as was the test interpretations

(Crites, 1981b) and responses to student journals (Schmidt & Davison, 1983). Furthermore, the dimension along which the interventions are ordered is seldom developmental but rather a contemporary attribute such as learning aptitude or motivation. At this point in the history of developmental counseling it may be more profitable for the counselor to rely on past personal experiences and the experience of trusted colleagues with an intervention rather than waiting for empirical evidence as the basis for a match.

The third "need" focuses the counselor's attention on *two dimensions of development*, the horizontal and the vertical. It reflects the application of an important idea from Piaget's work, the concept of horizontal *decalage*, which refers to the process of horizontal elaboration (i.e., within-stage rather than across-stage development) in which the capacity to use the highest level cognitive operations is gradually expanded to include a wider range of content areas. For example, clients in the exploration stage will be using their resources to master the full array of developmental tasks within that stage as well as preparing to move to the next stage.

Thus, the counselor and client are concerned with developmental change of two kinds: vertical acceleration up the developmental continuum and horizontal elaboration within the multiple tasks of the stage level. These two changes are roughly analogous to the two forms of career maturity according to Savickas' (1984) analysis: Career maturity I is a unidimensional assessment of the degree of progress on developmental tasks compared to expected degree of progress and Career Maturity II is a multidimensional assessment of degree of coping success with the full array of stage-appropriate developmental tasks.

There are relatively few interventions that represent planned efforts to encourage horizontal and vertical movement. Horizontal elaboration is probably best illustrated by classroom or workshop curricula that attempt comprehensive coverage of the career developmental tasks within a single stage. Examples are a life-role planning program for adolescents (Amatea & Cross, 1986), a Life Planning Workshop for college students (e.g., Mencke & Cochran, 1974), a college decision-making course based on developmental theory (Stonewater & Daniels, 1983) or Schlossberg's (1984) Career Transition Workshop for adults. The elaboration principle is also applied in the frequent repetitions advocated for values clarification activities whether within a classroom (e.g., Simon, Lowe, & Kirschenbaum, 1972) or within a computer program such as SIGI (Katz, 1973).

The barrier to implementing the third "need" is uncertainty about whether to move horizontally or vertically as the next step in the counseling process. Put another way, the timing of vertical moves is an issue. When should the "plus one staging" idea be applied? When should support be given by persuading the client to attempt another within-stage developmental task? What consideration should be given to client development relative to their peer group?

SUMMARY

Developmental career counselors are distinguished from those in other approaches because their thinking about career is based on traditions rooted in principles from developmental psychology. Developmentalists share a common language and preferences among counselor roles. The developmental theories counselors implore are those derived from world views represented by organismic and transactional metaphors. This leads to basic assumptions about human development, for example, that development is a self-constructive process, and concepts, such as stage, used to organize counselor's orientation to client career experiences. Although specific techniques are not clearly associated with developmental career counseling, two strategic principles apparently guide counselor actions: Developmental career counselors favor description and interpretation techniques leading to new client insights and they attempt to adapt their techniques to the client's developmental level.

The developmental career counseling approach can best be characterized as in its infancy although it has shown growth since the time of Crites' (1974a) review. Theoretical and empirical advances in developmental psychology during the past three decades have not, as yet, been translated completely into *models* that career counselors can readily apply in their daily work. The ideas in developmental theory seem to have considerable promise for enriching developmental career counselor's understanding of the dynamics of careers and the impact of counseling interventions. But the translation is very difficult work largely because the ideas are so abstract and broadly subsumptive.

As with learning theory and trait–factor theory approaches, the tools of the social scientist's laboratory may be modified into *methods* for the developmental career counselor's office. This work has shown some progress, but the methods are expensive both in terms of money and time. These costs are often difficult to justify to a profession that seems to share a societal value for efficiency and quick solutions to social and personal problems.

RERERENCES

Amatea, E., & Cross, E. G. (1986). Helping high school students clarify life role preferences: The life styles unit. *The School Counselor, 33*, 306–313.

Astin, H. S. (1984). The meaning of work in women's lives: A sociopsychological model of career choice and work behavior. *The Counseling Psychologist, 12,* 117–126.

Beilin, H. (1955). The application of general developmental principles to the vocational area. *Journal of Counseling Psychology, 2,* 53–57.

Blocher, D. H., & Siegal, R. (1981). Toward a cognitive developmental theory of leisure and work. *The Counseling Psychologist, 9,* 33–44.

Bolles, R. (1988). *What color is your parachute?* Berkeley, CA: Ten Speed Press.

Borow, H. (1961). Vocational development research: Some problems of logical and experimental form. *Personnel and Guidance Journal, 40,* 21–25.

Brammer, L. M., & Shostrom, E. L. (1982). *Therapeutic psychology: Fundamentals of counseling and psychotherapy* (4th ed.). Englewood Cliffs, NJ: Prentice-Hall.

Brandel, I. W. (1982). Puzzling your career: A self-responsibility, self-acceptance approach to career planning. *Personnel and Guidance Journal, 61,* 225–228.

Campbell, R. E., & Cellini, J. V. (1981). A diagnostic taxonomy of adult career problems. *Journal of Vocational Behavior, 19,* 175–190.

Carlsen, M. B. (1988). *Meaning-making: Therapeutic processes in adult development.* New York: Norton.

Carter, H. D. (1940). The development of vocational attitudes. *Journal of Consulting Psychology, 4,* 185–191.

Chadbourne, J. W., Rosenberg, H. J., & Mahoney, J. T. (1982). Defining decision making patterns: A tool for career-life planning. *Personnel and Guidance Journal, 61,* 51–53.

Chusid, H., & Cochran, L. (1989). Meaning of career change from the perspective of family roles and dramas. *Journal of Counseling Psychology, 36,* 34–41.

Cochran, L. (1983). Seven measures of the ways that deciders frame their career decisions. *Measurement and Evaluation in Guidance, 16,* 67–77.

Crites, J. O. (1974a). Career counseling: A review of major approaches. *The Counseling Psychologist, 4,* 3–23.

Crites, J. O. (1974b). A reappraisal of vocational appraisal. *Vocational Guidance Quarterly, 22,* 272–279.

Crites, J. O. (1974c). Career development processes: A model of vocational maturity. In E. L. Herr (Ed.), *Vocational guidance and human development* (pp. 296–320). Boston: Houghton Mifflin.

Crites, J. O. (1978). *Theory and research handbook for the Career Maturity Inventory.* Monterey, CA: CTB/McGraw-Hill.

Crites, J. O. (1981a). *Career counseling: Models, methods and materials.* New York: McGraw-Hill.

Crites, J. O. (1981b) Integrative test interpretation. In D. H. Montross & C. J. Schenkman (Eds.), *Career development in the 1980s: Theory and practice.* Springfield, IL: Charles C. Thomas.

Elkind, D. (1974). *Children and adolescent: Interpretive essays on Jean Piaget* (2nd ed.). New York: Oxford University Press.

Elkind, D. (1980). Child development and counseling. *Personnel and Guidance Journal, 58,* 353–355.

Erickson, E. (1964). *Insight and responsibility: Lectures on the ethical implications of psychoanalytic insight.* New York: Norton.

Fingarette, H. (1963). *The self in transformation: Psychoanalysis, philosophy and the life of the spirit.* New York: Harper & Row.

Fryer, D. (1931). *The measurement of interests.* New York: Holt.

Ginzberg, E. (1972). Toward a theory of occupational choice: A restatement. *Vocational Guidance Quarterly, 20,* 169–176.

Ginzberg, E. (1984). Career development. In D. Brown, L. Brooks, & Associates (Eds.), *Career choice and development* (pp. 169–191). San Francisco: Jossey-Bass.

Ginzberg, E., Ginsberg, S. W., Axelrad, S., & Herma, J. L. (1951). *Occupational choice: An approach to a general theory.* New York: Columbia University Press.

Goldman, L. (1983). The vocational card sort technique: A different view. *Measurement and Evaluation in Guidance, 16,* 107–109.

Gottfredson, G. D., & Holland, J. L. (1976). Using a typology of persons and environments to explain careers: Some extensions and clarifications. *The Counseling Psychologist, 6,* 20–29.

Gottfredson, L. S. (1981). Circumscription and compromise: A developmental theory of occupational aspirations. *Journal of Counseling Psychology Monograph, 28,* 545–579.

Gottfredson, L. S. (1985). Role of self-concept in vocational theory. *Journal of Counseling Psychology, 32,* 159–162.

Gribbons, W. D., & Lohnes, P. R. (1968). *Emerging careers.* New York: Teachers College Press, Columbia University.

Gribbons, W. D., & Lohnes, P. R. (1982). *Careers in theory and experience: A twenty-year longitudinal study.* Albany: State University of New York Press.

Gunnison, H., Shapiro, J., & Bradley, R. W. (1982). Inside the creative process of counseling: Vocational decision making takes place. *Personnel and Guidance Journal, 60,* 361–363.

Hall, D. T., & Associates. (1986). *Career development in organizations.* San Francisco: Jossey-Bass.

Hamachek, D. E. (1985). The self's development and ego growth: Conceptual analysis and implications for counselors. *Journal of Counseling and Development, 64,* 136–142.

Harren, V. A. (1980). *Assessment of Career Decision-Making (ACDM) Preliminary Manual.* Carbondale, IL: Author.

Havighurst, R. J. (1980). Social and developmental psychology: Trends in influencing the future of counseling. *Personnel and Guidance Journal, 58,* 328–333.

Hunt, D. E. (1975). Person-environment interaction: A challenge found wanting before it was tried. *Review of Educational Research, 45,* 209–230.

Ivey, A. E., & Gonsalves, O. F. (1988). Developmental therapy: Integrating developmental process into the clinical practice. *Journal of Counseling and Development, 66,* 406–413.

Janis, I. L., & Mann, L. (1977). *Decision making: A psychological analysis of conflict, choice and commitment.* New York: The Free Press.

Jepsen, D. A. (1974). The stage construct in career development. *Counseling and Values, 18,* 124–131.

Jepsen, D. A. (1975). Occupational decision development over the high school years. *Journal of Vocational Behavior, 1,* 225–237.

Jepsen, D. A. (1984a). The developmental perspective on vocational behavior: A review of theory and research. In S. D. Brown & R. W. Lent (Eds.), *Handbook of counseling psychology* (pp. 178–215). New York: Wiley.

Jepsen, D. A. (1984b). Relationship between career development theory and practice. In N. C. Gysbers & Associates (Eds.), *Designing careers* (pp. 135–159). San Francisco: Jossey-Bass.

Jordaan, J. P. (1974). Life stages as organizing modes of career development. In E. L. Herr (Ed.), *Vocational guidance and human development* (pp. 263–295). Boston: Houghton Mifflin.

Jordaan, J. P., & Heyde, M. B. (1979). *Vocational maturity during the high school years.* New York: Teachers College Press, Columbia University.

Kagan, N., & Krathwohl, D., & Griffin, G. (1966). *IPR-Interpersonal process recall.* East Lansing, MI: Michigan State University.

Katz, M. R. (1973). Career decision-making: A computer-based system of interactive guidance and information (SIGI). In Educational Testing Service, *Measurement for self-understanding and personal development, Proceedings of the 1973 Invitational Conference on testing problems*. Princeton, NJ: Educational Testing Service.

Kelly, G. A. (1955). *The psychology of personal constructs*. New York: Norton.

Kohlberg, L., & Mayer, G. (1972). Development as the aim of education. *Harvard Educational Review, 42*, 449–496.

Krumboltz, J. D., & Baker, R. D. (1973). Behavioral counseling for vocational decision. In H. Borow (Ed.), *Career guidance for a new age* (pp. 235–283). Boston: Houghton-Mifflin.

Krumboltz, J. D., & Thoresen, C. E. (1964). The effect of behavioral counseling in group and individual settings on information seeking behaviors. *Journal of Counseling Psychology, 11*, 324–333.

Langer, J. (1969). *Theories of development*. New York: Holt, Rinehart & Winston.

Lazarus, R. S., & Folkman, S. (1984). *Stress, appraisal, and coping*. New York: Springer.

Levinson, D. J., Darrow, C. N., Klein, E. B., Levinson, M. H., & McKee, B. (1978). *The seasons of a man's life*. New York: Ballantine.

Levy, L. H. (1963). *Psychological interpretation*. New York: Holt, Rinehart & Winston.

Liebowitz, Z., & Lea, D. (Eds.). (1985). *Adult career development: Concepts, issues and practices*. Alexandria, VA: AACD.

Loevinger, J. (1976). *Ego development: Conceptions and theories*. San Francisco: Jossey-Bass.

McGregor, A., & Cochran, L. (1988). Work an enactment of family drama. *Career Development Quarterly, 37*, 138–148.

Mencke, R. A., & Cochran, D. J. (1974). Impact of counseling outreach workshop on vocational development. *Journal of Counseling Psychology, 21*, 185–190.

Morrill, W. H., & Forrest, D. J. (1970). Dimensions of counseling for career development. *Personnel and Guidance Journal, 49*, 299–305.

Murray, H. A. (1938). *Explorations in personality*. New York: Oxford University Press.

Neff, W. S. (1985). *Work and human behavior* (3rd ed.). New York: Aldine.

Neimeyer, G. J. (1989). Applications for Repertory Grid technique to vocational assessment. *Journal of Counseling and Development, 67*, 585–589.

Nisbett, R., & Ross, L. (1980). *Human inference: Strategies and shortcomings of social judgment*. Englewood Cliffs, NJ: Prentice-Hall.

Okiishi, R. W. (1987). The genogram as a tool in career counseling. *Journal of Counseling and Development, 66*, 139–143.

Osipow, S. H. (1979). Career choices: Learning about interests and intervening in their development. In A. M. Mitchell, G. B. Jones, & J. D. Krumboltz (Eds.), *Social learning theory and career decision making* (pp. 106–111). Cranston, RI: Carroll.

Pask-McCartney, C., & Salomone, P. R. (1988). Difficult cases in career counseling: III – The multipotentialed client. *Career Development Quarterly, 36*, 231–240.

Perosa, S., & Perosa, L. (1983). The mid-career crisis: A description of the psychological dynamics of transition and adaptation. *Vocational Guidance Quarterly, 32*, 60–79.

Perry, W. (1970). *Forms of intellectual and ethical development in the college years*. New York: Holt, Rinehart & Winston.

Raynor, J. O. (1982). A theory of personality functioning and change. In J. O. Raynor & E. E. Entin (Eds.), *Motivation, career striving, and aging* (pp. 249–300). Washington, DC: Hemisphere.

Reese, H. W., & Overton, W. F. (1970). Models of development and theories of development. In L. R. Goulet & P. B. Baltes (Eds.), *Life-span development psychology: Research and theory* (pp. 115–145). New York: Academic Press.

Rest, J. (1974). Developmental psychology as a guide to value education: A review of "Kohlbergian" programs. *Review of Educational Research, 44*, 241–259.

Roe, A., & Siegelman, M. (1964). *The origin of interests*. Washington, DC: American Personnel and Guidance Association.

Rounds, J. B., Jr., & Tinsley, H. E. A. (1984). Diagnosis and treatment of vocational problems. In S. D. Brown & R. W. Lent (Eds.), *Handbook of counseling psychology* (pp. 137–177). New York: Wiley.

Salomone, P. R., & McKenna, P. (1982). Difficult career counseling cases: I–Unrealistic vocational aspirations. *Personnel and Guidance Journal, 60,* 283–286.

Sarbin, T. R., Taft, R., & Bailey, D. F. (1960). *Clinical inference and cognitive theory.* New York: Holt Rinehart.

Savickas, M. L. (1984). Career maturity: The construct and its measurement. *Vocational Guidance Quarterly, 32,* 222–231.

Schlossberg, N. K. C. (1984). *Counseling adults in transition: Linking practice with theory.* New York: Springer.

Schmidt, J. A., & Davison, M. L. (1983). Helping students think. *Personnel and Guidance Journal, 61,* 563–569.

Simon, S. B., Lowe, L. W., & Kirschenbaum, H. (1972). *Values clarification: A handbook of practical strategies for teachers and students.* New York: Hart.

Slaney, R. (1988). The assessment of career decision making. In W. B. Walsh & S. H. Osipow (Eds.), *Career decision making* (pp. 33–76). Hillsdale, NJ: Lawrence Erlbaum Associates.

Smelser, N. J. (1980). Issues in the study of work and love in adulthood. In N. J. Smelser & E. H. Erikson (Eds.), *Themes of work and love in adulthood* (pp. 1–26). Cambridge, MA: Harvard University Press.

Stonewater, J. K., & Daniels, M. H. (1983). Psychosocial and cognitive development in a career decision-making course. *Journal of College Student Personnel, 24,* 403–410.

Super, D. E. (1951). Vocational adjustment: Implementing a self-concept. *Occupations, 30,* 88–92.

Super, D. E. (1953). A theory of vocational development. *American Psychologist, 8,* 185–190.

Super, D. E. (1954). Career patterns as a basis for vocational counseling. *Journal of Counseling Psychology, 1,* 12–20.

Super, D. E. (1957a). The preliminary appraisal in vocational counseling. *Personnel and Guidance Journal, 36,* 154–161.

Super, D. E. (1957b). *The psychology of careers.* New York: Harper.

Super, D. E. (1963). Toward making a self-concept theory operational. In D. E. Super, R. Starishevsky, N. Matlin, & J. P. Jordaan (Eds.), *Career development: Self-concept theory* (pp. 17–32). New York: College Entrance Examination Board.

Super, D. E. (1969). Vocational development theory in 1988: How will it come about? *The Counseling Psychologist, 1,* 9–14.

Super, D. E. (1977). Vocational maturity in midcareer. *Vocational Guidance Quarterly, 25,* 294–302.

Super, D. E. (1980). A life-span, life-space approach to career development. *Journal of Vocational Behavior, 16,* 282–298.

Super, D. E. (1983). Assessment in career guidance: Toward truly developmental counseling. *Journal of Counseling and Development, 63,* 555–562.

Super, D. E. (1984a). Perspectives on the meaning and value of work. In Gysbers, N. C., & Associates (Eds.), *Designing careers* (pp. 27–53). San Francisco: Jossey-Bass.

Super, D. E. (1984b). Career and life development. In D. Brown, L. Brooks, & Associates (Eds.), *Career choice and development* (pp. 27–53). San Francisco: Jossey-Bass.

Super, D. E., Crites, J. O., Hummel, R. C., Moser, H. P., Overstreet, P. L., & Warnath, C. F. (1957) *Vocational development: A framework for research.* New York: Teachers College Press.

Super, D. E., & Nevill, D. D. (1986a). *The salience inventory.* Palo Alto, CA: Consulting Psychologists Press.

Super, D. E., & Nevill, D. D. (1986b). *The values scale.* Palo Alto, CA: Consulting Psychologists Press.

Super, D. E., Thompson, A. S., Lindeman, R. H., Jordaan, J. P., & Meyers, R. A. (1981). *The career development inventory.* Palo Alto, CA: Consulting Psychologists Press.

Tiedeman, D. V. (1961). Decision and vocational development: A paradigm and its implications. *Personnel and Guidance Journal, 40,* 15–20.

Tiedeman, D. V., & O'Hara, R. P. (1963). *Career development: Choice and adjustment.* New York: College Board.

Touchton, J. G., Wertheimer, L. C., Cornfeld, J. L., & Harrison, K. H. (1977). Career planning and decision making: A developmental approach to the classroom. *The Counseling Psychologist, 6,* 42–47.

Tyler, L. E. (1961). Research explorations in the realm of choice. *Journal of Counseling Psychology, 8,* 195–201.

Tyler, L. E. (1969). *The work of the counselor* (3rd ed.). New York: Appleton-Century-Crofts.

Tyler, L. E. (1978). *Individuality: Human possibilities and personal choice in the psychological development of men and women.* San Francisco: Jossey-Bass.

Vondracek, F. W., Lerner, R. M., & Schulenberg, J. E. (1986). *Career development: A life-span developmental approach.* Hillsdale, NJ: Lawrence Erlbaum Associates.

Widick, C. (1977). The Perry scheme: A foundation for developmental practice. *The Counseling Psychologist, 6,* 35–38.

Widick, C., Knefelkamp, L. L., & Parker, C. A. (1975). The counselor as developmental instructor. *Counseling Education and Supervision, 14,* 286–296.

Yost, E. B., & Corbishley, M. A. (1987). *Career counseling: A psychological approach.* San Francisco: Jossey-Bass.

5

Integrating the Social Learning Theory of Career Decision Making

John D. Krumboltz
Charles W. Nichols
Stanford University

Are theories about career choice and development all that different from each other? Does one have to choose sides and pick a favorite theory? What practical difference does it make which theory you favor? A central thesis of this chapter is that, although differing in emphasis and vocabulary, the major career theories are not in fundamental disagreement.

To make the case we first consider what a theory does. Then we review the basic concepts of the Social Learning Theory of Career Decision Making (SLTCDM). Next we compare the SLTCDM with three other career development theories. Finally, we present a broader living systems view of career decision making that is also essentially consistent with the SLTCDM, but provides a more comprehensive context for understanding decision-making processes and outcomes.

THE FUNCTIONS OF A THEORY

A theory is like a map. Both are intended to give us the big picture about a certain area of interest. They both help us understand the most essential characteristics of that area. Let us explore some other ways in which a map is similar to a theory.

A Representation of Reality

Both a map and a theory attempt to represent some portion of reality using words, symbols, numbers, colors, and/or figures. Neither the map nor the theory is reality itself—merely a representation of it. The various symbols are selected to represent various aspects of that reality in an understandable way.

Omission of Nonessentials

Consider a typical road map. It depicts and labels major highways, streets, cities, rivers, and lakes. It does not include trees, houses, rocks, flower beds, or pipelines. It deliberately omits certain features because the map maker believed them to be nonessential for the users of that map.

In the same way, a theory simplifies reality by ignoring a large number of variables. Reality is so complex that no single theory can adequately represent all of it. Each separate theory is an attempt to depict some small part of that reality and does so by deliberately ignoring other complexities. A theory is a deliberate oversimplification.

Distortion

To make the features of a certain territory clear a map exaggerates and distorts those features. For example, a major highway may be depicted in red ink on the map, whereas in reality the highway is a dirty gray color. The width of the highway is exaggerated on the map so that it is easily visible to the unaided eye.

In a similar way theories may stress the importance of certain variables by calling special attention to them—by giving them special names and by emphasizing their importance in words, figures and formulas.

Representation of the Unobservable

Just as a map may include invisible political boundaries (a county or state line), so a theory may include unobservable constructs and ideas believed to be important for understanding a particular phenomenon. The reality of some constructs is in the minds of the theory's adherents just as a political boundary is in the minds of those who observe it.

Scale

Maps differ in the size of the territory covered. Some maps depict a large area, for example, the entire world, on one sheet of paper. The scale must then be very small, perhaps 1 inch to 1,000 miles, and many details must be omitted. If a smaller territory is being represented, for example, the State of Colorado, the scale can be much larger, perhaps, 1 inch to 25 miles. Similarly, we could devise still larger scale maps to represent the city of Denver, the lot on which your house is located, and the floor plan of your living room.

In a similar way, theories vary in scale depending on the scope of the phenomenon with which they are attempting to deal. A theory attempting to explain the gravitational attraction of stars and planets would not begin to account for the ways in which human beings are attracted to different occupations.

Accuracy

Early map makers, working with incomplete information, made errors in their maps and misrepresented the physical features of the land just as theorists do now in their attempts to represent a reality they only partly understand. However, even a theory that is partially wrong can still be useful. The scientific ideal is to continue improving theoretical formulations to represent reality better. Over time errors get corrected, but in new sciences like psychology, much trial and error remains on the agenda.

Usefulness

A good map enables one to answer all sorts of different questions: How far is it from Clinton to Dubuque? Will I be looking into the sun if I drive there in the morning? How large is the population of Cedar Rapids?

Similarly a good psychological theory enables people to derive answers (right or wrong) to innumerable questions. Why do people commit crimes? How should I raise my child to be independent? What is the best treatment for generalized anxiety? How do people develop preferences for different occupations? How do we explain the manner in which Joe Doe became an accountant? What interventions are needed to help young people make wise career decisions?

Purpose

Maps vary in their purpose. A road map is useful for a motorist but not particularly valuable to a railroad engineer or an airline pilot. A map depicting average annual rainfall in various parts of the world might be useful to an agronomist or an environmentalist but of little value to a sociologist. A map is constructed to serve some purposes of its users.

In a similar way a theory is constructed to serve the specific purposes of its users—understanding a complex phenomenon, making predictions about future outcomes, or deciding on courses of action. Just as a map can be good for one purpose and not for another, so a theory can be good for one purpose and useless for another. It is not sufficient therefore to talk about good and bad theory without considering the purpose that the theory is designed to serve (Krumboltz, 1978).

THE SOCIAL LEARNING THEORY OF CAREER DECISION MAKING

The SLTCDM has been described in detail elsewhere (Krumboltz, 1979, 1981; Krumboltz, Mitchell, & Jones, 1976, 1978, 1980). Only a brief summary of the theory is presented here. The purpose of the SLTCDM is to explain how people come to be employed in a variety of occupations and to suggest possible interventions that might help people make satisfactory career decisions.

The most essential concept in this theory is the concept of learning. People acquire their preferences for various activities through a variety of learning experiences. They make sense of their activities because of ideas they have been taught or have learned through experience. They acquire beliefs about themselves and the nature of their world through direct and indirect educational experiences. They then take action on the basis of their beliefs using skills that they have developed over time. What follows is a closer look at the process.

Why Do People Prefer Certain Activities?

People develop their preferences by interacting with their environment in a long and complex series of experiences. Two kinds of learning experience are identified in the SLTCDM: instrumental and associative.

Instrumental Learning Experiences. Imagine Fred standing at home plate. Fred swings and hits a home run. His teammates cheer. Now imagine Sam coming up to bat next. Sam swings and misses. He misses the second pitch and the third pitch. Sam is out. His teammates say nothing. Which of these two boys is most likely to entertain dreams of becoming a professional baseball player?

If you said "Fred," then you are thinking along the same lines as the SLTCDM, which states that preferences are developed through the consequences of repeatedly trying a variety of activities. Through instrumental learning experiences people develop a preference for activities in which they succeed or are rewarded, and they tend to lose interest in activities in which they fail and for which they receive no reward or are punished.

Associative Learning Experiences.   Images are flashed before our eyes in a dazzling array. Television commercials associate mundane products with glamorous images. Television programs also depict certain occupations as glamorous and exciting. Influential people talk about certain industries as "hot": plastics, computers, or genetic engineering (depending on the year). Attractive pictures and words, when associated with certain industries and occupations, can create desirable images in the minds of observers. Negative words and pictures can represent other occupations as dull and boring.

Over the years each individual is exposed to millions of ways in which various occupations and activities are associated with positive or negative values. The associations are not necessarily consistent. Some are contradictory, and some are far more complex than a simple good or bad. Complex combinations of values involving prestige, financial reward, masculinity, variety, economic security, and altruism may be represented in various ways and to different degrees.

What Are the Consequences of These Learning Experiences?

Learning experiences do not have an automatic outcome. They are interpreted by each individual differently. People try to make sense of what they observe by constructing beliefs about themselves and about the world around them. They then use their beliefs to formulate their goals and guide their choices. Self-observation generalizations and task-approach skills are two consequences of these learning experiences.

Self-Observation Generalizations.   When Fred observes himself successfully hitting a home run, he may well say to himself, then or later, "I'm good at hitting a baseball." When Sam strikes out more frequently than most of his teammates, he is likely to be saying to himself, "I'm terrible at hitting a baseball." Each such statement is a self-observation generalization, a summary belief constructed by each individual based on a large number of prior learning experiences. It might be relatively accurate, or it could be harmfully mistaken.

Task-Approach Skills.   Through cognitive processes people are able to relate their observations of themselves to their environment. They make estimates of the degree to which they would be able to perform various activities in the real world. They develop work habits and problem-solving skills for coping with the world. They have beliefs about what they can and cannot do, and they have emotional reactions that accompany these beliefs. These relationships between the self-observation generalizations and the outside world are called *task-approach skills*. Included here are work habits, mental sets, perceptual and thought processes, performance standards and values, problem orientations, and emotional responses.

Some day Fred might relate his self-observation generalizations to his observations of the world around him in a task-approach skill something like this, "I do enjoy hitting a baseball and I do think I'm pretty good at it—but probably not good enough to make a career in the big leagues. Besides baseball is simply part of the entertainment industry, and I am more interested in applying my talents to improve the world. Even the best baseball players have short careers and need to find some other kind of work by the time they reach age 35. I think I'll look into some other possibilities."

Krumboltz (1988) has developed an instrument called the Career Beliefs Inventory to identify the kinds of beliefs and presuppositions that may interfere with people's ability to achieve their own goals.

Action Over Time. Over time this complex series of instrumental and associative learning experiences enables individuals to generate ever-changing self-observation generalizations and task-approach skills that provide the basis for career relevant action. Young people apply for and obtain part-time jobs. They develop new skills and habits. They get paid for their efforts. They learn which activities they like or dislike. Each job is a learning experience for the next job. Each experience builds on prior experiences.

In What Context Do These Learning Experiences Take Place?

Information Processing and Storage. Knowledge is accumulated over time through a complex combination of perception, information processing, and memory processes—known collectively as *learning*—which are still being outlined and debated. According to Bandura's social cognitive view (1986) people's conceptions about themselves and about the nature of things are developed and verified through four different processes: (a) direct recognition of the effects of their actions, (b) observation of the effects of someone else's behavior, (c) verbal instruction and discourse, and (d) self-generation of knowledge structures through reasoning processes. These processes are emphasized by the SLTCDM.

Each society and culture has a particular set of environmental conditions, economic opportunities, institutions for learning, political and social conditions that influence the nature of learning experiences. Self-observation generalizations and task-approach skills depend on the environment in which one is raised. The availability of schools and libraries, the quality of teachers, the presence or absence of war, the attitude of society toward differential sex roles for males and females, the societal birth rate, labor market conditions, political stability, and many other such factors create the context in which various types of learning experiences take place. Fred might aspire to be a baseball player if he grew up in the United States but a cricket player if he had grown up in England.

What Predictions Can Be Derived From This Theory?

A number of testable propositions have been advanced so far including the following:People will tend to prefer an occupation IF

1. they have succeeded at tasks they believe are like tasks performed by members of that occupation;
2. they have observed a valued model being reinforced for activities like those performed by members of that occupation;
3. a valued friend or relative stressed its advantages to them and/or they observed positive words and images associated with it.

A converse set of propositions can be stated as follows: People will tend to avoid an occupation IF

1. they have failed at tasks they believe are like tasks performed by members of that occupation;
2. they have observed a valued model be punished or ignored for activities like those performed by members of that occupation;
3. a valued friend or relative stressed its disadvantages to them and/or they have observed negative words and images associated with it.

Evidence relevant to the SLTCDM may be found in a number of references (Krumboltz, 1983; Krumboltz, Kinnier, Rude, Scherba, & Hamel, 1986; Krumboltz & Rude, 1981; Mitchell & Krumboltz, 1984a, 1984b, 1987).

SIMILARITIES WITH OTHER CAREER
DEVELOPMENT THEORIES

The general thesis of this chapter is that for all practical purposes different career development theories are not as different as most descriptions of them would have us believe. Certainly they use different terms, but to what extent are those terms simply synonyms for the same basic concepts, and to what extent do they represent different, but not contradictory, terrain?

There are certainly differences between theories, and we risk the charge of oversimplification in emphasizing similarities and minimizing differences here. However, there are more serious dangers in the belief that each career development theory is distinct. Some counselors seem to believe that they must subscribe to one theory or another. They believe that by advocating one theory, they deny the validity of others.

Other counselors like to maintain an "eclectic position," picking and choosing concepts from different theories—sometimes apologetically, sometimes not—to suit their particular purposes. In the following, we compare the SLTCDM with the theories proposed by Super, Holland, and Gottfredson. Because of space restrictions we drastically abbreviate the discussion of each theory while providing references to the more complete descriptions.

Super's Self-Concept Theory

Super (1953, 1955, 1957, 1963, 1964) and Super, Starishevsky, Matlin, and Jordaan (1963) maintained that the occupational choice of an individual is a function of the self-concept of that individual at the time of decision. Super has posited that people go through a series of stages in which the self-concept is successively refined.

In Super's view the similarity of a person's interests and abilities to the interests and abilities of people in a particular occupation increases the likelihood that a person will enter that occupation and will be happily employed there. Super did not specifically describe the ways in which learning experiences create differential interest and differential skills as does the SLTCDM. Neither did he describe how people learn how similar their abilities and interests are to those of people in different occupations. He did describe developmental patterns as evolving. The fact that he did not specifically describe the sequence of learning experiences that produces them does not necessarily mean that he denied the importance of learning experiences in creating interests and skills. If asked, he would probably endorse the notion that people indeed learn their interests and skills, but that it was not the purpose of his theory to describe these mechanisms.

Super's notion of the self-concept is very similar to the SLTCDM notion of the self-observation generalization. Super recognized that the self-concept changes and develops throughout life as a result of experience. The SLTCDM version posits that the self-observation generalization is refined through successive learning experiences in which people observe the degree to which their performance corresponds with their self-perception and that they then modify the self-perception accordingly. Of course, in some individuals, the self-perception becomes distorted as a result of faulty learning experiences of various types.

Regardless of the specific language used, however, both theories recognize that a growing and changing self-concept results from a series of learning experiences. These learning experiences can include identification with models, in Super's terms, or vicarious learning experiences in terms of the SLTCDM. They can result from direct experience or, in the SLTCDM's terms, instrumental learning experiences. Super discussed the influence of role playing—whereas the SLTCDM discusses the influence of positive and negative reinforcement from direct performance trials. Super also discussed the notion of reality testing, another variation of the same process.

Stages of development are a part of Super's theoretical notion, and he has suggested six developmental tasks beginning with the crystallization of a vocational preference and ending with readiness for retirement and decline. The SLTCDM depicts a continuous passage of time in which learning experiences occur but does not break down time into discrete labeled stages.

The notion of stages implies that there is some invariant sequence of behaviors that occurs at a certain period of one's life, that the sequence always occurs in the same order, and that rather rigid boundaries can be identified to distinguish the stages from each other. Super probably would not claim that the stages are all that sharply delimited and would certainly recognize the porous nature of the stages he has proposed. Indeed, in the fluid economy of the present decade, people at age 45 or 50 may well need to crystallize a vocational preference again if their present job has become obsolete. So at any given age, the same process may need to begin anew. For this reason, the SLTCDM does not delimit the passage of time by specifying discrete stages.

However, if Krumboltz were asked whether there are certain patterns of behavior more likely to occur with 14- to 18-year-olds than with 25- to 35-year-olds, he would certainly agree. On the average there are indeed certain common developmental tasks that occur more often at one age than other. The absence of stage specifications in the SLTCDM is a way of recognizing the fluid nature of learning experiences and the changing requirements of the occupational world. Stages are simply handy labels that could be attached to the time line in the SLTCDM—if someone wanted to think in those terms.

The two theories agree on the basic notion of persons successively refining their self-concept over time and applying it to their present world of work.

Vocational exploratory behavior is a key concept in both formulations. Jordaan (1963) was most articulate in emphasizing the way in which vocational exploration designed by the individual can produce learning experiences to either confirm or deny the present self-concept. The same general notion is advocated by the SLTCDM, which suggests that career beliefs need to be identified, examined, and subjected to testing by the person who holds them.

The distinction between self-observation generalizations and task-approach skills in the SLTCDM is parallel to the distinction between "psychtalk" and "occtalk" in Super's theory as described by Starishevsky and Matlin (1963). *Psychtalk* refers to the tendency of individuals to think about themselves (e.g., "I am a good baseball player," "I always tell the truth," "I work well with others"). *Occtalk* concerns the relationship between the psychtalk and the occupational and educational world. An occtalk statement might be, "I plan to become an accountant because I like numbers and because I work diligently and precisely and prefer to avoid excessive contact with people."

The term *incorporation* was used to indicate the degree of similarity between the psychtalk and the occtalk and the degree to which there is a realistic congruence. Although not using a term such as *incorporation*, the SLTCDM clearly provides for career deciders to test the adequacy of their conceptualizations with the real world. Thus, both theories posit that the career decider makes statements about the nature of the educational and occupational world, that these statements may be more or less accurate, that there are ways of testing the adequacy of these statements, and that actions and decisions to enter a particular occupation are based on the perceptions that individual holds.

Holland's Hexagon

Holland (1959, 1963, 1966, 1971, 1973) has generated a theory, instrumentation, and procedures that have had a powerful influence on career counseling. As the result of extensive factor analytic studies, Holland identified six orientations to describe people's interests: realistic, investigative, social, conventional, enterprising, and artistic. These six orientations can be represented in the form of a hexagon with the most different orientations at opposite sides of the hexagon and the most similar orientations adjacent to each other.

Holland did not describe in any detail how people come to develop the interests that characterize their particular orientation. However, if we were to ask Holland how interests were generated, he would undoubtedly indicate that people learn their interests as a result of interacting with the environment. The general learning model proposed by the SLTCDM could be used to explain how people come to develop any combination of these six orientations. By the same token, the SLTCDM does not specifically posit the existence of six orientations but does not deny the validity of these constructs either. If Krumboltz were asked about the usefulness of these six orientations, he would express his admiration for the research work that led to the hexagon model but would point out that there are sharp differences and distinctions within each orientation that must not be overlooked.

Holland posited a "level hierarchy," which is a function of one's general academic aptitude and self-evaluation. The self-evaluation in Holland's conception is similar to the notion of the self-observation generalization in the SLTCDM and differs from it only in its degree of specificity. Self-evaluation in Holland's conception refers to a more general assessment, whereas the SLTCDM's self-observation generalization pinpoints self-evaluation of specific behaviors and characteristics.

Holland also posited that occupational environments are characterized by these same six general orientations and that people attempt to match their own orientation profile to the orientation of particular occupations. The more similar the fit, the higher the "congruence." The SLTCDM specifically describes the influence of cultural, economic, and social influences on the opportunity structure and the availability of resources. It points out how the availability of schools and libraries, for example, can influence people's eventual occupational choice. Holland represented the same idea in a more macro manner by categorizing people and environments into six orientations and then calculating the degree of congruence.

Holland also contributed the concept of *self-knowledge*, which refers to the extent to which individuals possess accurate information about their own interests and abilities. Self-knowledge to Holland is similar to the self-observation generalization of the SLTCDM, which in turn is similar to the self-concept of Super.

According to Holland, a good occupational choice depends on accurate self-knowledge as well as accurate occupational knowledge. Again, he did not describe exactly how this knowledge is acquired, but we must certainly assume that it is acquired through learning and is not genetically imprinted. Some of his research (e.g., Holland, 1962) involved checking the similarity between the attitudes of students in the National Merit sample and their parents. He found some similarities between the attitudes held by mothers and the students' personal orientations. He also found that fathers' stated goals for their children were related to the basic orientation of their sons and, to a somewhat smaller degree, their daughters. Clearly, Holland recognized the transmission of values from parents to children although he did not specifically describe the mechanisms by which such attitudes and values are transmitted.

As a result of extensive research by Holland and his associates as well as by independent investigators, it has become quite clear that there is indeed a relationship between the orientations of individuals and the occupations that they choose. The correlations are far from perfect, however, and there is still much to be learned about the influences that affect career choice.

Holland's primary method of gathering data is by asking people about their preferences for named occupations. Subjects seem to have relatively stable stereotypes about occupations. One might well ask how occupational stereotypes are learned, but Holland's theory is not concerned with this question. The SLTCDM would suggest that stereotypes are learned primarily through associative learning experiences, the pairing of occupational names with images received through direct and vicarious experiences.

Although emphasizing different features of vocational development, the SLTCDM and Holland's theory do not basically disagree. Both would recognize that as a result of learning experiences people develop characteristic ways of viewing themselves and the world around them. Both stress that individuals seek to find a fit between the real world and their view of themselves. The better the fit, the happier the individual.

Gottfredson's Theory of Occupational Aspirations

A more recent theory on occupational aspirations has been proposed by Linda Gottfredson (1981). Gottfredson suggested that occupational aspirations are created in a four-stage manner: (a) orientation to size and power at ages 3–5; (b) orientation to sex roles at ages 6–8; (c) orientation to social valuation at ages 9–13; and (d) orientation to the internal unique self at ages 14 and over. Basically, she posited that certain aspects of the self and environment are more salient at some ages than at others. The SLTCDM, by contrast, does not divide the time line of development into distinct stages because learning experiences of different types can be influential at any age. Nevertheless, both theories clearly describe the increasing refinement of discriminations and conceptions with increasing age.

The most creative contribution of Gottfredson's theory is the notion that the attraction of a particular occupation is primarily a function of it's "sextype" rating and prestige level. She drew a grid in which the sextype rating of occupations is displayed along the horizontal axis from the most masculine occupations (e.g., miner) at the left to the most feminine occupations (e.g., manicurist) at the right. The prestige ranking of each occupation is displayed along the vertical axis, with the least prestigious occupations (e.g., groundskeeper) rated toward 0 at the bottom and the most prestigious occupations (e.g., federal judge) rated toward 100 at the top. Every occupation can then be placed on the grid.

Gottfredson proposed that each individual develops a "zone of acceptable alternatives" on this grid—a subset of occupations that are within the range of masculinity–femininity desired by the person and also within upper and lower limits of prestige deemed acceptable. The more idealistic aspirations are at the top of the zone, whereas more realistic aspirations are toward the bottom of the zone. Vertical boundary lines separate occupations that may be deemed either too masculine or too feminine for the taste of the person.

Gottfredson did not describe how people learn about these masculine or feminine characteristics of occupations, nor did she attempt to describe how people learn what prestige levels are ascribed to each occupation. The SLTCDM describes the mechanisms by which such learnings are acquired, but has not gone so far as to categorize the specific factors that influence most people at each age level. The SLTCDM lists the social factors that infringe on the choices of young people (e.g., labor market conditions, availability of libraries and industries, quality of education, neighborhood, and family background.) This environmental context creates the conditions from which learning experiences are developed. The SLTCDM describes how the learnings are acquired, whereas Gottfredson's theory describes how the products of that learning are organized. Although each theory focuses on different aspects of the process, they are not fundamentally in disagreement.

Gottfredson emphasized the importance of the "self-concept," which is similar to the SLTCDM's concept of the self-observation generalization. Gottfredson stressed the importance of the "gender self-concept," which is described as the "most strongly protected aspect of self" (p. 572), then mentions the social class and ability self-concept as being second in importance to the gender self-concept in influencing occupational aspirations. Thus, there is a strong need to pick an occupation that fits one's gender self-concept (suitably masculine or feminine) and also one's need for social class (prestige level). These primary requirements for a job take precedence over interest level, which essentially fine tunes preferences within the zone of acceptable alternatives decreed by the gender and prestige grid. According to Gottfredson, interest inventories that ask about expressed preferences in specifically named occupations are as effective as they are in predicting occupational placement because the names of occupations include connotations of sextype and prestige as well as interests.

Gottfredson pointed out that individuals must "compromise" their aspirations with the reality of the job market, a process that the SLTCDM designates as a task-approach skill. Gottfredson described a hierarchy of self-concepts—first gender, then social valuation, as being important. "The theory proposes that when people have to compromise—as they often do—between sextype, prestige, and field of work, they will most readily sacrifice field of work" (p. 575).

Gottfredson described the "effort-acceptability squeeze" in which demands for performance may exceed one's ability to satisfy them—again, a variation of what SLTCDM categorizes under the label of task-approach skill.

In summary, both theories present a picture of youngsters developing increasing sophistication and finer discriminations over a period of time. They generate as a result of learning experiences a set of acceptable occupational aspirations, some of which may or may not be realized as a result of the socioeconomic and cultural conditions existing at the time their choices are to be made. Compromises must be made between self-conceptions that may be ideal and the realistic work place. Gottfredson said that sacrifices are made first in the field of interest, second in the prestige level, and third in sextype, whereas the SLTCDM leaves open the possibility that different individuals may sacrifice on a different basis depending on specific circumstances. Both theories clearly recognize the role of self-concepts, presuppositions, and stereotypical beliefs that influence the career decision process. Both advocate that counselors need to access such beliefs.

We have examined the overlap of three theories of career choice and development in an attempt to highlight their congruence with the SLTCDM. Although significant overlap exists, each of these four theories also describes different aspects of the career choice and development process not covered by the others. In terms of our map analogy, each theory covers the same geographic area (i.e., career development), but each highlights some parts of the terrain while leaving other parts unspecified. Because our predictions of occupational choice are so far from perfect, there is still a significant portion of the terrain not covered adequately by any of these theories. Consequently, in the next section we offer a different view of the territory with the hope of adding more scope and detail to our evolving "map."

A LIVING SYSTEMS VIEW OF CAREER DECISION MAKING

The fundamental determinants of career choice and career progression are the same as those that determine choice and development in other domains of human involvement. Although one's thoughts, actions, and objectives will be uniquely a function of their current context and of their past experience, certain basic person processes can be identified that have the potential to influence behavior in every context.

The past two decades in psychology and related fields have seen a dramatic increase in the exploration of these basic processes. A significant portion of these studies are relevant to career decision making and development, but the specialized nature of research during this period has made it extremely difficult to integrate these findings into a coherent view of human preference and choice behaviors.

Recently, Donald Ford (1987) has organized much of these data and resulting mini-theories into a conceptual framework that "puts the person back together again," and in so doing, provides us with a means of expanding our understanding of career choice and progression. We feel that Ford's Living Systems Framework (LSF) can be a useful heuristic for understanding the determinants and complexities of career preference and choice. It also serves as a way to imbed the SLTCDM and other decision-making frameworks into a broader theoretical context.

> The Living Systems Framework (LSF) is designed to represent all aspects of being human, not merely a particular facet of behavior or personality. Therefore, the LSF is composed of a variety of integrated component conceptualizations (e.g., of motor behavior and memory). It describes how the various "pieces" of the person—goals, emotions, thoughts, actions, and biological processes—function both semi-autonomously as a part of a larger unit (the person) in coherent "chunks" of context-specific, goal-directed activity (behavior episodes). It also describes how these specific experiences "add up" to produce a unique, self-constructed history and personality (i.e., through the construction, differentiation, and elaboration of behavior episode schemata), and how various processes of change (self-organization, self-construction, and disorganization-reorganization) help maintain both stability and developmental flexibility in the organized patterns that result (steady states). Thus, the LSF cannot be easily characterized in terms of traditional theoretical categories. Rather, it is a way of trying to understand persons in all of their complexly organized humanness. (Ford & Ford, 1987, pp. 1–2)

The LSF outlines many of the variables and processes that, because they are basic to human functioning, will also influence career choice and development. By understanding the LSF, we can add detail to our theoretical map of career related behavior.

In the Living Systems perspective, as in the SLTCDM, decision making is a central aspect of the on-going process of career development that ultimately will determine the direction of one's career. Any single decision or sequence of choices can change the course of one's career even if these seem insignificant at the time. There are many documented instances where a minor decision changed the course of one's life (see Bandura, 1986 for examples and a discussion of the influences of fortuitous life events).

During any given day, a person makes thousands of decisions of varying scope requiring vastly different amounts of attention and conscious processing. Some decisions (e.g., putting the left or right sock on first) are habitual and therefore largely automatic. Others involve more extensive consideration (e.g., deciding how to organize an important report), whereas still others are major career or life-choice points requiring weeks or months of information gathering and deliberation (e.g., accepting a job in a different state).

If there is a single concept that can anchor one's understanding of the decision-making process, it is that a person acts to bring about desired consequences and avoid undesired outcomes. This reflects the fundamental goal-directedness of human behavior. In the LSF, goals are not just conscious objectives, as they are in the goal-setting literature and in lay usage. Rather, goals are cognitive representations of desired states and outcomes that may or may not be consciously acknowledged or targeted. Goals can be context-independent (e.g., wanting to feel safe, wanting to feel powerful) or context-specific (e.g., winning a golf game, getting promoted to vice president).

The idea that goals are not necessarily conscious is important and deserves further explanation. At the physiological level, goals function out of awareness, and generally out of conscious control. For example, body processes are organized to maintain a body temperature of 98.6 degrees. This temperature is a goal of the system. At a cognitive level, we develop a complex network of goals, many of which have not been verbally labeled. These representations of desired and undesired states and outcomes guide our behavior whether we consciously acknowledge them or not. We may choose consciously to consider certain objectives, such as deciding to run 3 miles a day, or we might act without a clear understanding of exactly what we are trying to accomplish.

Objectives that were once conscious can drop from awareness through habit formation. For example, we pick up the dry cleaning because it is ready to be picked up, without reviewing the many advantages of wearing clean pressed clothes to work. We run to answer the telephone because we anticipate the possibility of good news or an enjoyable conversation without deciding this consciously in advance. As behaviors are repeated, the purposes that they serve drop from awareness and the "choice" to act becomes automatic. Our behaviors serve our goals whether we are consciously aware of this fact at the time or not.

Through experience, observation, and thought, one develops an organized system of desired and undesired consequences. Decision making is the process of selecting goals, determining strategies to attain them, and maintaining progress toward those goals. Most other processes serve either to constrain or to facilitate one's attempts at goal satisfaction. For example, a lack of self-confidence will influence the goals one selects to pursue. Value and belief systems define appropriate and inappropriate means for goal pursuit. Situational factors may provide certain unique opportunities for goal attainment or prohibit action. Genetic endowments such as height, motor coordination, or intelligence tend to make some goals easier to accomplish, and others more difficult, whereas an inaccurate representation of reality can misinform and cause one to make erroneous assumptions about probable consequences.

The Living Systems Framework

The LSF specifies in detail the many structures, processes, and functions that combine to generate human behavior. These include sensory input, information processing and memory, goals, evaluative thought processes, planning, problem solving and behavior coordination, emotional arousal and attentional processes, transactional skills and informational exchange processes, physical structure and biological processes, and four categories of environmental influencers. Readers interested in gaining a deeper understanding of the Framework, and an understanding of the full complexity of human functioning are referred to the original volumes (Ford, 1987; Ford & Ford, 1987).

According to the LSF, the primary and most direct influences on decision making are (a) one's accumulated knowledge about the world and about one's self (information processing and storage); (b) one's entire set of desired and undesired outcomes (directive cognitions); (c) evaluative thought processes that determine what one can or should try to accomplish right now (regulatory evaluations); and (d) thought processes that determine strategies for how to accomplish current objectives and coordinate action (control processes).

In the fields of cognitive science, intelligence, personality, and learning, there are a number of different terms used to represent the cognitive processes involved in learning: *memory, encoding, decoding, classifying, categorization, symbolic representation, personal constructs, schemata, episodic memory, plans, scripts, cognitive structures, knowledge acquisition processes, input, concepts, propositions,* and *neural organization networks.* In reviewing the literature pertinent to these ideas, Ford (1987) suggested a distillation of these processes into seven innate basic mental processes that provide the means to accumulate information, three kinds of symbols through which experience is transformed into coded mental schemata, three general ways to accumulate information from the flow of behavior, and three types of information-memory units through which one stores behavioral programs. In the LSF these processes are collectively termed *information processing* and *information storage.*

Information processing and memory processes serve as a central library containing personal files of experience, knowledge about how things function, how one should behave in certain circumstances, what other people are like, one's own model of self, and other bits of information accumulated through direct experience, observation, instruction, and reasoning. (Although we use the "file drawer" metaphor for simplicity, it should be noted that recall of information seems to involve the reconstruction of information more than simple retrieval.) Current choices are based largely on this store of information and understanding. A decision about a career in sales, for example, is based largely on one's conception of what a salesperson does and what consequences are likely to result from these activities. A decision to sign up for a particular college course depends on one's perceptions of what is required; what will happen in that class; what personal demands it will require; and what purposes, academic or otherwise, it is likely to serve. These kinds of knowledge are developed through one's history of learning experiences and reasoning operations.

Because information processing and storage functions generate the base on which choices are evaluated, inaccuracies or inconsistencies in this store of information can lead to unexpected results.

> If the guiding information is contradictory and not coherently organized, the behavior it organizes will similarly be contradictory and somewhat disorganized. Terms like confused, ambivalent, uncoordinated, and conflicted illustrate the kinds of subjective feelings people have when their current behavior is being influenced by poorly organized or contradictory information. (Ford, 1987, p. 335)

In any career intervention a counselor must evaluate the accuracy, completeness, and coherence of the client's informational system. The effect of erroneous assumptions has been illustrated by Krumboltz

(1983) in his discussion of private rules in career decision making. Providing feedback about skills, personal competencies, and the accuracy of personal beliefs or providing specific information on jobs and the labor market realities are all ways a counselor can add new information to the system or help one reorganize past knowledge.

Directive Cognitions. The second major influence on decision making is representations of desired and undesired outcomes. These images provide purpose and direction to behavior. As individuals develop, they learn that certain things or specific transactions are enjoyable, and others are uncomfortable. For example, they like being with Mom, they like playing with a particular toy, and they dislike taking a bath. As one gets older, a great number of outcomes and experiences come to be desirable or undesirable. We often think of these simply as likes and dislikes. The SLTCDM views these likes and dislikes as the consequences of learning experiences.

Without images of desired consequences, our world would be emotionless, and our representations of cause-and-effect relationships would have no personal significance. Desire is the awareness of a valued goal or goal object. Interest can be understood as the recognition of an opportunity to pursue a desired goal. In general, opportunities to pursue desired goals are motivating, and the attainment of valued outcomes is satisfying. Anxiety and fear result when one perceives the likelihood of attaining undesired outcomes.

There is a long history of attempts to define basic directive variables. These began with lists of instincts thought to underlie and direct one's actions (e.g., McDougall, 1933). As the instinct view lost popularity, need taxonomies were proposed as basic determinants of behavior. Perhaps the most well-known of these is Murray's (1938) list of 28 needs including the need for achievement, the need for superiority, and the need for understanding. There are other examples of need taxonomies, including Maslow's (1943, 1970) hierarchy of human needs and a number of other domain-specific lists of motives (e.g., Dawis, Lofquist, & Weiss, 1968; Vroom, 1964).

These taxonomies were found to be inadequate for a number of reasons, each relating to the need or instinct models that supported them. Mediating cognitive and environmental processes were important determinants of behavior not adequately specified in these models. The LSF separates and defines many of these elements that had confounded previous attempts to define primary directive variables. In the LSF, the directive function is served by cognitive representation of goals, and behavior is the result of the interaction of goals with other cognitive and environmental influences. This view makes it possible to propose a list of basic directive thoughts (i.e., goals) unconfounded by other cognitive variables. Ford and Nichols (1987) have proposed such a list which has been reprinted in Table 5.1.

Although the taxonomy in Table 5.1 proposes major categories into which personal goals can be grouped, there are virtually an unlimited number of context-specific goals within these categories. Each is distinguished by the uniqueness of the person and the context to which it applies.

In career counseling, understanding client goals and helping the client clarify goals and resolve goal conflicts is an important part of information giving and problem solution. As we see once the other LSF functions have been defined, goals will play a key role in determining what one chooses to do, both in small ways and at major career decision points.

There is some clinical and theoretical evidence that many people have highly organized systems of goals in which the achievement of subordinate goals leads to the attainment of more superordinate, and thereby, more important goals (Nichols, 1986, 1990). These superordinate, or core goals, are ultimate emotional consequences that transcend any particular context. For example, "a desire to feel superior" is context-free, whereas "wanting to win this game of golf" is a goal that can only be achieved in a specific context. Core goals are very important to a person, and may be pursued through an extensive system of instrumental subgoals whose attainment leads to the attainment of the core goal. In some cases, people have reported that the majority of their strong emotional highs and lows can be traced back to a small set of idiosyncratic core goals such as, "a desire to feel respected," or "a desire to feel free and unconstrained."

Defining a client's set of core goals can help a counselor understand a client's most potent motives. When people can pursue their goals, they will experience feelings of interest, excitement, satisfaction, and meaningfulness. If people are involved in activities that do not provide opportunities for goal attainment, they will be likely to feel a lack of motivation toward the activities.

Because core goals are expressed as emotional consequences relatively independent of a specific context, they have a negative side. For example, if it is extremely important for an individual to "feel unconstrained and experience a sense of freedom," feeling limited by a situation or constrained in some way will be strongly aversive. For another person, however, the absence of choice and control in a situation might not be particularly bothersome, or may even be desirable in some situations. When a person anticipates the attainment of a strongly undesired state or outcome, the natural reaction is to want to

TABLE 5.1
A Taxonomy of Human Goals (from Ford & Ford, 1987)

Desired Within-Person Consequences

Affective Goals

Entertainment	Having fun, Avoiding boredom, Seeking heightened arousal
Tranquility	Peace of mind, Serenity, Avoiding stress
Happiness	Feelings of joy, satisfaction, or well being
Bodily sensations	Experiencing particular bodily sensations, Experiencing physical movement
Physiological well–being	Experiencing desired physiological states, Feeling healthy

Cognitive Goals

Exploration	Curiosity, Intellectual stimulation, Learning
Understanding	Ordering, Categorizing, Explaining, Making sense
Intellectual creativity	Inventing new ideas, Expanding one's limits
Positive or confirmatory self-evaluations	Self-efficacy, Self-esteem, Self-acceptance, Self-worth

Subjective Organization Goals

Unity	Seeking coherence, harmony, or oneness
Transcendence	Rising above ordinary experience, Pursuing an idealized state, Spiritually

Desired Person-Environment Consequences

Social Relationship Goals

Self-assertion	Maintaining or promoting the self
Individuality	Uniqueness, Separateness, Individual identity
Self-determination	Personal control, Freedom, Autonomy
Superiority	Social status or importance, Dominance, Winning, Comparing favorably with others
Resource acquisition	Obtaining support, assistance, advice, and validation from others
Integration	Maintaining or promoting other people or social groups
Belongingness	Attachments, Intimacy, Friendship, Community, Social identity
Social responsibility	Fulfilling social roles, Keeping interpersonal commitments, Accepting legitimate social control
Equity	Fairness, Justice, Reciprocation, Comparing equally with others
Resource provision	Providing support, assistance, advice, and validation for others

Task Goals

Mastery	Improving one's performance, Meeting a standard of achievement
Task creativity	Inventing new processes or products
Management	Handling routine tasks, Organizing people or things, Being productive
Material gain	Obtaining or accumulating money or tangible goods
Safety	Avoiding threatening or depriving circumstances

avoid the threatening situation. If the negative side of the core goal is experienced, the person will feel a strong urge to get out of the situation. If these undesired outcomes cannot be avoided, the person will feel anxiety, stress, and depression.

From a therapeutic standpoint, strong positive or negative feelings about a work-related activity are often due to the attainment or frustration of core goals. It is for this reason that a knowledge of a client's goals—both context-specific and context-independent goals—is so useful in either troubleshooting discontent or targeting potentially satisfying work.

Regulatory Evaluations. The information-processing and storage (IP&S) functions of thought provide a model of the world and of one's relation to it. Directive cognitions are stored representations of desired and undesired goals. Both of these are storage functions; they provide access to information constructed from past experience and thinking. We have hundreds of potential goals, possibly thousands, which cannot all be pursued simultaneously. Only a small number can be pursued at any time. Regulatory thought processes determine which goals are currently important. These processes include setting priorities among competing current desires, evaluating the importance of current demands, determining personal capabilities in the current circumstances, anticipating and evaluating probable consequences of different potential actions and their utility, evaluating the flow of behavior and maintaining progress toward goals, and determining when to start and stop a given activity.

Regulatory processes also include judgments of what is good, useful, correct or socially acceptable, personally acceptable, morally and ethically appropriate, and legal. Thus, when we speak of a conscience causing a person to feel guilty, we are speaking of a regulatory process. Thoughts of this nature combine to influence one's choice of behavior. In a sense, the regulatory function serves as the chief executive in charge of decision making. The formulation of a behavioral plan to accomplish the selected objective and the coordination of physical activity are controlled by a separate function: the control function.

Feelings of confidence and personal agency are also the result of regulatory evaluations. Perceptions of self-efficacy are subsequently derived from the sum of regulatory evaluations of competence in particular situations. Bandura's extensive examinations of the mechanisms of self-efficacy describe this aspect of regulatory functioning; people will generally not choose a course of action if they do not feel capable of accomplishing it.

The chief executive is always closely attending to current behavior, matching it against current desires, against perceived competencies, and against values and standards of performance. Maintaining progress toward currently desired outcomes is the objective. Any deviations from this course are noted, and plans are altered through control functions. The regulatory evaluations are the heart of decision-making processes. They draw on past experience and stored self-perceptions to guide current behavior toward desired goals and away from undesired outcomes. In the SLTCDM the task-approach skill is the outcome of this regulatory process.

Although we tend to think of the evaluative processes just described as conscious, regulatory thoughts can and often do become habitual and therefore can function autonomously outside of one's awareness. Habitual regulatory cognitions are just as powerful as those that are consciously attended to and are frequently harder to change. When we react "without thinking," or when we decide what to do without giving the choice much thought, we are relying on habitual regulatory thought processes. This ability makes it much easier to function in the world by avoiding the unnecessary reevaluation of already familiar circumstances, but it can also result in inaccurate beliefs or problematic behavior.

Regulatory processes also shape one's store of information. Certain outcomes are decreased or increased in attractiveness due to regulatory evaluations of their current desirability. These new valences then modify the stored perceptions of how important a particular goal is in general (directive cognitions). Similarly, as the regulatory function receives feedback from current actions, conclusions are reached about one's competence in this set of circumstances. This new information is then stored for later reference (IP&S).

The regulatory function can be difficult to grasp at first. Some examples may help to illustrate the effect of regulatory processes. Sarah is a senior in college. She wants to be a lawyer because she has always thought lawyers are highly respected and make a lot of money (she developed this perception of lawyers from her history of learning experiences related to lawyers through IP&S processes). It is important to her to be respected and have money (directive cognitions). Thus far, these thoughts have not influenced her behavior, but on registration day she notices a law school preparation class being offered. Faced with this option, she now must evaluate the desirability of taking this class. These thoughts are primarily regulatory cognitions, and include her estimation of her ability to succeed in the class and her expectations of the consequences if she fails to do well, her evaluation of the relative desirability of other classes she might take if she did not take the law class, her expectation that her friends will think she is just following a popular trend, and her thoughts about how pleased her parents will be that she is doing something to prepare for her future career. After considerable deliberation, she elects to sign up for the class. At mid-semester she discovers that the work is too stressful and she is concerned that she might not be able to succeed in law school (a regulatory reevaluation of her competence based on performance feedback). Because law is her only current career option, she is upset by this, and seeks out the help of a career counselor.

In this case, it was a regulatory evaluation of competence that caused the problem, but had she done well, still other regulatory evaluations could have caused her to question her decision. For instance, she could have determined that representing criminals whom she believes are guilty would go against her personal values.

Notice in this example how the directive, regulatory, and memory functions play off each other. Regulatory evaluations draw on directive representations of desired outcomes and memory stores that are, in turn, modified by regulatory evaluations and by behavioral consequences in a continuous, iterative flow. Many of the outcomes one comes to desire attain this status through regulatory processes that assign value to an outcome. For example, an outcome that is uninteresting to a 3-year-old (e.g., a good paying job) becomes significant over time as it is perceived as a means to other desired ends.

Emotions, particularly strongly felt emotions, can facilitate or take the place of regulatory evaluations. Emotions evolved to serve as a way to organize survival-oriented behavior. For example, along with the experience of fear, there is an urge to get out of the situation, and there is a preparatory physiological response that readies the body to run or fight. Thus, the emotion of fear serves the purpose of avoiding danger in situations where a lengthy cognitive analysis could be fatal. Other primary emotions function in similar ways, but energize different patterns of response.

When we say we want to do something but then act another way, the cause is often our emotional organizing forces overpowering our conscious regulatory intentions. Understanding that emotions and conscious intentions are separate systems that can serve the same function helps explain why people sometimes "do the same old thing" even though they do not want to, or why they react in ways they had hoped they wouldn't. The development of the basic emotions and their influence on behavior is described in detail in the Ford volume and in other texts on emotion.

Control Functions. Regulatory, directive, and information processing and storage functions combine to generate an intention (e.g., an intention to go to the store today, or a decision to investigate new job possibilities). Control processes coordinate the thought and behavior needed to carry out one's intentions. Control processes include reasoning and problem solving related to the method for accomplishing a particular objective, behavioral planning, and the actual coordination of physical movement.

Regulatory processes and control processes work in close coordination. In an episode of behavior, regulatory processes first select an objective, then control processes determine a means of attaining the objective by analyzing the situation and the behavioral tools available for use. This initial strategy is then evaluated by regulatory processes to determine whether it is consistent with values and other boundary conditions. Control processes then oversee the implementation of the strategy within the current situation. Progress is monitored by both regulatory and control functions. Regulatory thoughts evaluate the effectiveness of the behavior relative to the desired outcome and its appropriateness given the boundary conditions (e.g., values, rules, etc.). Control processes compare the actual execution of behavior with stored behavioral programs and behavioral episode schemata. A regulatory determination that the behavior is not achieving its intended purpose, or is violating certain conditions, will cause control processes to modify current behaviors or future plans.

It is this interplay of regulatory and control processes that most immediately guides current behavior. Both rely on memory and stored representations of goals during evaluation, planning, and execution phases, but the coordination and guidance of activity is largely carried out by regulatory and control processes.

In terms of decision making, the control function is much like a second level of decision making. The first level is the regulatory evaluation of *what* should be pursued. The second level is the determination of *how* to pursue it. When we speak of making decisions, we typically lump these two aspects together.

Control processes draw from a store of skills and knowledge about contextual behavior. Many of our past behaviors are coded as scripts (Tomkins, 1979), for example, how to order in a restaurant, what to say when we answer the phone, how to answer a particular job interview question. In the LSF, this procedural knowledge accumulates into files called behavior episode schemata (BES). Each episode of behavior we encounter—either directly, through observation, or through imagination—is stored in memory. Behavior episodes that share common features or serve similar purposes are stored together and become BES. For example, Tom's father always slammed doors when he was angry. Tom watched this many times, and began slamming doors himself on occasion when he was angry as a teenager. Now as an adult, he routinely slams doors when he is angry about something. Tom developed a "door-slamming" BES of how to act when angry by watching and then by doing. Each door-slamming episode strengthens and elaborates the BES until it becomes entrenched and habitual. Tom does this now without thinking.

Many of our behaviors are learned in this way. We can therefore modify our BES by acting differently, by reasoning and by imagining different behaviors. However, BES that are well formed and relatively invariant can be difficult to change or to avoid activating. Many career problems, as well as life problems, are the result of dysfunctional BES, or of the misapplication of a BES that would be appropriate in another context. For example, a manager may be having problems at work with her subordinates because she is dictatorial in a cooperative organization. Her BES of how to manage is different from her workers' expectations. To adapt, she will have to learn and practice new behaviors in order to modify her existing "managerial" BES. Note that at home, or with peers, she may have a similar style, indicating that her managerial BES is a subset of a larger "how to deal with people" BES, or she may act very differently with family and peers indicating that her "managerial" BES is limited to particular work contexts.

One's total store of BES are the base from which current behavior is constructed. BES do not necessarily determine behavior, but they are a potent influence in determining behavior. The modification and elaboration of BES and the generation of new BES are called learning, growth, change, or creativity.

In general, strategies are formulated to attain goals within boundary conditions and within the constraints of a particular context. One's repertory of past behaviors is drawn upon to construct current behavior. If past strategies are flawed, or applied without regard for the uniqueness of different environments, problems can result. These can range from not achieving the target outcome to achieving it, but with unexpected and troublesome side effects.

Other Components of the LSF

Ford referred to the IP&S, directive, regulatory, and control functions collectively as the governing functions. Although they are the key functions responsible for career choice, they interact with and are dependent on three other processes: arousal, transactional, and physiological/biochemical. Arousal processes provide the energy for action, for emotional responding, for intensity of affect, for attentional processes and for the governing processes. Arousal and governing functions together produce what is commonly referred to as motivation. Transactional functions include the intake of information through sensory channels and the expression of intention through bodily movement, vocalizations, and expressions. Furthermore, all major functions exist within a physiological/biochemical system that both potentiates and constrains behavior. Height, intelligence, and coordination are all products of this system.

Using the LSF to Diagnose Sources of Career Problems

Because a person is a system, and because decision-making processes are a central aspect of human behavior, any component of that system can have an influence on decision-making processes. To identify the source of a problem, one needs to examine the system. Because the governing functions are most frequently the determining factors in selection, a counselor should first explore the contribution of these processes to the presenting problem. If the source of the problem does not appear to be within these four functions, other aspects of the system should be examined.

Problems Due Primarily to the Governing Functions. We know that a person is trying to achieve desired consequences and avoid undesired ones. When clients present a problem or express emotional distress, it is likely that they are either having difficulty identifying an appropriate goal, having difficulty achieving a desired goal, facing the possibility of achieving an undesired goal, or currently trying to cope with an undesired outcome. Distress can also be caused primarily by chemical imbalances in the body, or by emotional dysfunction, but in most cases, the origin of the problem can be traced to one of these four goal-related scenarios.

People can be having difficulty achieving a goal because they have designed an ineffective strategy (control processes), which, itself, may be due to a flawed representation of the situation and cause–effect relationships involved (information processing and storage). People can also have problems achieving a desired goal because they believe they do not have the confidence to execute the necessary behaviors (regulatory processes). Determining the set of goals that are involved in the distress and trying to identify which are terminal goals and which are instrumental goals is an important first step in counseling.

Usually, a context-specific goal will be instrumental to a context-independent goal. For example, a man may want to get a job with IBM (context-specific, instrumental goal) because he believes that this will give him a feeling of job security (terminal, context-free goal). People use instrumental context-specific goals to achieve their context-independent emotional goals. The instrumental–terminal relationships people perceive influence what they do. People may find stock brokering attractive because they see it as a way to make quick money and attract members of the opposite sex. They may be consciously aware of this perception, or they may never have verbalized it. They may be successful, and their expectation may come to pass, or their expectation may be unrealistic given their skills, or given the state of the stock market. A counselor can help by clarifying a person's organization of instrumental and terminal goals so that the client can be clear about why he or she is attracted to a certain option and can better evaluate chances for success.

If the terminal–emotional goals can be identified, other contextual goals can be explored that could potentially serve these goals, thus increasing a person's options. With a number of choices, each objective can then be evaluated to determine the suitability of the day-to-day requirements of the job. It is common for people to focus on the ultimate objective and forget to evaluate what actually happens on a day-to-day level. It may be that the targeted goal is both desirable and possible to attain, but the 3 years of work it will take to get there will not be intrinsically enjoyable.

Evaluations of perceived competence are a significant factor in one's choice of action. It is important to assess this regulatory evaluation. A lack of confidence can keep a person from initiating attempts to achieve a desired goal. In the extreme, all important goals are too risky to pursue, and the person pulls away from that which is most desirable. Remember that any emotional goal will have an opposite negative side. Pursuing a desired emotional goal means risking failure, and the attainment of the negative. Individuals with low self-efficacy may be focused more on how to avoid negative outcomes than on how to achieve positive outcomes. Individuals with this motivational orientation put most of their effort into protecting themselves, and they rarely strive for the things that would be most satisfying because they do not want to risk the undesirable negative outcomes.

As one's confidence increases, one's perception of the likelihood that desirable outcomes can be obtained increases. This perception then leads to behavior designed to achieve these goals. A person's value structure provides the boundary conditions that limit the choice of acceptable behaviors. For example, people can feel that a goal can be achieved only through honest means that will not hurt anyone else, or that they must do what their parents feel is best, or that they must not violate certain religious commandments. These evaluative conditions can sometimes be overly stringent, thereby limiting one's choices substantially.

It is possible for a person to have reasonable goals, self-confidence, and facilitative boundary conditions, but have a poorly devised strategy or plan for attaining the goal (i.e., control processes). For example, a person may have learned that a certain interview style will impress interviewers when in fact it actually makes a bad impression. Or a person may feel that the best way to break into broadcast journalism is through graduate school in journalism, when in fact, a better way may be a 1-year internship with a working journalist.

Faulty strategies are usually based on faulty information, on the misapplication of learned patterns of behavior, or on a misinterpretation of the current situation. One's store of information and experience will be used to construct behavioral plans. If a person has limited experience, he or she will have a more difficult time developing effective strategies. People with a narrow range of experience will only have this to draw on to formulate current plans. If the targeted goal requires some other skills or knowledge not in memory, then their strategy is more likely to fail.

Problems Due Primarily to Transactional Functions. If governing processes appear not to be the cause of some people's problems, it may be that they are having difficulty processing information through their senses, or they may be having trouble expressing themselves. An example can help illustrate how transactional processes can be sources of career problems.

Rick was 38 years old, had just been fired, and wanted some help finding a job where he would have stability and could feel as if he could do a good job. He reported that most of his difficulties in past jobs have involved managing people and running meetings. He had been fired twice before, and had eventually gone to Alcoholics Anonymous with a drinking problem that developed from his attempts to control his job stress with alcohol. Despite this, he had compiled an impressive resume and appeared intelligent in the initial interview.

Rick's difficulties were analyzed by examining the contribution of each LSF function to his difficulties in an attempt to understand the source(s) of his problem. His current employment goals seemed appropriate, and his past managerial intentions and strategies seemed reasonable. He was intelligent and demonstrated logical and insightful reasoning. His desire to avoid being fired another time was appropriate given his history of experiences, and his emotional state matched his subjective experience. In exploring his self-perceptions of competence, he described feeling very stupid at times, and he often found himself not being able to understand what was going on around him. He had low self-esteem but felt that he was good at some things.

Intelligence testing revealed a significant inability to process auditory information and a letter reversal problem typical of dyslexia located in the visual intake system. Hearing tests indicated a congenital high frequency loss in both ears that made it difficult for him to track conversations when the speaker talked quickly, talked in a high pitch, or when more than one person talked at one time. When these results were presented to Rick, he was able to attribute many of his past difficulties in school, at work, and even in relationships with women to these limitations. He had difficulty hearing women because their vocalizations were often in the higher pitch range.

He was fitted with a hearing aid and was able to process conversation much more easily. The recognition that many of his bad experiences were due to these physical limitations made it possible for him to reinterpret many of his past difficulties, raise his perceptions of self-confidence, target a job in which he could compensate for his disabilities and rely on his strengths.

Problems Due Primarily to Arousal Functions. Problems with arousal functions include depression, hostility, stress, distractibility, and burnout (i.e., emotional exhaustion). Another frequent problem is repression of internal emotional signals that can lead to generally low levels of motivation because arousal functions provide the energy for behavior. In the following example this type of arousal dysfunction was responsible for a woman having problems selecting and committing to career goals.

Sally came for counseling because she wanted help selecting career goals. She was having trouble deciding on a direction herself. After initial sessions, it turned out that as a result of a long history of physical and emotional abuse as a child, she had learned that expressing emotion typically brought about some abusive parental response. Whenever Sally had expressed a desire for something, her father had intentionally denied her request. In order to avoid the abuse, she began to hide her emotions and to avoid expressing a preference for things. Over many years these protective strategies resulted in her being unable to want things for herself or to commit to any particular course of action with heartfelt desire. Treatment involved her coming to realize that now, as an adult, she could feel and express her preferences, desires, and emotions without fear of painful consequences. As she began to understand this through the repetition of positive experiences in different contexts, she became able to assign value to activities and goals and to commit to them without fear. Once this happened, she was able to set career goals for herself in which she felt invested and to work toward them.

Dysfunction in the arousal subsystem can be complex and can require significant amounts of time to correct. Arousal problems generally have a pervasive influence on the governing functions. Without commitment that is fueled by affect, motivation is generally low, and long-term persistent goal-directed action is less likely.

Problems Due Primarily to Biological Functions.   Chemical imbalances are difficult to diagnose without the help of a medical professional, but it is possible that a career problem can have its roots in either hormonal or neurotransmitter imbalances. One would suspect this if there seemed to be no clear evidence that the problem was due to governing, arousal, or transactional functions. Chronic low blood sugar levels, organic depression, premenstrual syndrome, and the early stages of organic dementing syndromes such as Alzheimers and Parkinson's disease are all examples of disorders that can affect one's career functioning and decision making.

LSF Summary

To recap, decision making is most directly influenced by the four governing functions: information processing and storage, directive, regulatory, and control processes. These cognitive processes are inextricably linked to and interact with arousal processes, with transactional abilities, and with the physiological substrate from which all behavior ultimately emanates. A thorough understanding of the difficulties a career client can have in making decisions or in guiding the direction of his or her life depends on a thorough understanding of human living system functioning. An abbreviated, but useful, understanding of decision making for most career interventions can be obtained by focusing on the interplay of the four governing functions with the knowledge of their interrelatedness to the other subsystems and with the environment.

In terms of our map analogy, the LSF allows a career theorist to have a more comprehensive view of the decision-making terrain. Although the LSF does not specify the full complexity of human decision making, it provides us with a map of a larger area than we generally consider in current theories of career behavior.

PRACTICAL IMPLICATIONS

The emphasis on learning experiences in all these theories should cause parents, educators, television executives, and members of the public to pay close attention to the kinds of experiences we are providing for young people. Parents and teachers need to insure that each child experiences a sufficiently large number of positive learning experiences to encourage future learning and to enable the child to see positive alternatives in the future. The television industry needs to pay closer attention to the type of models they provide for young people.

Counselors, teachers, and parents who help young people plan their futures need to inquire into the beliefs and assumptions that young people have developed through their past learning experiences. Youngsters need help in examining the accuracy of these beliefs. Some beliefs are based on one particularly vivid experience that may or may not be representative of the occupational world at large. It is difficult for a youngster alone to evaluate whether his or her skills are adequate for learning the tasks that lie ahead. For example, some people make assumptions that they should only accept a job if they already know how to do it. They overlook the fact that at one time everyone had to learn the beginning skills.

Educational researchers, counselors, teachers, and parents need to encourage the development and testing of enjoyable and stimulating new learning experiences to help young people find out about themselves and the world of work. Administering tests and inventories that measure interests, beliefs, and skills can be useful. Devising creative simulations and computer programs to represent occupational tasks would be one way of making career exploration more attractive. Young people need help in seeing the relationship between school experiences and the work world. More importantly, schools need to make their curricular offerings more relevant to important career and life skills.

The learning process is never over. One's first job is just a training ground to accumulate learning experiences for the future. Learning continues, skills are built, and self-observation generalizations are modified as a result of the successes and failures on every job. Each individual needs to learn that the process of career development never ends. It is a life-long task to refine one's perception of self, to relate one's own self-perceptions to career demands, and to make some sense out of the mysterious world we are privileged to share.

REFERENCES

Bandura, A. (1986). *Social foundations of thought and action: A social cognitive theory.* Englewood Cliffs, NJ: Prentice-Hall.

Dawis, R.V., Lofquist, L.H., & Weiss, D.J. (1968). *A theory of work adjustment (a revision). Minnesota Studies in Vocational Rehabilitation.* (Vol. I). Minneapolis, MN: Work Adjustment Project, Department of Psychology, University of Minnesota.

Ford, D.H. (1987). *Humans as self constructing living systems: A developmental perspective on personality and behavior.* Hillsdale, NJ: Lawrence Erlbaum Associates.

Ford, M.E., & Ford, D.H. (Eds.). (1987). *Humans as self-constructing living systems: Putting the framework to work.* Hillsdale, NJ: Lawrence Erlbaum Associates.

Ford, M.E., & Nichols, C.W. (1987). A taxonomy of human goals and some possible applications. In M. Ford & D. Ford (Eds.), *Humans as self-constructing living systems: Putting the framework to work* (pp. 289–311). Hillsdale, NJ: Lawrence Erlbaum Associates.

Gottfredson, L.S. (1981). Circumscription and compromise: A developmental theory of occupational aspirations. *Journal of Counseling Psychology, 28,* 545–579.

Holland, J.L. (1959). A theory of vocational choice. *Journal of counseling psychology, 6,* 35–45.

Holland, J.L. (1962). Some explorations ot a theory of vocational choice: I. One- and two-year longitudinal studies. *Psychological Monographs, 76,* (26, Whole No. 545).

Holland, J.L. (1963). Explorations of a theory of vocational choice and achievement: II. A four-year prediction study. *Psychological Reports, 12,* 547–594.

Holland, J.L. (1966). *The psychology of vocational choice.* Waltham, MA: Blaisdell.

Holland, J.L. (1971). A theory-ridden, computerless, impersonal, vocational guidance system. *Journal of Vocational Behavior, 1,* 167–176.

Holland, J.L. (1973). *Making vocational choices: A theory of careers.* Englewood Cliffs, NJ: Prentice-Hall.

Jordaan, J.P. (1963). Exploratory behavior: The formulation of self and occupational concepts. In D.E. Super, R. Starishevsky, N. Matlin & J.P. Jordan (Eds.), *Career development: Self-concept theory.* New York: CEEB Research Monograph No. 4.

Krumboltz, J.D. (1978). This Chevrolet can't float or fly. In J.M. Whiteley & A. Resnikoff (Eds.), *Career counseling* (pp. 139–145). Monterey, CA: Brooks/Cole.

Krumboltz, J.D. (1979). A social learning theory of career decision making. In A.M. Mitchell, G.B. Jones, & J.D. Krumboltz (Eds.), *Social learning and career decision making* (pp. 19–49). Cranston, RI: Carroll Press.

Krumboltz, J.D. (1981). A social learning theory of career decision making. In D.H. Montrose & C.J. Shinkman (Eds.), *Career development in the 1980s: Theory and practice* (pp. 43–66). Springfield, IL: Charles C. Thomas.

Krumboltz, J.D. (1983). *Private rules in career decision making.* Columbus, OH: National Center for Research in Vocational Education, The Ohio State University.

Krumboltz, J.D. (1988). *Career beliefs inventory.* Palo Alto, CA: Consulting Psychologists Press.

Krumboltz, J.D., Kinnier, R.T., Rude, S.S., Scherba, D.S., & Hamel, D.A. (1986). Teaching a rational approach to career decision making: Who benefits most? *Journal of Vocational Behavior, 29,* 1–6.

Krumboltz, J.D., Mitchell, A.M., & Jones, G.B. (1976). A social learning theory of career selection. *The Counseling Psychologist, 6*(1), 71–81.

Krumboltz, J.D., Mitchell, A.M., & Jones, G.B. (1978). A social learning theory of career selection. In J.M. Whiteley & Arthur Resnikoff (Eds.), *Career counseling* (pp. 100–127). Monterey, CA: Brooks/Cole.

Krumboltz, J.D., Mitchell, A.M., & Jones, G.B. (1980). A social learning theory of career selection. In T.L. Wentling (Ed.), *Annual review of research in vocational education* (Vol. 1, pp. 259–282). Urbana, IL: University of Illinois.

Krumboltz, J.D., & Rude, S. (1981). Behavioral approaches to career counseling. *Behavioral Counseling Quarterly, 1,* 108–120.

Maslow, A. (1943). A theory of human motivation. *Psychological Review, 50,* 370–396.

Maslow, A. (1970). *Motivation and personality* (2nd ed.). New York: Harper & Row.

McDougall, W. (1933). *The energies of men.* New York: Charles Scribner's Sons.

Mitchell, L.K., & Krumboltz, J.D. (1984a). Research on human decision making and counseling. In S.D. Brown & R.W. Lent (Eds.), *Handbook of counseling psychology* (pp.

238–280). New York: Wiley.

Mitchell, L.K., & Krumboltz, J.D. (1984b). Social learning approach to career decision making: Krumboltz theory. In D. Brown & L. Brooks (Eds.), *Career choice and development: Applying contemporary theory to practice.* San Francisco, CA: Jossey-Bass.

Mitchell, L.K., & Krumboltz, J.D. (1987). The effects of cognitive restructuring and decision-making training on career indecision. *Journal of Counseling and Development, 66,* 171–174.

Murray, H.A. (1938). *Explorations in personality.* New York: Oxford University Press.

Nichols, C.W. (1986). *A study of the organization of salient human goals.* Unpublished manuscript, Stanford University, Stanford, CA.

Nichols, C.W. (1990). *An analysis of the sources of dissatisfaction at work.* Unpublished doctoral dissertation, Stanford University, Stanford, CA.

Starishevsky, R., Matlin, N. (1963). A model for the translation of self-concept into vocational terms. In D.E. Super, R. Starishevsky, N. Matlin & J.P. Jordaan (Eds.), *Career development: Self-concept theory.* New York: CEEB Research Monograph No. 4.

Super, D.E. (1953). A theory of vocational development. *American Psychologist, 8,* 185–190.

Super, D.E. (1955). Personality integration through vocational counseling. *Journal of Counseling Psychology, 2,* 217–226.

Super, D.E. (1957). *The psychology of careers.* New York: Harper & Row.

Super, D.E. (1963). Self-concepts in vocational development. In D.E. Super, R. Starishevsky, N. Matlin, & J.P. Jordaan (Eds.), *Career development: Self-concept theory.* New York: CEEB Research Monograph No. 4.

Super, D.E. (1964). A developmental approach to vocational guidance. *Vocational Guidance Quarterly, 13,* 1–10.

Super, D.E., Starishevsky, R., Matlin, N., & Jordaan, J.P. (Eds.). (1963). *Career development: Self-concept theory.* New York: CEEB Research Monograph No. 4.

Tomkins, S.S. (1979). Script theory: Differential magnification of affects. In R.A. Dienstbier (Ed.), *Nebraska Symposium on Motivation 1978.* Lincoln: University of Nebraska Press.

Vroom, V. (1964). *Work and Motivation.* New York: Wiley.

6

Career Counseling: A Social Psychological Perspective

Fred J. Dorn
Memphis State University

Because counselors were initially encouraged to consider social psychological variables in their research methodologies (Goldstein, 1966), practitioners and researchers have enthusiastically pursued the examination of counseling as a process of interpersonal influence. This is reflected in the growing body of literature on the social psychological approach to counseling (see Corrigan, Dell, Lewis, & Schmidt, 1980; Dorn, 1984a; Heppner & Dixon, 1981, for reviews) that has frequently been referred to as the social influence model (SIM).

Some proponents of the social influence model (Dorn, 1986a; Heesacker, 1986a; Stoltenberg, 1986) have suggested that counseling is a process of attitude change. Clients seek counseling because they are in a static state of behavior. This static state of behavior has resulted from the individual attributing his or her difficulty to factors over which he or she does not have control. For example, if we consider a career counseling case, one frequently hears from college students that they are unable to identify an appropriate college major because the economy is unstable. As a result, they delay selecting a major (a static state of behavior) with the anticipation that economic stability will provide some insight about a particular major. The economy of our nation, however, is a factor far beyond any one person's control.

My basic intent in this chapter is to present a rationale for utilizing social influence theory in career counseling. Overall, an emphasis is placed on how the career counseling process can be examined from a social psychological perspective and how career counseling practice and research can be enhanced. Initially, an overview of the social influence model is presented. This overview is followed by an integration of career counseling and social influence theory principles. Additional support for addressing career counseling from a social psychological perspective is extrapolated from the literature; and finally, ideas regarding possible areas of investigation that blend social influence theory and career counseling are presented.

THE SOCIAL INFLUENCE MODEL: AN OVERVIEW

As was previously noted, the basic assumption in the social influence model is the belief that clients seek counseling because they are in a static state of behavior. This static state of behavior results from clients attributing their difficulties to factors that are beyond their control. The counselor working within the social influence framework attempts to assist the client in moving toward a more active state of behavior. This is usually accomplished through the counselor's encouragement to the client to reattribute his or her difficulties to factor(s) that he or she has control over. For instance, as was previously mentioned, the college student who is undecided about a major will be encouraged to reattribute his or her indecisiveness to a lack of awareness of self and the world of work rather than to a fluctuating economy. This process of reattribution should provide the client with a greater sense of control over his or her circumstances and a rationale for engaging in new and different behaviors.

Analogue research on the social influence model has demonstrated that clients are more willing to accept the counselor's suggested reattributions if the counselor is perceived as an expert who is trustworthy and socially attractive (Corrigan et al., 1980). Perceived expertness emerges as a result of the counselor's credibility and reputation in the community, specialized training, and ability to dispute the client's opinions with knowledgable arguments. Perceived counselor trustworthiness evolves from the client's realization that the counselor is working for the client's benefit. The perceived attractiveness of the counselor results from his or her compatibility, similarity, and positive regard for the client.

It is important to note, here, that although counselors are in the process of attempting to introduce new information to the client for the purposes of initiating a reattribution process, clients are reacting to this information in a variety of ways. In essence, the introduction of this new information will challenge the client's world view (Claiborn, 1986) and more than likely lead to a state of cognitive dissonance within the client. This dissonance is a result of the discrepancy that exists between the client's attributions regarding his or her difficulty and the new attributions that were introduced by the counselor. The dissonance is a product of two cognitive elements that are inconsistent; the client's attributions and the counselor's attributions. The "existence of dissonance is accompanied by psychological discomfort (in the client) and when it arises, attempts are made to reduce it" (Zimbardo, 1960, p. 86). Therefore, when the counselor introduces alternate factors to which the client can reattribute his or her difficulties, the client will attempt to reduce this dissonance. There are five ways in which clients can attempt to reduce this dissonance. These are: (a) convince the counselor to accept their initial attributions, (b) discredit the counselor's attributions with contradictory information, (c) seek additional information and opinions in an effort toward supporting initial attributions, (d) imply that the initial reason for seeking counseling was not important, and (e) reattribute their difficulties to the factors that the counselor introduced. As was previously noted, clients are more likely to accept the counselors suggested reattributions if they perceive the counselor as expert, trustworthy, and socially attractive.

The three counselor dimensions of expertness, trustworthiness, and social attractiveness collectively contribute to the social power of the counselor. The social power of the counselor emerges when the counselor's behavior generates some kind of change in the client's thoughts, feelings, or behavior (Strong & Matross, 1973). There are five specific social power bases the counselor can establish when working in a social influence framework. These are expert, referent, legitimate, informational, and ecological (Goodyear & Robyak, 1981). Expert power is established when the client perceives the counselor as an expert. A referent power base is established when the client perceives the counselor as socially attractive. Legitimate power results from the social status the counselor holds in society as a helper. Informational power results from the counselor's familiarity with informational resources that the client will find advantageous. An ecological power base comes from the counselor's suggestions on how the client can control his or her personal environment.

Assessing Counselor Social Power

The Counselor Rating Form (CRF) developed by Barak and LaCrosse (1975) is the most widely used measure for assessing the counselor dimensions of expertness, trustworthiness, and attractiveness (Dorn, 1984a). The CRF is a semantic differential measure that contains 36 bipolar items. These items are separated into three subscales with each scale reflecting one of three counselor dimensions of expertness, trustworthiness, and attractiveness. Each one of the items contains two adjectives that anchor ends of a 7-point Likert scale. One adjective is positive and the other is negative. The items for each of the three subscales are randomly ordered and randomly anchored; thus negative and positive adjectives are on either side of the Likert scale so as to prevent set responses from occuring.

All of the studies cited in the literature review employed the CRF. It is important for readers to note, however, that although the Counselor Rating Form possesses intuitive appeal in terms of assessing counselor social power (Heesacker & Heppner, 1983), it is unclear whether the three dimensions are in fact independent or whether they collectively contribute to a single global dimension. A recent investigation by Tracey, Glidden, and Kokotovic (1988) seems to suggest that the three dimensions are a reflection of both general satisfaction with counseling as well as a response to perceived counselor charisma.

Integrating Career Counseling and the Social Influence Model

The basic task of identifying, selecting, and pursuing a career path is an ambiguous and confusing process for many individuals. In part, this ambiguity and confusion can be attributed to the fact that there is really little formal and tangible direction provided to most individuals when they are faced with the task of selecting a career path. Thus, many people rely on what little information they have gathered from their respective environment. Generally, the core dimensions of this information reflect a solid work ethic that suggests that career selection, satisfaction, and success are generated through responsibility, stability, and when necessary, mobility.

Unfortunately, the information obtained and utilized by these same individuals often times proves to be ineffective. As a result, counselors often encounter clients with career concerns who are frustrated, confused, and overwhelmed because the attitudes that they have relied on (which were developed according to this inaccurate information), in an attempt to implement their own career development, have not brought the expected end result.

The examination of the career development process from this perspective provides one with a basis for proposing that the central issue is the client's attitudes. These attitudes lead to specific behaviors and if these behaviors are ineffective then it becomes necessary for new attitudes to be formulated so that new behaviors can be utilized.

Attitudes that have been developed and refined over a period of time are not easily changed (even those that prove to be self-defeating). Therefore, the process of assisting clients in abandoning existing attitudes and formulating new attitudes about career development is a process of persuasion.

Recently, Dorn (1987a) proposed that career counselors begin to organize these ineffective career development attitudes around specific "career myths." The conceptualization of irrational beliefs regarding the career development process has been proposed by other authors as well (Lewis & Gilhousen, 1981; Rosenberg, 1977; Thompson, 1976). This was the first attempt, however, to propose that client attitudes about the career development process be considered within the context of the social influence model. The rationale for this recommendation rests with Claiborn's (1986) observation that "the concept of attitude refers broadly to assumptions, constructs, and expectancies that determine the way one sees the world. That world view, in turn, is the immediate determinant of behavior: people respond not to reality itself but to their perception or cognitive construction of reality" (p.34). In addition, Dorn (1985) had found that there is a fairly strong relationship between the "external barrier" construct as measured by the Career Decision Scale (Osipow, Carney, Winer, Yanico, & Koschir, 1976) and the Survey of Career Attitudes (Woodrick, 1979), which has been used in the assessment of client's subscription to career myths (Dorn & Welch, 1985).

The Survey of Career Attitudes (SCA) is a 50-item questionnaire that consists of statements about the career development process. Respondents are asked to indicate whether they agree or disagree with each statement. The degree to which an individual does not adhere to various career myths is indicated in the number of items they answer correctly. The responses are grouped into factors that indicate whether the individual adheres to any of the following 13 different career myths:

1. once a career decision has been made it should not be changed;
2. certain careers are best for only one sex;
3. college is the best route to a career;
4. experts know what careers are best for people;
5. there is a perfect job for each person;
6. time will tell what is the best career;
7. the harder a person tries, the quicker he or she can make a career decision;
8. work is the most important thing in a person's life;
9. career planning is an exact science;
10. a person can succeed at anything he or she wants;

11. happiness is contingent on career success;
12. a person's worth is measured by the career he or she has selected; and
13. interests and aptitudes are synonymous.

There is little empirical support for career myths as ineffective career development attitudes simply because this area of career behavior is relatively unexplored by researchers. A review of the literature revealed only two published studies on career mythology with one (Dorn & Welch, 1985) focusing on the existence of such attitudes in a suburban middle-class Caucasian community and the other study (Pinkney & Ramirez, 1985) comparing the differences in the degree to which Chicano and Caucasian high school students subscribed to career myths. In the first study, which utilized the SCA, it was found that high school students subscribed to all but four of the proposed myths. The myths they did not adhere to were: once a career decision has been made it should not be changed, certain careers are best for only one sex, there is a perfect job for each person, and a person's worth is measured by the career he or she has selected.

In the Pinkney and Ramirez (1985) study an adapted version of the SCA was utilized with several items added for the express purpose of attempting to identify career myths that may have been culturally specific. The results of this investigation revealed that not only did the Chicano population subscribe to more career myths but that they also adhered to several career myths that were culturally specific (i.e., the loss of cultural identity as a result of career success).

A word of caution should be expressed here about the SCA. Although the measure has been utilized in a few research investigations it is in need of psychometric refinement. As was noted by Dorn and Welch (1985), in their examination of a high school population, although

> the measure seems to possess acceptable degrees of reliability and validity, the results of this study do raise some questions. For example, because the sample easily met the established criterion level on three of the myths and equaled another, one can speculate about whether these myths exist or if the items on the measure are sufficiently discriminating. Issues such as these and others related to test construction warrant further investigation. (p. 141)

Therefore, it is imperative that career counseling practitioners and researchers examine the social psychological literature for guidance and direction. It is tantamount that the appropriate methodologies for assessing attitudes, attitude formation, and attitude change be utilized so that career counseling researchers can establish a strong foundation for determining the role that attitudes about the career development process play in eventual career behavior. It is necessary to answer questions such as: how and when are attitudes about the career development process developed and under what conditions can these attitudes be influenced?

If we consider some of the proposed "career myths" that are assessed through the Survey of Career Attitudes such as "work is the most important thing in a person's life" and "once a career decision has been made it should not be changed," one could speculate that such attitudes are a reflection of the family environment. In contrast, a myth such as "college is the best route to a career" may reflect not only family environment but community environment as well. Especially, if a comparison is made between two communities such as an affluent suburban community and a semi-skilled labor community. More important, a myth such as "happiness is contingent upon career success" may reflect a more broadly based environment such as American society.

Furthermore, it is necessary for career researchers to determine what these attitudes are, how they are formed, and what purpose the formation and maintenance of these attitudes serve for the individual. For some individuals, work serves an important role (central) in their lives, whereas for others it serves a peripheral role (i.e., the acquisition of income for the express purpose of engaging in leisure activities).

Some additional issues that need to be addressed are: determining the degree to which these expressed attitudes are consistent with behavior and under what conditions these attitudes are inconsistent with behavior. For instance, if we consider the behavior of selecting a college major, the prevailing attitude among many people is to select a major based on the assumption that certain occupational fields will provide greater employment opportunities than others. This would be an example of consistency between attitude and behavior. In contrast, if we assume that the prevailing attitude in the work force is that people dislike their work, why is it that they do not change their career field or occupational environment?

In addition, given these two examples, under what conditions are attitude-behavior consistencies more likely to exist and when do they break down? Is this a function of specific personality variables? As well, how discrepant must the contrasting attitude be and how strong must the counselor's social power be in order for attitude change to occur? Finally, are career attitudes what lead to career behavior or does career behavior lead to career attitudes?

It is also important for us to consider the relationship that exists between client's career attitudes and their self-perception. Fazio (1987) has noted that in terms of self-perception theory, people are usually induced to formulate attitudes through verbal inquiry. Therefore, as a result when a person is asked to express an attitude, they engage in self-perceptual analysis in an effort toward formulating specific attitudes. If an individual has been responding to inquiries (over a long period of time) regarding career plans and career goals, it becomes easily understood how well developed and deep-seated these attitudes are. It is even more apparent why the resistance to reformulating these attitudes is so great, even in the presence of tangible evidence that contradicts the implementation of anticipated career plans. For example, many experienced career counselors know that even factual information such as poor academic performance and low standardized test admission scores do not dissuade clients, who have a professional career in medicine or law in mind, due to a long-standing self-perception of involvement in that particular career field. These difficult career cases are encountered quite frequently by career counselors and such individuals were highlighted by Salomone and McKenny (1982).

A REVIEW OF THE LITERATURE

The existing literature on social influence and career counseling is sparse. In addition, early studies provide one with the impression that the inclusion of a career concern or the resemblance to career counseling was more for the purpose of examining a specific social influence principle rather than for the purpose of examining career counseling. For example, Binderman, Fretz, Scott, and Abrams (1972) were interested in determining whether clients would be willing to accept discrepant vocational test results from counselors with a high degree of perceived credibility as opposed to a counselor with low-perceived credibility. The results of this study basically revealed that clients are more willing to accept discrepant test results from counselors with a high degree of credibility, which suggests that the counselor dimension of expertness enables counselors with high credibility to influence clients.

In a similar study, Guttman and Haase (1972) trained counselors in expert and inexpert roles and had clients visit with these counselors in a high or low credibility appearing office (i.e, diplomas, books) to discuss vocational test results and career alternatives. The unexpected finding in this study was that clients indicated that although they felt more comfortable with the inexpert counselor they were able to recall more specific information about their test results with the expert counselor.

Several years later, Dixon and Claiborn (1981) considered the client quality of "perceived need" that was defined as a two-component characteristic comprised of a request for help and a commitment to change. Participants in the study were assigned to one of two groups according to their perceived need for career counseling. High-perceived need individuals were instructed to write down a list of reasons why it is important to think about and make a career decision, whereas low-perceived need individuals listed the college courses they had completed.

All participants were involved in three sessions of both group and individual career counseling. During this segment of the study each individual was informed about the various career counseling services available at the university counseling center. However, in addition half of the participants in each of the perceived need conditions was also asked to sign a written contract indicating their commitment to pursue career counseling through these services. Results of that study revealed that those individuals in the high-perceived need and high commitment to change condition exhibited the highest degree of compliance with seeking career counseling services. The authors concluded, however, that these results were more of a reflection on commitment to change rather than on perceived need.

A year later, Kerr (1982) published a study that focused some attention on the environmental conditions in which career counseling occurs and the likelihood of clients returning for further exploration. Three room types frequently found in career counseling environments: a professional counselor's office, an institutional interview room, and a career resource center were used in the study. In addition, participants were exposed to either a peer or a professional counselor, both reflecting common practice in career counseling.

Individuals participating in the study were assigned to one of six conditions (setting and counselor). Results of the study indicated that clients interviewed in the career resource center were more likely to return and that there were no differences due to the counselor role. This lead Kerr to conclude that career counseling settings should include an "air of opportunity" because a well-stocked career resource center is perceived as stimulating, which increases the likelihood of further career exploration.

In a far more comprehensive investigation, Kerr, Olson, Claiborn, Bauers-Gruenler, and Paolo (1983) examined the forces of client opposition and resistance and the counselor dimensions that can be utilized effectively in response to these client behaviors. These authors differentiated between client resistance and opposition by suggesting that resistance is the client's negative attitudes toward the process of counseling, whereas opposition is the client's disagreement with the content of the counselor's influence attempts that in this case was encouragement toward vocational exploration. Furthermore, they suggested that the counselor dimension of expertness would be most effective in overcoming client opposition and that counselor attractiveness would be most effective in overcoming client resistance.

In an effort toward assessing whether the counselor dimensions of expertness and attractiveness are effective in overcoming opposition and resistance, Kerr and her associates conducted both an analogue study and a field-based study. The subjects in both experiments were asked to complete a vocational measure which assessed attitudes toward vocational exploration (opposition to the content of counseling) and a counseling measure that assessed attitudes toward the process of counseling (resistance). These same individuals were then exposed to either an expertness- or attractiveness-based counseling interaction. Posttest measures were then administered in an effort toward assessing changes in the subjects' attitudes toward the content and process of counseling.

The results of both experiments supported the distinction between opposition and resistance in counseling as well as the effectiveness of utilizing either an expertness or attractiveness dimension to influence these attitudes. In addition, as Kerr et al. (1983) noted, these studies

> represent a first attempt to examine the restraining forces in the (social influence) model, opposition and resistance, as client variables. In addition, as client variables, opposition and resistance can exist prior to counseling or they can develop in response to the counselor's behavior. Whatever there source, they consist of attitudes held by the client and, as such, must be overcome by the same influence processes to which they constitute a barrier. (p. 330)

There have been several concerns expressed about the research that has been conducted on social influence theory as it relates to counseling. Among these are the absence of clients from actual counseling settings (Heppner & Dixon, 1981) and the failure to acknowledge the role that client characteristics play in the social influence process (Dorn, 1984c).

In an attempt to address some of these issues, the effects of a group counseling intervention structured according to social influence principles was assessed in two separate studies. In the initial study (Dorn, 1987b), clients who presented themselves at the university counseling center expressing concern about selecting a college major were referred into a structured group intervention. This intervention was known as the Choice of Major Workshop and it focused on social influence concepts such as perceived social power as reflected in counselor expertness and social attractiveness (Atkinson & Carskaddon, 1975; Kerr & Dell, 1976; Schmidt & Strong, 1970), perceived need (Dixon & Claiborn, 1981), interpretation (Claiborn, 1982; Claiborn, Ward, & Strong, 1981; Strong, Wambach, Lopez, & Cooper, 1978), and reattribution (Forsyth & Forsyth, 1982).

Clients in the study meet for two 2-hour sessions over a 1-week period. During these sessions, attention was directed at generating a sense of self-awareness in clients in terms of their interests and how these interests related to specific college majors. Attempts were also made to provide students with appropriate occupational information and with some direction in terms of how they could become more aware of specific career options through campus resources.

The participants in the study completed the Counselor Rating Form (Barak & LaCrosse, 1975) after the first session and the Career Decision Scale after each session. The results of the study indicated that male and female counselors were perceived similarly in terms of social power by both male and female clients. This is an interesting result because social influence research has found that male counselors are usually rated higher than female counselors on the dimension of expertness and that female clients usually rate counselors higher than male clients.

In terms of actual treatment, statistical analyses that compared pre- and posttest mean scores, revealed that the intervention increased participants scores on the Certainty about a College Major scale and decreased scores on the Indecision about a College Major, Lack of Structure for a Vocational Decision, and Approach-Approach in Making a Career Decision scales. Unexpected findings in the study were that as a result of participating in the intervention clients scores on the Personal Conflict scale increased and scores on the External Barrier against a Vocational Choice decreased slightly for females. These findings indicate that the structured group program heightened some specific issues for both male and female participants and these were different for each gender. More specifically:

> the difference in the increase of scores for male and female participants also may be attributable to the different external barriers that men and women experience during the career development process. Perhaps the slight increase in scores for men was related to their expectation that they might fail to receive approval from significant others by selecting a major in which they had interest (i.e, education) rather than one that is viewed as practical (i.e., engineering). This may have also been the case for female participants, but more important, they may have perceived the external

barriers for certain majors (i.e., engineering) to be greater than for others (i.e., education) because of their desire to experience other dimensions of life such as marriage and family. (p. 126)

Unfortunately at this time, these results cannot be attributed specifically to social influence principles but rather to a group career counseling intervention structured according to social influence principles. Future investigations should include the comparison of this type of intervention with more traditional approaches to career counseling.

In the second study (Dorn, 1989a), utilizing the same structured group counseling intervention, an attempt was made to acknowledge the role that client characteristics play in the social influence process. In this particular case, will the client characteristic of motivation contribute to the social influence process through a higher degree of career certainty for participants in the study? Again, students expressing concern about selecting a major were referred to the Choice of Major Workshop. During this study, however, each individual was asked to complete the Expectations About Counseling (EAC; Tinsley, Workman, & Kass, 1980) questionnaire. The EAC consists of 13 scales, one of which assesses the client's degree of motivation for and personal commitment to the counseling process. The rationale for examining client degree of motivation resulted from previous evidence in the literature (Heppner & Heesacker, 1982), which indicated that client motivation contributed to perceived counselor social power and client change (Dorn, 1983).

As was the case in the earlier study, clients were also asked to complete the Counselor Rating Form after the first session and the Career Decision Scale (CDS) after each session of the workshop. Again, statistical analyses revealed that there were no differences in the perceived social power of male and female counselors by male and female clients.

Participants in this study were divided into two groups, those designated as high motivated and those designated as low motivated. Assignment to either group was based on whether the individual's motivation score was above (high) or below (low) the median score (45 out of a possible 56) for the entire group. Further analyses on this data revealed that significant differences existed between the two groups on the characteristic of motivation but no differences were evident due to client gender.

Comparisons of the pre- and posttest data were made in an effort toward determining whether high-motivated clients became more career certain and less career indecisive then low-motivated clients. The results of these comparisons revealed no differences between high- and low-motivated clients on the six factors of the CDS. Additional analyses, however, revealed that there were significant differences between pre- and posttest scores for all participants on the certainty and indecision scales as a result of participating in the group intervention.

There were several possible explanations for these unexpected results posed by the authors. Among these were that it was assumed that the client characteristic of motivation was stable, and that this quality may have fluctuated in quality as a result of participation in the group career counseling intervention, that the distinction between high and low motivation was artificial because the median score of 45 was high, and that the length of the intervention was not long enough to produce the expected results.

Perhaps the most comprehensive overview of how social influence principles can be utilized in a career counseling context was presented by Dorn (1988) in a case study format. In that particular article, the career concerns of a young pre-med student were conceptualized in terms of attitudes and attributions and how these contributed to her career indecisiveness and static state of behavior.

The young women described attributed her moderate academic performance to poor study skills. During the first session, however, it became apparent to the counselor that she was not particularly interested in pursuing a medical career. She was hesitant to abandon this career avenue, however, out of concern that her family would not approve. (All members of her immediate family—parents and siblings— were either established as physicians or in the process of completing medical training.)

Across a five-session individual career counseling intervention, data was collected through the Career Decision Scale (Osipow et al., 1976) and the Counselor Rating Form (Barak & LaCrosse, 1975). An examination of this data across the five counseling sessions reveals not only fluctuations in terms of career decision making but also marked changes in terms of her perceptions of the counselor on the three dimensions of social power.

There are several interesting points that can be made about the data obtained from this case study. First and foremost, the client's perceptions of the counselor dimension of trustworthiness remained constant across all five sessions. In contrast, however, the dimensions of expertness and attractiveness fluctuated across sessions.

These changes in perception were noted to correspond directly with the content and the intensity of the counseling relationship. More specifically, it was during the second and third counseling session that the greatest degree of affect was displayed by the client. It was during these sessions that she struggled with obtaining approval from her family and (at the possible expense of this approval) pursuing her own interests and goals, which were more closely related to prevention through health and wellness rather than through the traditional healing approach. Thus, the counselor's challenge to these long-term attitudes, which were painful for the client to maintain, were possibly managed by the client through a discrediting process (expertness) and an emotional distancing (attractiveness).

These clinical observations were supported by the data that was obtained on the six factors of the Career Decision Scale. The scores on Uncertainty of Career, Lack of Structure for a Vocational Decision, External Barrier against a Vocational Choice, and Approach-Approach in Making a Choice scales increased by the third session, whereas scores on the Certainty about a Career and Personal Conflict remained the same. By the fifth session, the client had accepted some of the counselor's suggested reattributions and had begun developing some alternate career plans. As a result, scores on the Certainty about a Career scale increased and scores on all other scales, including Personal Conflict dropped. In addition, scores on the expertness and attractiveness dimensions increased. Interestingly enough, however, although the client's perception of the counselor returned to the original level on the expertness dimension, it did not on the attractiveness dimension.

These results were interpreted to suggest that scores on the factors measured by the CDS increased and decreased with the perceived social power of the counselor. Caution was expressed, however, in terms of interpreting results because there are issues that can be raised about the case study method and the generalizability of the results. Still, the results of the study offer support and direction for investigations that integrate social influence theory and career counseling.

FUTURE DIRECTIONS

At best, it seems appropriate to suggest that research on the integration of social influence theory and career counseling is at the preliminary stages of development. Therefore, the opportunities for inquiry are plentiful and the possibilities robust in terms of integrating theory with practice in career counseling.

The following discussion focuses on some specific concepts in social influence theory that have direct applicability to career counseling. The development of research efforts in these areas will provide practitioners with a stronger foundation for understanding the interactional aspects of the career counseling process as well as extend the conceptualization of the social influence process in general.

Social Power

As indicated earlier, the Counselor Rating Form is used to assess client's perceptions of counselors on the three dimensions of expertness, trustworthiness, and attractiveness. Although there is some debate as to whether these three factors are independent of one another, there is consensus that collectively, these three dimensions contribute to the perceived social power of the counselor. What remains unexplored, however, are the various kinds of social power and how these might be utilized more effectively during different stages of the career counseling relationship.

The reader is reminded that the five social power bases are expert, referent, legitimate, informational, and ecological. Furthermore, the expert power base is established as a result of the perceived expertness of the counselor, whereas the referent power base emerges as a result of the perceived social attractiveness of the counselor. The legitimate power base results from the counselor's standing in the community as a helper and the ecological power base develops from the counselor's awareness of how the client can control his or her own environment. The informational power base develops as a result of the counselor's awareness of the various informational resources that the client will find useful.

When one considers these five social power bases and the examination of career counseling at various stages and in different forms of service delivery, a number of intriguing questions present themselves. For example, during the initial stages of the career counseling process which social power bases should be utilized? Are there additional factors (i.e., client variables) that may enhance or diminish the impact of the selected power base?

A review of the social influence literature reveals a fair amount of research being directed at the expert and referent social power bases but little attention has been directed at the legitimate, informational, and ecological power bases. It would be useful for researchers to assess the role that the informational power base plays in the delivery of counseling services because occupational information is utilized so often during career counseling. In addition, there is merit in determining whether different social power bases are more useful in group career counseling service delivery rather than with individual counseling because such a large portion of career counseling occurs in structured groups.

There is a small body of literature that has developed around the issue of counselor's preferences for specific social power bases in the counseling relationship (Robyak, 1981; Robyak, Goodyear, & Prange, 1987;

Robyak, Goodyear, Prange, & Donham, 1986). The rationale for exploring this particular dimension of the counseling relationship rests
with the observation that generally, counselors preferences for specific
power bases develop as a result of trial and error. Therefore, it is not
unlikely that a counselor's preference for a specific power base may be
interferring with therapeutic outcome and effectiveness simply because
there is a lack of congruence between the counselor's influence attempts
and the client's perceptions (or expectations) for the counselor's source
of power. The consideration of counselor's preference for specific power
bases has implications for career counseling.

Initially, it is unclear at this point whether the outcome of the career
counseling relationship would be more effective if it was initiated
through an expert or referent power base. The reader will recall that
earlier it was noted that the expert and referent social power bases
would be differentially effective in overcoming opposition and resistance in career counseling. The reader will recall as well that the authors
(Kerr et al., 1983) suggested that the referent power base would be most
effective in overcoming client resistance to the process of counseling,
whereas the expert power base would be most effective in overcoming
opposition to the content of counseling. Does this suggest then that if a
client is seeking out career counseling, and is not resistant to the content
of counseling (vocational exploration), and that the counselor has a
preference for utilizing a referent power base, that early termination is
likely? The reason for posing such a question is not based on a desire to
present mute questions for speculation but rather an attempt to determine whether much of career counseling does not continue due to an
inconsistency between the client's expectations and the counselor's
preferences. It may be that most individuals looking for career counseling services have a high need for direct contact and specific information and that the counselor who utilizes a referent, rather than an expert
power base, in an attempt to establish a relationship, fails to establish a
relationship because there is an incongruence between the counselor's
preferences and the client's expectations for where that social power
should emerge. As well, it may be that career counseling is thought of
too often as an information-giving enterprise and as a result, whereas
counselors rely on the expert power base in an attempt to provide clients
with the important facts, clients may be interested in a relationship that
provides them with insight about who they are and what they might
pursue in terms of a career path.

Recently, several authors (Blustein, 1987; Brown, 1985; Brown
& Brooks, 1985; Lowman, 1987) have proposed both the benefits and the
necessities of infusing personal counseling into the career counseling
process. The examination of clients' perceptions of where they perceive

counselor social power emerging in counseling relationships that are identified as strictly personal, strictly career, and an integration of career and personal counseling should provide both practitioners and researchers with some direction in terms of assessing whether career and personal counseling are different types of counseling interventions.

In addition, it would be useful to learn whether the client's perception of the counselor's social power shifts across time in the counseling relationship. As well, counselors need to determine whether the utilization of specific power-based influence attempts are helpful or detrimental to the establishment of the counseling relationship in the early stages.

An examination of the results of the career counseling case study (Dorn, 1988) reveals that the perceived expert and referent social power fluctuated across sessions. Still, in that particular case the degree of perceived referent power never exceeded the degree of perceived expert power.

Client Variables

The social influence process is a reciprocal one. Practitioners and researchers acknowledge that although the counselor is intent on attempting to influence the client, the client is also interested in pursuing an influence pattern with the counselor. As a result, it is extremely important for researchers interested in the social influence model to include in their methodology specific client variables that may have some bearing on the counselor's perceptions of the client. For example, there has been some evidence to suggest that client motivation has a reciprocal impact on counseling relationships. This was the conclusion reached by Heppner and Heesacker (1982) when they found that clients with a high degree of motivation for counseling perceived their counselors as more attractive than those clients who had a lower degree of motivation. Similarly, those counselors who were perceived as attractive, indicated that they felt the greatest degree of social power over their clients. The question that remains unanswered here, however, is who is responsible for initiating the end result. In other words, does high client motivation lead to perceived counselor attractiveness or does counselor attractiveness, either physical or social, generate motivation in clients?

There is a fairly substantial body of literature that supports the notion that counselors are influenced by many surface qualities of clients (Wills, 1978), for example, physical appearance, and that clients make an effort at presenting themselves in a strategic and purposeful manner during counseling. Friedlander and Schwartz (1985) outlined five major self-presentational strategies that clients usually employ in counseling. They are facework, ingratiation, supplication, self-promotion, and intimidation. The authors noted that the first strategy, facework, is a defensive posture, whereas the remaining four strategies are assertive.

Facework is the individual's attempt to avoid blame or disapproval by placing oneself in a different light. For example, a client in search of a career path may blame his or her present career situation on a previous advisor or perhaps on a family member. This strategy provides the client with an opportunity to create an impression of victimization that could elicit a sympathetic response from a counselor.

Ingratiation, the most common assertive strategy, is usually employed when the client is relating to a person who they perceive to be both powerful and in control of important reinforcers. The intent of the individual who utilizes ingratiation as an impression management strategy is to encourage the target individual to like him or her. The individual utilizing this strategy, however, is simultaneously attempting to disguise his or her intent. One might consider clients who present themselves in a manner that demonstrates attentiveness to the counselor but also respect for his or her comments during the session, as employers of an ingratiation strategy.

The client strategy of supplication has been referred to by Friedlander and Schwartz (1985) as the strategy of last resort. The client exploits his or her own weaknesses and makes an attempt to arouse feelings of nurturance, obligation, and protection on the part of the counselor. The client who bemoans his or her career circumstances with statements about lack of interests, skills, and aptitudes and the eventual outcome of "destined to be a career failure" is an example of the client who utilizes the strategy of supplication. He or she is the client who fosters dependency and makes attempts to influence the counselor into assuming responsibility for his or her career decision making.

The individual utilizing the self-promotion strategy is a person who initially attempts to portray a sense of ambivalence toward counseling. This is the individual who, although seeking career counseling, implies that his or her presence in the counselor's office is more a reflection of curiosity about the possibility of "careers with potential" rather than a real need for career counseling services.

Self-promotion is the client's attempt to mask insecurity about him or herself and his or her career direction. The skillful client who employs the self-promotion strategy will be adept at self-promotion through others. Comments such as "my friends see me as multitalented" and "my teachers say I have a great career ahead of me" assist the individual because he or she believes these comments will enable him or her to avoid being perceived as arrogant and self-centered.

Intimidation is the last, and most assertive strategy utilized by clients. Clients usually employ this strategy when the counseling relationship is nonvoluntary. Therefore, career counselors may envision the intimidating client as one who is experiencing difficulty in the work environment (i.e., outplacement) and has been placed in a counseling situation. It is important to recognize that "intimidation does not necessarily involve active or aggressive threats. Incipient hostility, passive resistance, or the suggestion of emotional collapse can be equally effective" (Friedlander & Schwartz, 1985, p. 493).

Still, these client strategies reflect on only half of the social influence process. One of the major tasks facing practitioners and researchers who are interested in applying the social influence model to counseling is the identification of those counseling strategies, and the social power bases from which they emerge, that are effective in reducing the influence potential of these client strategies.

More important, it may be far more advantageous to conceptualize the social influence process as something other than a rugged struggle (Dorn, 1984d). Perhaps counseling practitioners should examine the relationship from the perspective of what contributes to the ease of the process.

For instance, social influence researchers generally agree, as was discussed earlier, that the counselor dimensions of expertness, trustworthiness, and social attractiveness contribute to counselor social power. Social power in this context is viewed as a positive counselor quality and it is employed for the specific benefit of the client. In terms of social influence theory then, we generally know what qualities counselors need to display in order to generate positive outcome. What practitioners and researchers are not aware of presently, is what clients can do to contribute to positive outcome.

Recently, there has been an effort to identify those characteristics and qualities that clients bring to the relationship that contribute to outcome. Some examples of these qualities and behaviors are self-disclosure, topic initiation, eye contact, and the more broadly defined quality of motivation. Several researchers have reported that counselors are more inclined to respond favorably to clients who exhibit these appropriate behaviors in counseling (Jennings & Davis, 1977; Lewis, Davis, Walker, & Jennings, 1981), they are more likely to engage these clients (Tryon, 1985), and they are more likely to evaluate them positively (Wachowiak & Diaz, 1987). These findings are simply a reflection of the reciprocal effect that was reported by Heppner and Heesacker (1982). The major finding in that study was that "highly motivated clients perceived their counselor to be attractive. The counselors of these same clients perceived their clients to also be highly attractive. These same counselors who perceived their clients as attractive also believed that they held the greatest degree of social power over these same clients" (Dorn, 1984b, p. 344). What was unclear in that study and what is still unclear at this point is the identification of what specific qualities contribute to the positive perceptions of clients.

In his review of counselors and therapist's perceptions of clients, Wills (1978) proposed that positive perceptions fall into one of three dimensions: client motivation, client capability, and client social attractiveness. Client motivation is reflected in a person's desire to benefit from counseling and the willingness to do those things that are necessary for deriving a benefit from counseling. Client capability is reflected in the individual's ability to function in the counseling relationship. The socially attractive client is an individual who possesses the interpersonal skills that generate a desire on the part of the counselor to engage the client in counseling.

Wild and Kerr (1984) are the only researchers who have made any attempt to translate this reciprocal process to career counseling. In their investigation they generated a creative reversal of the standard process that is so often employed in social influence research.

A training program was developed for high school students in the area of job interviewing skills. Operating from the assumption that counselors can be trained in persuasion skills (Kerr, Claiborn, & Dixon, 1982), these authors taught the individuals in their study specific behaviors that would enhance employers perceptions of them.

After the training sessions, each individual was interviewed for a hypothetical job as were individuals from a control group. The interviewers were asked to rate the high school students on an abbreviated version of the Counselor Rating Form. Results of the study indicated that those individuals who received the training program were perceived as far more persuasive and more likely to be hired for the position for which they interviewed.

The results of this study have some interesting implications for career counseling. Initially, they suggest that the identification of specific client behaviors is warranted. Second, they present a rationale for providing clients with training before entering the counseling process.

The identification of specific client behaviors by career counselors and researchers will lead to the determination of the types of client behaviors that are perceived more positively by counselors. For example, Schwartz, Friedlander, and Tedeschi (1986) recently concluded that clients are perceived by counselors as more motivated and attractive when they assume responsibility for their presenting concerns than when they attribute their difficulties to circumstances or other people. Often clients seeking career counseling attribute their difficulties to situations and others. Is the presentation of career concerns more likely to elicit a different response from counselors (i.e., no differences between assuming responsibility and not assuming responsibility simply because counselors have a tendency to view career problems as being less within the control of the client and more a result of the poor fit that exists between the person and the occupational environment)? Again, posing such a question is more of an attempt to assess whether the perceptions and the processes are similar or dissimilar when the client's presenting problem is career or personal.

The rationale for proposing that clients be provided with training prior to entering the counseling process is linked to the observation that little is done to assist clients in their efforts toward being successful in counseling. Rather, much of what happens in the early stages of the counseling relationship is a result of chance because many clients lack the basic awareness and understanding of how they might benefit from their counseling experience. More important, although "most counseling approaches require that the client take an active role in the counseling process (these same approaches) do not specify how the client is to learn those behaviors which he or she is held theoretically responsible" (Lewis et al., 1981, p. 313). Conversely, counselors have received extensive training in self-presentation and impression management and they utilize this training to enhance the perceptions of their clients.

A review of the literature revealed several approaches to client pre-training that produced positive results. These pre-training programs consisted of role induction (Friedlander & Kaul, 1983), self-instruction modules and role-play audiotapes (Shaw, Wittmer, & Orr, 1985), and videotaped orientations (Smith & Quinn, 1985; Wilson, 1985; Zwick & Attkinson, 1985). An examination of these types of programs should provide guidelines and direction for those practitioners and researchers interested in integrating career counseling and social influence theory. Furthermore, the utilization of these programs might provide the impetus that is necessary for linking specific client behaviors with the previously proposed client dimensions of motivation, capability, and social attractiveness and the impact that these client dimensions have on counselor perceptions. Finally, it may be that these pre-training experiences provide clients with a sense of involvement in the counseling experience that is so vital to promoting attitude change.

There are proponents of the application of the social influence model to counseling (Heesacker, 1986a; McNeill & Stoltenberg, 1989; Stoltenberg, 1986) who assert that the client variable of "personal involvement" is particularly relevant to the attitude change process. Employing what is known as the Elaboration Likelihood Model (ELM) of attitude change

(Petty & Cacioppo, 1981, 1986), these researchers have attempted to determine the role that "personal involvement" plays in attitude change. This model has particular relevancy to what has been discussed thus far in this chapter because the model incorporates client attitudes, counselor social power, and client variables.

Proponents of the ELM suggest that there are two routes to persuasion; the central route and the peripheral route. More important, the individual's level of personal involvement with the attitude under consideration determines whether the central route or the peripheral route is selected by recipients of the persuasive message. In addition, because the issue presented is of particular relevance and is important to the message recipient, he or she is more likely to attend to the message, process the content of the message, and evaluate the quality of the message. As well, proponents of the ELM have suggested that attitude change that occurs through the central route is greater, the change in attitude is more persistent over time, and the change in attitude influences behavior.

Research on the application of the ELM to career counseling situations is sparse (Heesacker, 1986b; Stoltenberg & Davis, 1988; Stoltenberg & McNeill, 1984), but the results support the notion that the social influence process is far more complex than originally proposed. The limitation in all three of these studies is the fact that client attitude change could not be attributed to client level of personal involvement. A close examination of one of these studies (Stoltenberg & McNeill, 1984) reveals that it is not the construct of "personal involvement" that is a limitation but rather the manner in which it was operationally defined. For example, in that particular study low personal involvement was defined by high career decisiveness and high personal involvement was defined by low career decisiveness. The rationale for defining involvement in this manner was based on the assumption that those individuals who were less career decisive would be more motivated to engage in the relevant thinking that is necessary for the processing of information through the central route. Experienced career counselors and researchers realize, however, that career indecisiveness does not necessarily lead to a sense of motivation or involvement toward making a career decision.

Still, the dileniation between peripheral and central route processing of information in terms of attitude change does have some particular relevancy to career counseling. It may explain the lack of results some interventions produce as well as provide us with some insight into the temporary changes that are observed in some clients. In addition, the ELM provides a basis for understanding the resistance that practitioners experience with clients when alternate career paths are proposed.

The major task facing career counselors and researchers who are interested in applying the ELM to specific interventions is defining *personal involvement*. More importantly, of particular relevancy to career counselors is determining how they might successfully promote personal involvement in clients. The study by Kerr et al. (1983) clearly outlines the dynamics involved in client opposition and resistance to counseling and it appears that in terms of career counseling the construct of personal involvement is related to the content aspect of the counseling relationship. In otherwords, low client personal involvement is a function of opposition to considering the actual process of vocational exploration or alternate career paths. If career counselors could promote high personal involvement in the vocational exploration process or receptivity to alternate career paths then client opposition would be reduced. Further exploration into the attitude change literature should provide career researchers with more direction. For example, the proposed notion that failure to engage in attitude change will be accompanied by negative consequences may be worth exploring. Many career counselors have observed the high degree of personal involvement that second semester college juniors exhibit when their failure to declare a college major poses an obstacle to graduation. In practice, perhaps more appropriate and far less negative consequences can be developed in an effort toward heightening personal involvement, attitude change, and behavior change.

Interpretations

The examination of career counseling as a process of interpersonal influence involves more than counselor perceptions and client perceptions. As well, it is necessary to determine the effectiveness of specific verbal interventions and client's reactions to these verbal interventions.

The verbal intervention that has been referred to most frequently in the social influence literature is that of "counselor interpretation." Historically, interpretation has emerged from psychodynamic theory and from information-processing theory (Spiegel & Hill, 1989).

According to psychodynamic theorists, interpretation is an effective technique because it generates change in the client by stimulating insight that produces more reality-oriented feelings and subsequent behavior change. Information-processing theorists on the other hand suggest that counselor interpretation provides the client with additional information that had not been considered previously. In addition, the discrepancy that exists between the counselor's point of view and the client's point of view should generate change in the client that results in him or her adopting a viewpoint that is more closely aligned with the counselor's viewpoint.

Previously in this chapter, it was noted that the process of career development can be a confusing and ambiguous enterprise for many people. Due to a lack of information or a preponderance of misinformation, many people seek career counseling in the hope of obtaining some specific direction. The verbal intervention of interpretation appears to have some applicability to the career counseling process simply because it can provide the career counselor with an opportunity to assist the client with some understanding about his or her experiences. As Claiborn (1982) has stated with the verbal intervention of interpretation "rather than reflect, the counselor relabels client experience; rather than reconstruct client material, the counselor reconstrues it" (p. 442).

Integrating the observations made by Claiborn (1982) and Spiegel and Hill (1989) can provide practitioners and researchers with an excellent two-step working model for utilizing interpretation within a social influence context with career counseling. Initially, the "relabeling" of client's experience fits neatly into the psychodynamic point of view because interpretation according to psychodynamic theory generates reality-oriented feelings. Therefore, during the initial stages of career counseling interpretation might be utilized in an effort toward assisting the client in developing self-acceptance. In addition, interpretation may assist the client in beginning to realize that it is external factors rather than internal factors that have contributed to his career difficulty and these experiences are reflected in the career development process of others as well.

From an information-processing point of view, counselor interpretation provides the client with additional information that had not been considered previously. Therefore, when the counselor reconstrues or translates the client's experiences into a language the client can understand, the client is provided with a sense of direction and control over his or her career development. Thus, providing support for the observation that "interpretations are used less to establish the source of the client's problem than to describe the client's present behavior and experiencing and to point out the interpersonal effects of these" (Claiborn, 1982, p. 440).

A review of the literature on the utilization of interpretation within a social influence context in counseling is sufficient enough to warrant support for both its use in practice and in research. The initial effort in assessing the role that interpretation plays in the social influence process was conducted by Strong et al. (1978). Employing three different interpretations to explain procrastination behavior to clients, they attempted to determine whether an interpretation that emphasized the client's control over his circumstances would be more effective than one that did not. The results of the study indicated that client control over individual circumstances increased client motivation and behavior change.

Subsequent investigations revealed a variety of findings, all of which provide support for the use of counselor interpretation. Among these findings were as follows

1. that interpretation provides clients with a greater sense of direct control over their circumstances (Hoffman & Teglasi, 1982);
2. clients with internal locus of control respond better to interpretation (Forsyth & Forsyth, 1982);
3. interpretations that provide clients with several options are more positively perceived when compared with interpretations that offer restricted options (Wright & Strong, 1982);
4. slightly discrepant interpretations as opposed to large discrepant interpretations are more effective (Claiborn et al., 1981);
5. interpretations that carry a positive connatation, thus relieving the client of responsibility and attributing the client's circumstances to external factors, are received more positively by clients as opposed to negative connatation interpretations (Beck & Strong, 1982); and
6. paradoxical interpretations stimulate client motivation and behavior change (Feldman, Strong, & Danser, 1982).

More recently, research on interpretation has demonstrated that the actual content of the interpretation was irrelevant during the early stages of counseling (Claiborn & Dowd, 1985) and that propositional interpretations (use of the counselor's theory to describe relationships among events in a client's life) rather than semantic interpretations (relabeling the client's experience using the counselor's theory) are directly linked to perceived counselor expertness (Strohmer, Biggs, & Bradshaw, 1985). Finally, in a rather creative effort that linked specific client variables (dogmatism and locus of control) to receptivity and resistance to counselor interpretation, Jones and Gelso (1988) examined client responses to tentative and absolute interpretations. They hypothesized that resistant type clients (defined for the purposes of the study as dogmatic and external locus of control) would prefer an absolute interpretation, whereas internal nondogmatic clients would prefer a tentative interpretation. The results of the study revealed however, that both resistant and non-resistant clients preferred the tentative interpretation.

The counselor behavior of interpretation is the last and perhaps the most potentially far-reaching variable discussed in this chapter. Previously it was noted that specific client attitudes about the career development process lead to either an active or a static state of client behavior. The interpretation of the client's experience by the counselor is the central component that links together counselor social power and client variables. In addition, client change is dependent on counselor interpretation as well. Therefore, it is imperative that career practitioners and researchers begin developing various interpretations of the career development process in an attempt to assess client responses to them.

The only example in the literature of an interpretation related to the career development process is the one offered by Dorn (1987b). This interpretation stressed direct control over one's circumstances by developing an awareness of self and the world of work (Forsyth & Forsyth, 1982) but it was used simply as a means of facilitating the structured group intervention.

Some questions that might be considered in terms of interpretation are: Do some career clients prefer absolute interpretations? Are some interpretations strengthened by increased counselor social power or specific client variables? Are specific interpretations needed for specific client types? Is the link between attitudes about career development and subsequent behavior strong or weak?

The last question is of particular importance because the theoretical orientations in which interpretation is based suggest that client insight and awareness will result. Still, client insight and awareness do not necessarily lead to actual behavior change. There are many individuals who are very much aware of the negative qualities associated with their own career circumstances but are resistant to change. Therefore, perhaps the important link between generating insight and subsequent behavior change is promoting client personal involvement.

SUMMARY

The integration of social influence theory and career counseling offers some intriguing possibilities for both practitioners and researchers. An examination of the career counseling literature reveals that historically the focus of attention has been on the assessment of specific individual traits and on the identification of certain stages of development. In addition, more recently, there has been too much emphasis on identifying the differences between career counseling and personal counseling (Dorn, 1986b, 1989b) and not enough emphasis on the similarities that exist between these two types of services. Equally important, it may be that the lack of interest and enthusiasm that some counselors express about career counseling (Gelso et al., 1985; Pinkney & Jacobs, 1985) is as much a statement on the lack of creativity that reflects career counseling interventions and the lack of process-oriented research that describes career counseling interventions. The blending of the social influence model with career counseling offers both practitioners and researchers a creative conceptualization of the career counseling process. Furthermore, the utilization of social psychological principles in the examination of the career counseling process will infuse some vitality into this area of the counseling discipline.

Some authors (Leary & Maddux, 1987) have enthusiastically supported the emerging relationship between social psychology and clinical practice. Still, of all the possible applications to clinical practice described by these authors (i.e., marriage and family therapy), the one application they failed to acknowledge was career counseling. It is almost as if career difficulty is viewed as a necessary evil in everyday life and although clinicians continue to emphasize the interpersonal aspects of dysfunctional behavior, they fail to recognize that career difficulties are a reflection of dysfunctional behavior. It is high time that those interested in career behavior reaffirm the importance of good person–environment fit and highlight the eventual psychological difficulties that can emerge from poor person–environment fit.

Career counseling practitioners and researchers have historically relied on concepts and constructs from other disciplines in their attempt to understand career behavior. It appears as if it is time to venture from the shore in an attempt to revitalize interest in this all important aspect of human behavior.

REFERENCES

Atkinson, D., & Carskaddon, G. (1975). A prestigious introduction, psychological jargon, and perceived counselor credibility. *Journal of Counseling Psychology, 22,* 180–186.

Barak, A., & LaCrosse, M. (1975). Multidimensional perception of counselor behavior. *Journal of Counseling Psychology, 22,* 471–476.

Beck, J., & Strong, S. (1982). Stimulating therapeutic change with interpretations: A comparison of positive and negative connatation. *Journal of Counseling Psychology, 29,* 551–559.

Binderman, R., Fretz, B., Scott, N., & Abrams, N. (1972). Effects of interpreter credibility and discrepancy level of test results on response to test results. *Journal of Counseling Psychology, 19,* 399–403.

Blustein, D. (1987). Integrating career counseling and psychotherapy: A comprehensive treatment strategy. *Psychotherapy: Theory, Research, and Practice, 24,* 794–799.

Brown, D. (1985). Career counseling: Before, after, or instead of personal counseling. *Vocational Guidance Quarterly, 33,* 197–201.

Brown, D., & Brooks, L. (1985). Career counseling as a mental health intervention. *Professional Psychology: Research and Practice, 6,* 860–867.

Claiborn, C. (1982). Interpretation and change in counseling. *Journal of Counseling Psychology, 29,* 239–243.

Claiborn, C. (1986). Social influence: Toward a general theory of change. In F. J. Dorn (Ed.), *The social influence process in counseling and psychotherapy* (pp. 31–42). Springfield, IL: Charles C. Thomas.

Claiborn, C., & Dowd, T. (1985). Attributional interpretations in counseling: Content versus discrepancy. *Journal of Counseling Psychology, 32,* 188–196.

Claiborn, C., Ward, S., & Strong, S. (1981). Effects of congruence between counselor interpretations and client beliefs. *Journal of Counseling Psychology, 29,* 101–109.

Corrigan, J., Dell, D., Lewis, K., & Schmidt, L. (1980). Counseling as a social influence process: A review. *Journal of Counseling Psychology, 27,* 395–441.

Dixon, D., & Claiborn, C. (1981). Effects of need and commitment on career exploration behavior. *Journal of Counseling Psychology, 28,* 411–415.

Dorn, F. (1983). A parallax view of counseling: The social influence model. *Personnel and Guidance Journal, 61,* 633–635.

Dorn, F. (1984a). *Counseling as applied social psychology: An introduction to the social influence model.* Springfield, IL: Charles C. Thomas.

Dorn, F. (1984b). The social influence model: A social psychological approach to counseling. *Personnel and Guidance Journal, 62,* 342–345.

Dorn, F. (1984c). The social influence model: A cautionary note on Counseling Psychology's warm embrace. *Journal of Counseling Psychology, 31,* 111–115.

Dorn, F. (1984d). The social influence model: A social psychological approach to counseling. *Personnel and Guidance Journal, 62,* 342–345.

Dorn, F. (1985). *An examination of the relationship between the Career Decision Scale and the Survey of Career Attitudes.* Unpublished manuscript.

Dorn, F. (1986a). The social influence model: An overview. In F.J. Dorn (Ed.), *The social influence process in counseling and psychotherapy* (pp. 3–15). Springfield, IL. Charles C. Thomas.

Dorn, F. (1986b). Needed: Competent, confident, and committed career counselors. *Journal of Counseling and Development, 65,* 216–217.

Dorn, F. (1987a). Dispelling career myths: A social influence approach. *School Counselor, 34,* 263–267.

Dorn, F. (1987b). Career counseling: A social influence approach. *Journal of College Student Personnel, 28,* 122–127.

Dorn, F. (1988). Utilizing social influence in career counseling: A case study. *The Career Development Quarterly, 36,* 269–280.

Dorn, F. (1989a). An examination of client motivation and career certainty. *Journal of College Student Personnel, 30,* 237–241.

Dorn, F (1989b). Career counseling in the university counseling center: A professional dilemma. *NASPA Journal, 26,* 212–218.

Dorn, F., & Welch, N. (1985). Assessing career mythology: A profile of high school students. *School Counselor, 33,* 136–142.

Fazio, R. (1987). Self-perception theory: A current perspective. In M. Zanna, J. Olson, & P. Herman (Eds.), *Social influence: The Ontario symposium* (Vol. 5, pp. 129–150). Hillsdale, NJ: Lawrence Erlbaum Associates.

Feldman, D., Strong, S., & Danser, D. (1982). A comparison of paradoxical and nonparadoxical interpretations and directives. *Journal of Counseling Psychology, 29,* 572–579.

Forsyth, N., & Forsyth, D. (1982). Internality, controllability, and the effectiveness of attributional interpretations in counseling. *Journal of Counseling Psychology, 29,* 140–150.

Friedlander, M., & Kaul, T. (1983). Preparing clients for counseling: Effects of role induction on counseling process and outcome. *Journal of College Student Personnel, 24,* 207–214.

Friedlander, M., & Schwartz G. (1985). Toward a theory of strategic self-presentation in counseling and psychotherapy. *Journal of Counseling Psychology, 32,* 483–501.

Gelso, C., Prince, J., Cornfeld, J., Payne, A., Royalty, G., & Wiley, M. (1985). Quality of counselor's intake evaluations for clients with problems that are primarily vocational versus personal. *Journal of Counseling Psychology, 32,* 339–347.

Goodyear, R., & Robyak, J. (1981). Counseling as an interpersonal influence process: A perspective for counseling practice. *Personnel and Guidance Journal, 60,* 654–657.

Guttman, M., & Haase, R. (1972). Effect of experimentally induced sets of high and low expertness during brief vocational counseling. *Counselor Education and Supervision, 11,* 171–178.

Heesacker, M. (1986a). Extrapolating from the Elaboration Likelihood Model of Attitude Change to Counseling. In F.J. Dorn (Ed.), *The social influence process in counseling and psychotherapy* (pp. 43–54). Springfield, IL: Charles C. Thomas.

Heesacker, M. (1986b). Counseling pretreatment and the Elaboration Likelihood Model of attitude change. *Journal of Counseling Psychology, 33,* 107–114.

Heesacker, M., & Heppner, P. (1983). Using real-life client perceptions to examine psychometric properties of the counselor rating form. *Journal of Counseling Psychology, 30,* 180–187.

Heppner, P., & Dixon, D. (1981). A review of the interpersonal influence process in counseling. *Personnel and Guidance Journal, 60,* 542–550.

Heppner, P., & Heesacker, M. (1982). Interpersonal influence process in real-life counseling: Investigating client perceptions, counselor experience level, and counselor power over time. *Journal of Counseling Psychology, 29,* 215–223.

Hoffman, M., & Teglasi, H. (1982). The role of causal attributions in counseling shy subjects. *Journal of Counseling Psychology, 29,* 132–139.

Jennings, R., & Davis, C. (1977). Attraction enhancing client behaviors: A structured learning approach for "non-yavis Jr." *Journal of Consulting and Clinical Psychology, 45,* 135–144.

Jones, A., & Gelso, C. (1988). Differential effects of style of interpretation: Another look. *Journal of Counseling Psychology, 35,* 363–369.

Kerr, B. (1982). The setting of career counseling. *The Vocational Guidance Quarterly, 30,* 210–218.

Kerr, B., Claiborn, C., & Dixon, D. (1982). Training counselors in persuasion. *Counselor Education and Supervision, 22,* 138–148.

Kerr, B., & Dell, D. (1976). Perceived interviewer expertness and attractiveness: Effects of interviewer behavior, attire, and interview setting. *Journal of Counseling Psychology, 23,* 553–556.

Kerr, B., Olson, D., Claiborn, C., Bauers-Gruenler, S., & Paolo, A. (1983). Overcoming opposition and resistance: Differential functions of expertness and attractiveness in career counseling. *Journal of Counseling Psychology, 30,* 323–331.

Leary, M., & Maddux, J. (1987). Progress toward a viable interface between social and clinical-counseling psychology. *American Psychologist, 42,* 904–911.

Lewis, K., Davis, C., Walker, B., & Jennings, R. (1981). Attractive versus unattractive clients: Mediating influences on counselor's perceptions. *Journal of Counseling Psychology, 28,* 309–314.

Lewis, R., & Gilhousen, M. (1981). Myths of career development: A cognitive approach to vocational counseling. *Personnel and Guidance Journal, 60,* 296–299.

Lowman, R. (1987). Occupational choice as a moderator of psychotherapeutic approach. *Psychotherapy, Theory, Research, and Practice, 24,* 801–808.

McNeill, B., & Stoltenberg, C. (1989). Reconceptualizing social influence in counseling: The Elaboration Likelihood Model. *Journal of Counseling Psychology, 36,* 24–33.

Osipow, S., Carney, C., Winer, J., Yanico, B., & Koschir, M. (1976). *The Career Decision Scale.* Columbus, OH: Marathon Consulting.

Petty, R., & Cacioppo, J. (1981). *Attitudes and persuasion: Classic and contemporary approaches.* Dubuque, IA: William C. Brown.

Petty, R., & Cacioppo, J. (1986). *Communication and persuasion: Central and peripheral routes to attitude change.* New York: Springer-Verlag.

Pinkney, J., & Jacobs, D. (1985). New counselors and personal interest in the task of career counseling. *Journal of Counseling Psychology, 32,* 454–457.

Pinkney, J., & Ramirez, M. (1985). Career planning myths of Chicano students. *Journal of College Student Personnel, 26,* 300–305.

Robyak, J. (1981). Effects of gender on the counselor's preference for methods of influence. *Journal of Counseling Psychology, 28,* 7–12.

Robyak, J., Goodyear, R., & Prange, M. (1987). Effects of supervisors sex, focus, and experience on preferences for interpersonal power bases. *Counselor Education and Supervision, 26,* 299–309.

Robyak, J., Goodyear, R., Prange, M., & Donham, G. (1986). Effects of gender, supervision, and presenting problems on practicum students' preference for interpersonal power bases. *Journal of Counseling Psychology, 33,* 159–163.

Rosenberg, H. (1977). Games the vocationally undecided play. *Personnel and Guidance Journal, 56,* 229–231.

Salomone, P, & McKenny, P. (1982). Difficult career counseling cases: I – Unrealistic vocational aspirations. *Personnel and Guidance Journal, 60,* 283–286.

Schwartz, G., Friedlander, M., & Tedeschi, J. (1986). Effects of clients' attributional explanations and reasons for seeking help on counselors' impressions. *Journal of Counseling Psychology, 33,* 90–93.

Schmidt, L., & Strong, S. (1970). Expert and inexpert counselors. *Journal of Counseling Psychology, 17,* 115–118.

Shaw, D., Wittmer, J., & Orr, J. (1985). Pretraining clients in specific counseling communication skills. *Journal of College Student Personnel, 26,* 23–26.

Smith, D., & Quinn, S. (1985). The effects of two precounseling orientation presentations on client expectations of counseling. *Counselor Education and Supervision, 25,* 244–248.

Spiegel, S., & Hill, C. (1989). Guidelines for research on therapist interpretation: Toward greater methodological rigor and relevance to practice. *Journal of Counseling Psychology, 36,* 121–126.

Stoltenberg, C. (1986). Elaboration Likelihood and the counseling process. In F.J. Dorn (Ed.), *The social influence process in counseling and psychotherapy* (pp.55–64). Springfield, IL: Charles C. Thomas.

Stoltenberg, C., & Davis, C. (1988). Career and study skills information: Who says what can alter message processing. *Journal of Social and Clinical Psychology, 6,* 38–52.

Stoltenberg, C., & McNeill, B. (1984). Effects of expertise and issue involvement on perceptions of counseling. *Journal of Social and Clinical Psychology, 2,* 314–325.

Strohmer, D., Biggs, D., & Bradshaw, C. (1985). Perceptions of counselor expertness: The effects of interpretation content, discrepancy, and type. *Counselor Education and Supervision, 25,* 134–142.

Strong, S., & Matross, R. (1973). Change processes in counseling and psychotherapy. *Journal of Counseling Psychology, 20,* 25–37.

Strong, S., Wambach, C., Lopez, F., & Cooper, R. (1978). Motivational and equipping functions of interpretation in counseling. *Journal of Counseling Psychology, 26,* 98–107.

Thompson, A. (1976). Client misconceptions in vocational counseling. *Personnel and Guidance Journal, 55,* 30–33.

Tinsley, H, Workman, K., & Kass, R. (1980). Factor analysis of the domain of client expectations about counseling. *Journal of Counseling Psychology, 27,* 561–570.

Tracey, T., Glidden, C., & Kokotovic, A. (1988). Factor structure of the Counselor Rating Form-short. *Journal of Counseling Psychology, 35,* 330–335.

Tryon, G. (1985). The engagement quotient: One index of a basic counseling task. *Journal of College Student Personnel, 26,* 351–354.

Wachowiak, D., & Diaz, S. (1987). Influence of client characteristics of initial counselor perceptions. *Journal of Counseling Psychology, 34,* 90–92.

Wild, B., & Kerr, B (1984). Training adolescent job-seekers in persuasion skills. *Vocational Guidance Quarterly, 32,* 63–69.

Wills, T. (1978). Perceptions of clients by professional helpers. *Psychological Bulletin, 85,* 968–1000.

Wilson, D. (1985). The effects of systematic client preparation, severity, and treatment setting on dropout rate in short-term psychotherapy. *Journal of Social and Clinical Psychology, 3,* 62–70.

Woodrick, C. (1979). *The development and validation of an attitude scale to measure career myths held by college students.* Unpublished doctoral dissertation, Texas A&M University, College Station, TX.

Wright, R., & Strong, S. (1982). Stimulating therapeutic change with directives: An exploratory study. *Journal of Counseling Psychology, 29,* 199–202.

Zimbardo, P. (1960). Involvement and communication discrepancy as determinants of opinion conformity. *Journal of Abnormal and Social Psychology, 60,* 86–94.

Zwick, R., & Attkinson, C. (1985). Effectiveness of a client pretherapy orientation videotape. *Journal of Counseling Psychology, 32,* 514–524.

7

Computers and Career Counseling

Jack R. Rayman
Penn State University

Many career counselors are understandably squeamish about the prominent role that computers have come to play in the career counseling process. Vendor exhibits at counseling conventions bristle with computer hardware and software while conference program agendas are laden with the acronyms that we in the profession have come to identify with computer-assisted career guidance (CACG). Despite the increasingly high profile of computer usage within the profession, the questions persist. Is it reasonable and humane to utilize machines to deliver that most human of all services—counseling? It is sensible and advantageous to administer assessment devices and simulations by computer? Is computer-assisted career guidance really guidance or is it merely a cover for information storage and retrieval? If, indeed, computers are capable of establishing relationships with clients, aren't those relationships dehumanizing, shallow, substitutes for real therapeutic relationships—a sort of Pac Man therapy?

At the practical level, if some of the content of the counseling process can be accomplished by computers, which systems accomplish which processes best for which clients? Which systems are most cost efficient, and what impact does the use of computer-assisted guidance have on the cost and quality of counseling services? These are but some of the questions that confront career counseling practitioners as we approach the end of the decade. One thing is certain, more career counseling providers than ever before are utilizing computer-assisted guidance systems, and recent sales estimates from ACT (DISCOVER) and ETS (SIGI) suggest that this trend will continue. Although exact sales figures are understandably difficult to come by, informed estimates suggest that ETS (SIGI and SIGI PLUS) and ACT (the several versions of DIS-COVER) each have in excess of 1,000 sets of software in active use.

To clarify understanding it is probably useful to point out that there are three principal levels in which computer involvement in career counseling has been manifest. The first has been the simple use of computers in support of counselor work tasks that are principally administrative and clerical in nature (e.g., word processing, test scoring, data analysis, scheduling, attendance keeping, test administration, etc.). Although there has been an explosion in the variety and availability of this kind of software, and although these applications offer tremendous utility to the practicing career counselor, they are not the subject of this chapter.

The second level of computer involvement has been the utilization of computers to store and retrieve large volumes of occupational and educational information—the so called Career Information Systems (CIS). These systems differ from generic commercial software in two principal ways: First, they are supported by massive data files that must be updated on a regular basis, and second, they are available in both mainframe and micro versions for direct access by either counselor or client. These systems are of considerably more interest than simple counseling support software and receive some discussion in this chapter.

The third, and most interesting level of computer involvement has combined the massive informational databases of CIS with the delivery of career planning and counseling content to form computer-assisted career guidance (CACG) systems. A considerable body of knowledge about CACG has accumulated since the first primitive efforts to employ the computer in the counseling process in the 1960s (Sampson & Reardon, 1988; Sampson, Reardon, & Ryan-Jones, 1988a, 1988b). Indeed, several key counseling journals have devoted special issues to CACG and related subjects. Although this chapter draws heavily on those special issues and on the counseling literature generally, the special issues regarded as must reading by this author are listed here for the convenience of the reader.

- Computer Assisted Counseling. *The Counseling Psychologist, 11* (4), 1983.
- Computers in Counseling and Development. *Journal of Counseling and Development, 63* (3), 1984, November.
- A Special Issue on Computers and Career Development. *Journal of Career Development, 12,* 1985.
- Special Issue: Computer Applications in Testing and Assess-

ment. *Measurement and Evaluation in Counseling and Development,* *19* (1), 1986.
* A Thematic Issue on A Decade of Career Information Delivery Systems 1977 to 1987. *Journal of Career Development,* 14 (3), 1988.

This chapter was written to provide both the counseling practitioner and the counseling services administrator with an integrated update on the status of the use of computers in support of the career counseling process. It is divided into six sections. The first section provides a brief history of the development of computer-assisted career guidance, not a boring trip down trivia lane by an acronym spouting technocrat, but a minimal treatment of the key events in the development of computer-assisted career guidance (CACG). The second section provides a sketch of the theoretical bases for the content of those CACG systems now available. The content necessary for a CACG system, the content of currently available systems and some comparisons are outlined in the third section. A brief review of the rather modest evaluational studies that have been made of existing systems is given in the fourth section. The fifth part of this chapter addresses the difficult issue of integrating CACG systems into the career counseling process. Finally, in the last section I present and discuss current issues related to the use of computers in career counseling and comment on the significant contributions that CACG has made to the profession.

HISTORY OF COMPUTER-ASSISTED CAREER GUIDANCE

Although no exhaustive effort has been made to document the history of the use of computers in counseling and guidance, Rayman and Harris-Bowlsbey (1977) and later Harris-Bowlsbey (1984) have identified the key capabilities that made the computer a particularly attractive counseling and guidance tool.

Capability 1: Storage of Data Files

Sufficient and accurate information is the prerequisite of all good decision making; career counseling is the art of assisting individuals in the making of good, goal-directed decisions. Career counseling necessarily requires an enormous information base including data files on: occupations, educational programs, colleges, technical schools, financial aid, military programs, referral sources, and many others.

The computer and its associated file-storage devices specialize in the low-cost storage of massive data files and in the instantaneous recall of them. Furthermore, the computer offers the capability to keep these files updated, even on a daily basis, if and when new data become available.

Capability 2: Interactive Dialogue

The primary and most basic tool of counseling is interviewing, or interactive dialogue. The computer and its associated devices are capable of carrying on a structured interview with a client. Although currently available systems are not capable of totally "free responses," they are capable of simulating a counseling interview through the use of pre-structured programs. These interviews are different for different people based on user selection or a computer decision based on the user's possession or nonpossession of a combination of prescribed variables.

This capability means that the computer can deliver any pre-designed interview sequences that career counseling professionals can construct. Client perceptions of the flexibility and personalization of these sequences are limited only by the capabilities of the system developer. Furthermore these "interviews" are highly portable and can be held in homes, libraries, counseling offices, shopping malls, prisons, or anywhere a terminal can be placed.

Capability 3: Searching of Data Files

This is a capability unique to the computer. It allows the user to stipulate a series of search variables or criteria for the perusal of a file of options and, based on these criteria, it produces a list. More powerful, however, is its dynamic capability to allow the user to modify criteria in a variety of ways and become aware of how options change as parameters are altered. This capability allows the user to generate and explore a variety of options in a low-risk, nonthreatening way.

Capability 4: Assessment and Interpretation

The computer is capable of administering assessment instruments (interest inventories, personality inventories, ability measures, skill inventories, values inventories, etc.) and providing individualized, standardized interpretations to the user. The computer delivery of such instruments may be advantageous motivationally as well as being faster, more accurate, and available on a more timely basis than group administrations.

Capability 5: Individualization of Treatment

The combination of the capability for interactive dialogue and the on-line administration of a variety of assessment devices allows the computer to offer a fifth capability, that of providing alternative and individualized treatment to users based on a prescriptive analysis of their needs. For example, administration of an aptitude battery could lead to computer-assisted instruction in areas of specific content weakness identified by the on-line assessment.

Rayman, Bryson, and Bowlsbey (1978) have identified several "commonly held perceptions" of the computer that may have contributed as much to its acceptance as a guidance tool as the previously described verifiable capabilities.

Nonthreatening. Although the thought of using a computer is intimidating to some people, once used the computer is generally perceived as being nonthreatening. It is not thought of as being in a "one-up position" the way counselors often are, because in the end it is only a machine. Thus, many clients are less hesitant to interact with a computer than they are with a counselor (Rayman et al., 1978). In this way the computer exhibits its own form of "unconditional positive regard."

Bias Free. The computer does not bias its response on the basis of the personal characteristics of the client and therefore is perceived as being relatively bias free by most users. Black or White, tall or short, male or female, rich or poor, the computer responds the same. Of course, as a tool developed and programmed by humans, the computer has the potential to be as biased as its developers. However, conscientious, careful attention on the part of developers has minimized bias.

Control. The computer conveys a sense of control to the user. Seeking assistance from a counselor represents some modest loss of control. As a client you must sit through the session (in most cases). Most users feel totally in control of the computer, because they can move around through its content at will, and they have the ultimate control—they can walk away from it without even saying "excuse me."

Authoritative. Computer output whether on a cathode ray tube terminal or in printed form conveys a powerful sense of authority. The computer is often cited by clients as "the source" of information when in reality it is merely a medium posing as a source! A large-scale, nationwide survey conducted by Chapman and Katz (1981) revealed that of the four sources of career information valued most highly by school personnel, two are computerized information systems (CIS and GIS). Clearly, the medium and the message are merging in the eyes of many users.

Motivational. The computer, presumably because it provides nearly instantaneous reinforcement and is a glamorous medium has a powerful motivational impact on users. Studies have consistently confirmed that students who are provided with alternative ways to obtain vocational information will choose to use a computer system over books, audiovisual aids, and other traditional sources (Chapman, Norris, & Katz, 1973; Harris, 1972; Myers et al., 1972). The combination of these capabilities and positive perceptions together with the widely held (albeit inaccurate) belief that career counseling consists of little more than providing clients with timely, accurate information converged to virtually assure the acceptance of computer-assisted career guidance systems.

EVOLUTION OF THE USE OF COMPUTERS IN COUNSELING AND GUIDANCE

The evolution of the use of computers in counseling and guidance has been described by Rayman and Harris-Bowlsbey (1977) in generational terms. In this chapter, I draw on their generational scheme, expand it to include current developments, and summarize it in timeline form.

Batch-Processing: The First Generation

The first computer-based systems that were developed for use in counseling and guidance were batch-processing systems. In this type of system the user had no direct contact with the computer. The user completed a questionnaire on which the desired characteristics of a school or an occupation were indicated. This questionnaire was sent, with others, to a central location where a group of questionnaires were processed in a batch. As the student's selections on the optically scanned questionnaire were applied to the large files of information that computer-storage devices contained, a list of schools or occupations that had the combination of characteristics desired by the student was printed and then returned to the student, usually through his or her counselor. These systems were based principally on a trait–factor model of career development. The computer's role was principally that of storing large amounts of occupational–educational information and then retrieving it based on the clients completed questionnaire. Such batch-processing systems are largely a thing of the past though their basic principles still apply in the case of some computer-scored assessment devices.

On-Line Systems for Information Retrieval: The Second Generation

The second type of computer-based system that was developed was one in which the student was put in direct communication (on-line) with the computer (mainframe) by means of a phone line or cable and terminal devices, usually in the form of a typewriter terminal. This technology allowed the developers of computer-based guidance systems to capitalize on three new and very powerful capabilities: (a) the construction of highly interactive, although structured "interviews" that could take place between the student (who entered responses at the terminal) and the computer (that had text stored in its files); (b) the creation of computer-stored records for each user, so that data about the student could be used in the "interviews," and information about the student's use of the system could be added to the record for both student and counselor use (an on-line monitoring function); and (c) the development of very sophisticated strategies for searching through files that allowed the user to have constant knowledge of the effect of each choice made and the opportunity to "erase" some former choices or to redo file searches with different sets of characteristics.

Some second-generation systems like the Information System for Vocational Decisions (ISVD) were experimental and were never really implemented. Others like the Educational and Career Exploration System (ECES) were implemented on a small scale but never really enjoyed widespread distribution. Still others are in active use today.

As early as the mid-1970s, several hundred schools and agencies utilized such second-generation systems as Computerized Vocational Information System (CVIS), The Oregon Career Information System (CIS), Guidance Information System (GIS), and others. Much of the impetus for the development and implementation of these systems came through grants to individual developers from the U.S. Office of Education, various hardware vendors, and later (1976) through the establishment of the National Occupational Information Coordinating Committee (NOICC) and its state counterparts the State Occupational Information Coordinating Committees (SOICCs). Although NOICC's charge was to develop and implement a standardized "occupational information system" to serve the needs of vocational education and employment and training programs at the local, state, and federal levels, the influx of financial and technical resources that NOICC provided propelled CACG to the next generation.

Systems In Support of Career Development:
The Third Generation

The third generation of CACG systems grew naturally from the second. Some second-generation systems (most notably ISVD) were ahead of their times theoretically but died before technology became sophisticated enough to support them. Others like GIS were content with their niche as Computerized Information Systems (CIS) and through inertia or conscious decision remain mature second-generation systems. Nevertheless, ISVD, ECES, and to some extent CVIS provided a conceptual bridge to the third generation.

As the technological capabilities of the computer grew and the costs decreased, third-generation system developers exploited those capabilities in innovative ways. Rapidly increasing computer speed, telecommunication systems breakthroughs, enormously increased storage capabilities, and the mass distribution of the cathode ray tube terminal, all combined to greatly improve the speed, complexity, and interactivity of CACG systems. CACGs were moving beyond information storage and retrieval. The content of both SIGI and DISCOVER reflected the prevailing view that career development is a process. On-line assessment devices, various exercises and simulations, and instructional modules became imbedded components of the systems. Branching and alternative treatments were presented to clients depending on their responses to increasingly sophisticated interactions, and developers began to urge that CACG systems become integrated components of the larger career guidance program.

The Microcomputer: A Fourth Generation

The third generation of CACG saw the integration of career development theory. The rationale for CACG had become more than common sense and pragmatism and the content had become more than information storage and retrieval. Although other developers and systems were still in existence, practically it had become a two horse race. SIGI and DISCOVER emerged from the third generation as the dominant systems. The advent of the microcomputer signaled the start of the fourth generation. Both SIGI and DISCOVER quickly developed micro versions of their systems and mass marketed CACG as we know it today was born. A timeline of key events in the history of the development and use of computers in career counseling and guidance is presented in Table 7.1.

RELATIONSHIP OF CAREER DEVELOPMENT THEORY TO CACG

Historically the development of Computer-Assisted Career Guidance Systems relates to career development theory in two distinct ways. ECES

TABLE 7.1
A Timeline of Key Events in the History of the use of Computers in Career Counseling and Guidance

The First & Second Generations

1967	Computerized Vocational Information System (CVIS)
	Computerized Occupational Information System (COIS)
1968	The Information System for Vocational Decisions (ISVD)
1969	Educational and Career Exploration System (ECES)

The Third Generation

1973	System for Interactive Guidance Information (SIGI) (Original version)
1976	National Occupational Information Coordinating Committee and State Occupational Information Coordinating Committee (NOICC/SOICC) originating legislation
1976	DISCOVER (Mainframe version)
1978	Comprehensive Employment and Training Act (CETA)

The Fourth Generation

1982	DISCOVER becomes a Division of the American College Testing Program (ACT)
	DISCOVER for Microcomputers is introduced
	Job Training Partnership Act (JTPA)
1983	DISCOVER for Minicomputers
1984	DISCOVER for Organizations
1985	SIGI PLUS
	DISCOVER for Adult Learners
1987	DISCOVER for High Schools
	DISCOVER for Colleges and Adults

(Minor, 1970), ISVD (Tiedeman, 1970), and SIGI (Chapman et al., 1973) represent the efforts of theoretically oriented developers to design systems based on the best available theory. In the case of all three systems, formal systematic analyses were made of existing career development theory, of the counseling process as it existed at the time, and of the emerging capabilities of the computer to support that process. Systems were conceptualized on the basis of these analyses and eventually some elements of the systems were implemented. In these cases, counseling theory and process dictated the components and capabilities of the proposed computer-assisted guidance systems. Theory and function drove the development of these systems while the lagging capabilities of the computer prevented full implementation of ISVD.

Common sense and pragmatism drove the other approach. Career counselors and school guidance counselors recognized in the computer a tool that had the potential to "free" them of much of the drudgery that they had come to associate with guidance counseling. With unfavorable counselor:student ratios of 1:500 or worse, guidance counselors were hard pressed to deliver the quality and type of counsel they had been trained to provide. Guidance counseling has always drawn heavily on a huge informational database, and common sense and necessity dictated that delivery methods change to accommodate the multitudes. The capabilities of the computer were seen as a "way out of the wilderness." Developers like Harris (1968, 1970) and Impellitteri (1967) looked to the unique capabilities of the computer to "free" guidance counselors of the massive information storage and retrieval tasks that had come to dominate the profession. Systems were designed and built to do the work of the guidance counselor that unfortunately had come to include a large component of record keeping and information storage and dissemination. Only later were attempts made to expand the already operational computerized career information systems (CISs) with career planning and guidance content based on theories of career development. This second approach was analogous to the development of the Strong Campbell Interest Inventory. For more than 40 years the Strong Vocational Interest Blank was used as an empirically based tool with no real basis in theory. Then, in 1968, the Holland Theory became a part of the Inventory giving it a theoretical base. In the case of ECES, ISVD, and SIGI theory preceded practice. With the various Computer Information Systems (CISs), necessity and practice preceded the application of formal theory, and at least one of those systems (CVIS) evolved into a Computer-Assisted Career Guidance System (DISCOVER). No matter how the relationship evolved, the "big two" surviving CACGs (SIGI and DISCOVER) are immeasurably strengthened by their strong basis in career development theory.

Trait–Factor Theory

To some extent all guidance systems or career counseling processes, no matter what their theoretical leaning have their roots in the trait–factor theory of Frank Parsons (1909). In the words of Katz (1963), "the role of guidance is to reduce the discrepancy between untutored readiness for rational behavior and some hypothetical ideal state of knowledge and wisdom" (p. 25). Katz further suggested that to fulfill this role guidance procedures typically include attention to three major topics: (a) appraisal of the client, (b) information about options, and (c) strategies for decision making (Katz & Shatkin, 1983). To these three Katz added, (d) planning for appropriate action (implementation strategies). Undeniably, these four topics broadly define the content of career guidance no matter what the medium of delivery.

Classification Theory

Two theories of vocational choice have had a significant impact on the classification strategies utilized by CACG developers—those of Roe

(1957) and Holland (1973). Roe's "field" and "level" occupational classification system served as the basis for the occupational search strategies in computerized vocational information system (CVIS) and continues to be a simple but useful way to categorize occupations into a 48 cell level/field matrix.

The hexagonal occupational and personality classification system developed by Holland (1973) as an integral part of his theory of career choice is probably the most widely used occupational classification system in career counseling and guidance. Holland's SDS (1970) and his RIASEC classification system were key components in the original mainframe version of DISCOVER. The UNIACT Interest Inventory and the World of Work Map, integral components of DISCOVER since 1982, both grew out of the Holland theory. As Fig. 7.1 illustrates, Holland's classification system, ACT's Data/People/Things/Ideas World of Work Map, and Roe's occupational fields are closely related two-dimensional representations of

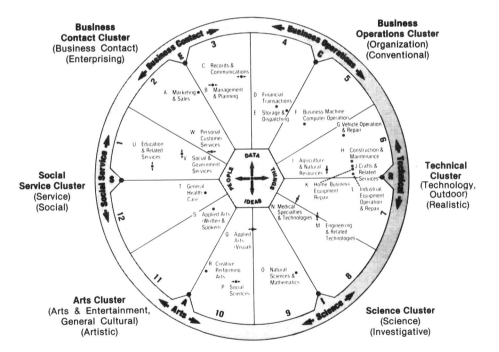

FIG. 7.1. The world-of-work map. The relationship among ACT job clusters, Roe and Holland types, and the data/ideas, people/things work task dimensions. Note: Job cluster titles are shown in boldface type. Roe and Holland titles related to the job cluster titles are shown in parentheses. Roe titles appear first. This figure is adapted from the DISCOVER for Colleges and Adults Professional Manual (1988, p. A–10) by permission of the American College Testing Program. Copyright © 1988 by the American College Testing Program.

the world of work. All have proven to have utility as occupational classification strategies and have influenced CACG developers.

Developmental Theory

The developmental theories of Ginzberg, Ginsburg, Axelrad, and Herma (1951) and Super (1957) have clearly had the greatest influence on the overall structure of both SIGI and DISCOVER. In particular, Super's life-stage conceptualization provides the basis for the linear, process nature of the overall design of both systems. Both SIGI and DISCOVER originally focused on the "exploration" and "establishment" stages of Super's "Growth-Exploration-Establishment-Maintenance-Decline" continuum. Rayman and Harris-Bowlsbey (1977) and Rayman, Bryson, and Day (1978) graphically depict this relationship between developmental theory and the original DISCOVER system in their *Vocational Guidance Quarterly* article entitled, "DISCOVER: A Model for a Systematic Career Guidance Program."

As Fig. 7.2 implies, the DISCOVER system is not only linear and process oriented, but the content of the individual modules of the system relates directly to the developmental stages identified by Super. The exercises and activities contained in these modules encourage and support the developmental tasks associated with each developmental stage.

Acknowledging the full life-span nature of career development ACT

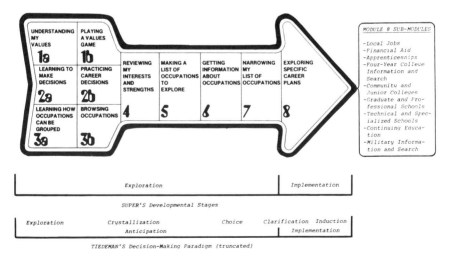

FIG. 7.2. DISCOVER: A model for a systematic career guidance program. Reprinted from Rayman et al. (1977).

has recently introduced DISCOVER for high schools (1987) and DIS-COVER for adults (1985), thereby extending their CACG services backward to include clients near Super's "Growth" stage and forward to include clients in the "maintenance" stage.

Decision Theory

The decision theory and conceptualizations of Tiedeman and O'Hara (1963) and Katz (1954, 1963, 1966) provided the decision paradigms on which computer-assisted career guidance systems were based. ISVD and DISCOVER draw on Tiedeman's Decision-Making Model as illustrated in Fig. 7.3. Harris-Bowlsbey (1984) described the model as follows:

> In the steps of the anticipation phase, the decider becomes aware of a need, reaches out into the environment to identify potential alternatives, envisions what it would be like to employ each of these alternatives, narrows the alternatives to a small number, assesses the valence of each, reaches a tentative choice, and painstakingly reviews the choice and itsanticipated consequences. These processes are primarily internal to the decider, and therefore, relatively low-risk. With induction, however, the decider takes a step of implementation, such as getting a job or entering a college. In this stage the decider conforms to the environment and attempts to behave in the patterns expected in that environment. In the reformation stage the decider begins to project him or herself into the environment and attempts to modify it. Finally, the integration stage is a compromising and a blending of the environment's press and the decider's will. (p. 147)

The content and sequence of the modules of the original DISCOVER system relate directly to the stages and phases of Tiedeman's Decision-Making Model as illustrated in Fig. 7.2.

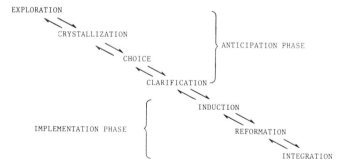

FIG. 7.3. A paradigm of the processes of differentiation and integration in problem solving (Tiedeman's decision-making paradigm). Adapted from Tiedeman and O'Hara (1963, p. 40) by permission of College Entrance Examination Board. Copyright © 1963 by the College Entrance Examination Board.

Similarly, SIGI's structure and content embody Katz's emphasis on values, information processing, and decision theory in a model of career decision making (Katz, 1954, 1963, 1966, 1974).

Career development theory has played a significant role in the development of CACG since its inception. Whether system development was based on a specific theory or whether development preceded theory construction, the evolutionary interplay between theory and system development has immeasurably enhanced the quality and utility of CACG.

DESCRIPTION OF SYSTEM CONTENT

As the preceding section suggests theory has dictated much of the conceptual content of CACG systems. The "actual" content of available CACG systems, however, consists of those assessment devices, activities, exercises, instructional materials, and informational resources that the developers have chosen as a means of delivering that conceptual content. A further element of the content of CACG systems are those special "system features," many of which are unique to the computer medium, and that may be as important to the efficacy of the total package as the other two forms of content. Because of space limitations and because of the realities of the marketplace the content of SIGI PLUS and DISCOVER (for colleges and adults) are described and compared here in outline form. In each case a generic description of the module or segment of content is provided (those with Roman numeral headings), the formal vendor title of that module of content is listed for both SIGI PLUS and DISCOVER (side by side in the interest of providing a ready comparison for the reader), the vendor's brief description of the module content is given, and finally, brief author comments regarding the handling of that segment of content are provided. With this technique of presentation an attempt has been made to succinctly compare and contrast the "big two" CACG systems. Finally, "system-wide" features employed by both systems are described, compared and contrasted.

I. Introduction and Suggested Sequence of Modules or Sections

DISCOVER	SIGI PLUS

1) *Beginning the Career Journey*
    –Teaches the steps of an effective career planning process assesses the user's position in the process
    –recommends DISCOVER modules based on the assessment
	1) *Introduction*
	    –Explains how simple the system is to use
	    –Gives an overview of the program and recommends a pathway suited to user's particular needs

The introductory module (section) of both systems is direct and user friendly. Both systems provide a brief overview of their respective system, collect minimal user demographic information, describe the "special function" keys, and recommend a sequence or pathway suited to the user's particular needs.

II. Instructional Module about the Organization of the World of Work

DISCOVER	SIGI PLUS
2) *Learning About the World of Work*	(No section with this type
–Teaches ACT's World of Work Map	of content)
–Provides user with an opportunity to browse programs of study and occupations by World-of-Work-Map categories.	

DISCOVER provides an instructional module that teaches ACT's World of Work Map. Although such content is not absolutely necessary to a guidance system, knowledge of an occupational classification scheme can have considerable value to a user because it breaks down the complex and confusing occupational world into manageable categories to which individuals can then relate important self-characteristics. The use of the World of Work Map also provides an important linkage to existing printed materials and thus facilitates integration into the larger institutional guidance program.

III. Assessment

DISCOVER	SIGI PLUS
3) *Learning About Yourself*	2) *Self Assessment*
–Interests	–Values
–Abilities	–Interests
–Values	–Skills
–Experiences	–Activities
(Allows entering results of inventories taken off-line)	

Both systems now provide multiple on-line assessment devices to assist the user in establishing linkages between personal interests, values, abilities, skills and experiences on the one hand, and occupations deemed most likely to mesh with these personal characteristics on the other. Although the devices used to accomplish these linkages appear to have face validity, not all have been subjected to the psychometric scrutiny that one might hope for (more discussion of this issue is provided in the fourth section of this chapter). It is, however, encouraging to note that SIGI PLUS acknowledges linkages to occupations other than on the basis of values alone. (This is, indeed, a "plus.") Although DISCOVER pioneered the multiple linkage approach, the SIGI PLUS values weighting exercise is, in this authors judgment, still one of the most intriguing structured exercises available in either system.

DISCOVER's capability to accept the results of commercially available inventories taken off-line represents a real advantage to the institution that wishes to provide some portions of the guidance content via a noncomputerized medium. Acceptance of off-line results also lends itself to more ready integration of the use of a CACG system into the fabric of the overall guidance program.

IV. Generating a List of Occupations Based Upon Personal Assessment

DISCOVER	SIGI PLUS
4) *Finding Occupations* –Identify a list of occupations based on a) on-line assessment b) scores from off-line assessment c) search of 8 job characteristics d) search by programs of study displays a prioritized list of the occupations derived	3) *Search* –Creates a personalized list of occupations based on values, skills and level of education –Allows a "negative" search, i.e., removes from the list occupations with features the user wants to avoid

These modules of both systems draw on the computer's most obvious strength. Results from the users on-line assessment are used to generate a list of occupations based on user responses. Both systems offer a "why not" function that allows the user to ask why a particular occupation did not show up on the list. This function, not available in earlier CACG systems, is a welcome variation that has the potential to significantly expand an individual's occupational understanding.

V. Occupational Infirmation

DISCOVER	SIGI PLUS
5) *Learning About Occupations* –provides extensive information about occupations of user's choice –assists the user to narrow the identified list to 10 or fewer	4) *Information* –Users get answers to as many as 27 questions about occupations –occupations can be compared 2 at a time

Both systems do an excellent job of providing the user with quality occupational information. Both vendors have learned that interactivity is important to maintain user interest and have used it effectively. SIGI PLUS provides the option of receiving the answers to specific questions about any two occupations at the same time. This seems a very helpful feature that was available in the early mainframe version of DISCOVER but that has since been dropped. DISCOVER offers the user the option to elect a lengthy three-page occupational description or a more concise two-page version directed to the printer only. This feature is another reason why this author regards the career information subsystem of DISCOVER to be more powerful than that of SIGI PLUS.

VI. Inventory of Personal Skills

DISCOVER	SIGI PLUS
(No module with this type of content)	5) *Skills* –Users learn what skills are needed in an occupation and whether they have those skills

This section allows the user to select an occupation and see, one at a time, up to 10 of the skills required to be successful in this occupation. The user then does a self-rating for each of these skills and may get a printout showing what skills are necessary for this occupation together with his or her self-ratings of those skills. The placing of personal skills in close juxtaposition with the skills identified as being necessary for success in an occupation is one of the strengths of SIGI PLUS. Although its data files are much less comprehensive, it seems to do a somewhat more focused job of leading the user to compare personal characteristics with those determined to be necessary for successful occupational membership and then leading the user to the decision point. In addition this module has a special section devoted to the exploration of the special skills and work style necessary to be a successful manager or supervisor.

Although DISCOVER deals implicitly with skills, SIGI PLUS, in this section, provides a more explicit skills inventory.

VII. Educational and Training Requirements

DISCOVER	SIGI PLUS
6) *Making Educational Choices* –user identifies possible paths of training for the 10 or fewer occupations stored in the user record –identifies programs of study related to each high-priority occupation	6) *Preparing* –Education and/or training requirements are described along with the skills needed for chosen occupations –Helps users estimate their chances of completing such preparation;

DISCOVER and SIGI PLUS deal with educational and training requirements insimilar ways. Both attempt to educate the user to the various pathways of training that might lead to occupational membership recognizing that there are often several pathways. Finally, an attempt is made to assist the user to determine the probability of being successful in pursuing these various pathways to occupational membership. This module in both systems provides a transition to what Tiedeman would call the "Implementation" phase of decision making.

VIII. Implementing Career Choices

DISCOVER	SIGI PLUS

7) *Planning Next Steps*
  –detailed information
  about colleges, graduate
  programs &
  military programs
  –financial aid
  –learn about job
  seeking skills
	7) *Coping*
	  –financial aid
	  –time management
	  –getting credit for experience
	  –finding day care facilities
	  (option to add local informa-
	  tion) (Some implementation
	  strategies are provided in
	  section 9 entitled, *Next Steps*.
	9) *Next Steps*
	  –Short-range goals are
	  established
	  –Steps are outlined to achieve
	  those goals
	  –Sample resumes are
	  provided

In these sections of SIGI PLUS and DISCOVER specific information is provided in support of implementation of choice. DISCOVER's strength here stems from its massive data files of information on thousands of educational institutions and the very powerful capability to employ sophisticated search strategies to access those data files. Both systems have extensive sections to assist the user with financial aid, obtaining credit for prior experience or learning, and placement-oriented exercises like developing job-seeking skills, resume preparation, and the like. This content is split between two sections entitled "Coping" and "Next Steps" in SIGI PLUS. This seems a rather curious bifurcation of similar content, but perhaps it is done to reduce the length of what otherwise would be a rather lengthy segment of straight information with limited interactivity. The "implementation" content of both systems is appropriate and has improved with updates.

IX. Deciding

DISCOVER	SIGI PLUS
(No module with this type of content)	1) *Deciding* –Directs users in weighing the potential rewards and chances for success in their chosen field.

Deciding is the section of SIGI PLUS that attempts to "push" the user one step beyond anything offered in DISCOVER. Through the use of a graphic representation called a "Deciding Square," the user can evaluate up to three career choices at a time, including the work they are currently doing. Lest users conclude that the decision made in this section is "cast in stone," the SIGI PLUS professional manual suggests that users should be reminded that "Best Choice" is only among those three, not in the whole universe of occupations. The content seems a useful way to provide the user with the opportunity to make a tentative, low-risk decision.

X. Long Range Career Planning

DISCOVER	SIGI PLUS
8) *Planning A Career* —Uses the "Career Rainbow" to graphically explain life roles and help the user to plan for the future	(No section with this type of content)
9) Making Transitions –Teaches users about the nature and importance of transitions in life/career development	(No section with this type of content)

The DISCOVER modules entitled, "Planning A Career" and "Making Transitions" represent an effort to explicitly extend the content of the system to address career development tasks associated with those stages of career development that Super has labeled "establishment" and "maintenance." These two modules are largely instructional. "Planning a Career" draws on Super's concept of a Career Rainbow to graphically explain life roles and assist the user to plan for the future. Making transitions draws on the work of Schlossberg to educate the user about the nature of transition, its role in life-long career development and the role that the person and the environment play in transition.

Although SIGI PLUS does not address "establishment" and "maintenance" stage career development explicitly (with specially designed modules), the overall process design of SIGI PLUS has relevance and utility for users throughout the life span.

System-Wide Features

Both DISCOVER and SIGI PLUS do an excellent job of utilizing the unique features of the computer medium to enhance the power, appeal, and utility of their respective systems. Some of the key system-wide features that do not relate to any specific guidance content of the systems are described here.

Print Function. Users of either system have the option of making hard copies of much of what they receive on the terminal screen. Past versions of such systems made the mistake of allowing users to print any frame of content, often leading to user over-printing of largely irrelevant material. Current versions of both SIGI PLUS and DISCOVER have remedied this problem in two ways: First, only certain frames of material can be printed (others are locked out). Second, both systems prompt users to print copies of data and text at key points to insure that users receive permanent records of particularly important items. SIGI PLUS has introduced two other particularly helpful print features: Each time a user elects to print out a portion of data or text, his or her name and the current day and date are printed in the upper right hand corner of the printout. This feature together with the "SIGI PLUS PRINTOUT CHECKLIST" which is a part of the users guide, encourages users to keep their printouts and file them in a specified order for future reference.

Both systems have significantly refined their approach to providing printouts to users in very positive ways.

Exit Function. Both systems employ a special function key to allow users to leave the system with one push of a key. As mentioned in an earlier section of this chapter, the perception of control conveyed by this feature is important functionally and motivationally. Pushing the F2 key on SIGI PLUS or the F3 key on DISCOVER takes the user immediately to a menu of the modules (sections) allowing movement to any other section or the opportunity to sign off.

Backup Function. Both systems have acknowledged the discrete, noncontinuous nature of computer delivered text by supporting a function key that allows the user to go back to the previous screen of text. This function conveys an important sense of control, continuity, and flexibility to users.

User Record Keeping. DISCOVER has always provided the user with the capability of returning to the system, recovering previously generated personal data, and proceeding to build on that personal record with continued use of the system. One must assume that this capability reflects, on the part of DISCOVER developers, more of a "process" view of career development—an understanding that users are unlikely to complete the process in one sitting, and will probably return several times to complete the process. Interestingly, ETS has recently announced that it too will provide this capability in its most recent version of SIGI PLUS.

Direct Access to Data Files. Both systems provide users with the opportunity to directly access occupational and other data files without using the guidance content of the systems. This capability can be a valuable feature for client users and counselors alike. The DISCOVER "Information Only" approach is supported by much more comprehensive data files than that of SIGI PLUS and its occupational file includes "crosswalks" to the Dictionary of Occupational Titles (DOT), the Standard Occupational Classification System (SOC), and the Guide to Occupational Exploration (GOE). This superior informational database no doubt reflects DISCOVER's developmental roots in CVIS (a career information system). Although the occupational data file that supports SIGI PLUS is a solid one, institutions seeking a strong computerized career information system will no doubt opt for DISCOVER that also includes information on more than 5,000 2- and 4-year colleges, technical and specialized schools, and graduate schools.

Localization. Both systems offer the leasing institution with the opportunity to develop limited local text and data files as indicated in the content descriptions given earlier. One particularly useful localization feature in both DISCOVER and SIGI PLUS is the capability to insert "bulletin boards" or local announcements at key locations throughout the systems. Thus, users might be reminded at the outset that their guidance or counseling office offers regular group sessions on "choosing a college major" or that "resume preparation workshops are available on a drop-in basis every Thursday from 4 to 5 p.m. in Room 12 of the Richards Building." DISCOVER also provides the option of inserting institutional counselor codes so that counselors can monitor their individual clients' use of the system and more readily integrate "off-line" counseling support. Localization options in both systems significantly enhance the relevance of the content and convey a sense that the systems are an integral part of the on-going career counseling and guidance program of the institution.

Ease of Operation. Because DISCOVER is a somewhat more complicated system with more frequent branching, a more elaborate information system and more nested options, it is potentially more confusing to operate. SIGI PLUS, on the other hand, unfolds in a more linear, crisper, cleaner, and direct way. Experience in our Career Center with both systems suggests that users require less standby support to use SIGI PLUS. One operational advantage of DISCOVER over SIGI PLUS is that nearly every user entry in DISCOVER requires only one key stroke, whereas many of the SIGI PLUS entries require two key strokes. For example, when users choose from among four multiple-choice options in SIGI PLUS they must enter their option (choice "B" for example) and then press the "enter" key. Although this appears to be a minor issue, it does unnecessarily complicate use.

Use of Color and Graphics. Both systems have made excellent use of color and graphics to enhance interest, appearance, and clarity. A comparison of either system with those of earlier generations confirms that a remarkable revolution has taken place. User appeal has been remarkably enhanced.

Counselor/Administrator Reports. DISCOVER has always had a data-collection component that provides the counselor/administrator with access to student-generated data. The latest version of DISCOVER provides eleven different types of reports including both evaluative and summative information. These reports can help to create useful ties and increase understanding between the counselor and user. Evaluative information may also be used to justify the continuation of system use. Finally, data from these reports can be quite helpful in conducting research.

The latest upgrade of SIGI PLUS (midwinter 1988–1989) includes a counselor report feature similar to that in DISCOVER. Although the exact nature of these reports is not yet known, the counselor/administrator report feature is certainly a desirable one.

Finally, it is evident to one who has followed the evolution of SIGI PLUS and DISCOVER, and it should now be evident to the reader, that these two systems have evolved to the point that they are currently more alike than they are different. Both have changed and improved with each update. Both vendors have listened well to users and responded in ways that have inevitably caused them to be similar in content both conceptually and actually, but each has its essential uniqueness and personality. They are products of a healthy competition one with the other, and in a sense they reflect the personalities of their primary developers and their parent-testing agencies.

SIGI PLUS in this author's judgment reflects the values of its primary benefactor—ETS. It is carefully crafted, understated, straightforward, direct, slightly unimaginative, and a bit overconfident. DISCOVER, on the other hand, is bold, slightly careless, pragmatic, expansive, and adventuresome with a populist flavor—somewhat characteristic of its publisher, ACT. An interesting parallel might be an Ivy League school and a public institution. SIGI has been the Harvard of the computer-assisted guidance systems. It has always been well endowed. It has always been located in Princeton and its father, Martin Katz, is a careful, confident, social scientist who appears to be a reluctant developer and entrepreneur. SIGI, like the only child of wealthy parents has always been secure, has lived in the lap of luxury and has enjoyed a steady, thoughtful growth.

DISCOVER on the other hand is the community college of computer-assisted guidance systems. Its roots were in the Middle West. It has always been quick to respond to user-suggested change and has a history of innovation. It has always tried harder. It has not enjoyed the luxury of security, but rather has moved from Dekalb, Illinois to Westminster, Maryland to Towson, Maryland and finally, as a division of the American College Testing Program, to Hunt Valley, Maryland. Its driving force, Joanne Harris-Bowlsbey, is principally a counseling prac-titioner, developer, and entrepreneur. DISCOVER, like the child of struggling, middle-class parents has always had to scramble to survive. It has never enjoyed the largesse of huge supportive grants, rather its support has come from the strong will and driving force of its principle developer and from the fact that it is based on sound theory. But perhaps more importantly the public resonated to it because of its pragmatic approach rooted in middle-class values.

The user, personal or institutional, cannot go wrong with either of these systems. Some of their differences have been pointed out here but most of the differences are subtle, even trivial. The fact is, consumers are faced with the option of two excellent systems grounded in solid career development theory and supported by the two largest testing agencies in the nation. Unless Houghton Mifflin's coupling of the Harrington-O'Shea career decision-making system (CDM) with their guidance information system (GIS) (a career information system) is more suc-cessful than this author anticipates, SIGI PLUS and DISCOVER will continue to be the class of the computer-assisted career guidance systems.

EVALUATIONAL STUDIES: A REVIEW

In their *Journal of Counseling and Development* article entitled, "Comput-erized Career Information and Guidance Systems: Caveat Emptor,"

Johnston, Buescher, and Hepner (1988) lament the fact that computer-assisted career information systems (CIS), computer-assisted assessment systems, and CACG systems have received little psychometric scrutiny. Indeed, in preparing this chapter, I found the evaluational literature to be thin at best. This lack of quality evaluation literature is predictable given the relatively short developmental history of CACG as outlined in an earlier section of this chapter. To the best of my knowledge all of the computer-assisted systems that have been developed (and are currently in operation), or are currently under development have received substantial resource support in the form of grants from private or public sources. Similarly, most of the evaluation studies have been carried out by the developers of the systems or their disciples under funding support provided by advocates for the efficacy of the systems (Bowlsbey, Rayman, & Bryson, 1976; Chapman et al., 1973; Garis & Harris-Bowlsbey, 1984; Harris, 1972; Norris, Shatkin, Schott, & Bennet, 1985). Not surprisingly, these studies support the efficacy of CACG, although in most cases the thrust of the evaluations has been formative in nature (i.e., the studies were designed to gather information from users to assist developers in modifying and improving later versions of their systems). The problem here is a simple one that is not unique to computer-assisted career guidance. Persons who have a strong vested interest in the development and successful marketing of a product, probably should not be involved in the evaluation of that product. Unfortunately, most CACG evaluations have been conducted by partisans.

The broad topic of evaluating the utilization of the computer in the counseling enterprise seems to have taken three forms: (a) evaluation of the computer as a delivery medium, (b) evaluation of the quality of the information provided by the systems, and (c) evaluation of the effects that utilization of the system have on users.

Evaluations of the Computer as a Delivery Medium

Most of the early evaluational studies focused on the computer as a medium of delivery (Chapman et al., 1973; Harris, 1972; Impellitteri, 1968; McKinlay & Franklin, 1975; Myers et al., 1972). Typical research questions asked in these early studies were: Did you enjoy working on the computer? Was the system useful? Would you recommend the system to a friend? Would you rather receive career information from a counselor, from a book, or from a computer? Did you understand the directions? Could you understand the words used by the computer? and so on. As was mentioned earlier, the emphasis here was clearly on insuring that the medium was being effectively utilized and on gathering user perceptions of the systems in the hope of improving subsequent versions of the systems. This early research, although extremely important and valuable to developers in improving their products, provided very little useful insight into whether or not CACG systems were effecting positive behavioral change in users. The following summary of findings from one such study is fairly representative of the findings of this genre of study (Rayman et al., 1978):

- Institutions that have implemented CVIS, CIS, ECES, and GIS all report widespread user appeal and acceptance.
- Students accept computer-based guidance systems with enthusiasm and do not feel dehumanized by them.
- When provided with alternative ways to obtain vocational information, students often choose to use a computer system over books, audiovisual aids, and other traditional sources.

Although the studies cited here make fascinating reading to those interested in the developmental history of CACG, they have little value to the practitioner or administrator concerned about the efficacy of currently available systems. It is one thing to know that users like using a system, understand how to use it, and do not feel dehumanized by it. It is quite another to know whether the information being conveyed is accurate and whether or not the user/system interaction is resulting in positive behavioral change. The medium is NOT the message.

Evaluations of the Quality of the Information (Data Files) in the Systems

Every counselor who has ever used a computerized career information system (CIS) has had the experience of looking up his or her own undergraduate institution on the system only to find that certain elements of the data file were inaccurate. Despite the impetus provided by the Association of Computer-Based Systems for Career Information (1982) to enhance and improve the quality and timeliness of occupational and educational data files, much remains to be done. The computer is a marvelous delivery system but as John Krumboltz (1985) pointed out:

> The computer, like a pencil, is a tool. It can be used for writing, for figuring, or for doodling. The computer, like a pencil, follows directions explicitly. Human beings with the aid of a computer, or a pencil, can turn out great works of literature, complex mathematical computations, or

artistic masterpieces. But without directions from a human being, the computer, like the pencil, is useless.

The computer can print out falsehoods without becoming any more conscience-stricken than a pencil. If the humans who give the directions have made intentional or unintentional mistakes, the report will be faulty. Advertisers make reference to "computer-designed automobiles," for example, to convey the image that their product is somehow superior to other products. We must avoid the presupposition that computer-assisted career guidance systems are necessarily better just because they are computer assisted. (p. 165)

Bruce McKinlay (1984), in his article entitled, "Standards of Quality in Systems of Career Information," identified the qualities that characterize good information. According to Franklin (1979, pp. 61–65), quality information is:

Accurate: Valid; true and verifiable.

Current: Applicable at the time of its use.

Relevant: Addresses topics of concern to the user.

Specific: Covers specific institutions, occupations, and local labor markets.

Comprehensive: Thorough; no gaps in its coverage.

Impartial: Leaves status distinctions to each user's values and judgment.

Cost Effective: Economical for system users.

The Association of Computer-Based Systems for Career Information (ACSCI) has adopted a set of 12 standards for career information. According to these standards, information in systems for career information should:

1. Cover 90% of total employment in the system's service area.
2. Have an empirical base.
3. Cover standard occupational topics ranging from job duties to factors influencing projected supply and demand.
4. Be demonstrably understandable in format, style, and language level and avoid racial, sexual, and status references.
5. Be based on current data and documented by research staff.
6. Be validated and updated at least yearly.
7. Be able to demonstrate an empirical relationship between user and occupational characteristics in any sorting mechanism.
8. Cover all significant instructional programs.

9. Describe educational program objectives, specialties, degrees conferred, sample courses and institutions.

10. List only licensed and accredited educational institutions.

11. Cover admissions, housing costs, financial aid, and student services in school information.

12. Enhance comparisons among schools. (ACSCI, 1982)

The good news is that a clear consensus is emerging regarding appropriate standards of quality for career information that is included in CACG systems. The bad news is that in a recent study by Bloch and Kinnison (1989) in which they systematically evaluated Career Information Systems in the broad areas of (a) comprehensiveness, (b) accuracy, and (c) effectiveness, none of the evaluated systems scored impressively. Clearly, the quality of the career information that makes up the data files of any computer-assisted career guidance system is critical to the overall efficacy of the system. The fact that users seem to attribute unusual powers of speed, accuracy, and authority to CACG makes it all the more essential that supportive data files be characterized by absolute integrity. All systems have a way to go to achieve this standard.

Evaluations of the Effects of CACG Systems on Users

Few really careful evaluations have been conducted of SIGI PLUS, DISCOVER, or any other CACG system. There are several compelling reasons why quality evaluations have lagged. First, none of the systems have been around that long. The systems have only been available in reasonably stable form for approximately 10 years. In comparison other career interventions like interest inventories have been in active use for more than 50 years. Not surprisingly, most of the energy and resources to date have gone into development and formative testing, not into formal evaluation. Second, outcome measures for complex career treatments have not been readily available. Although the My Vocational Situation (MVS), the Career Development Inventory (CDI), the Survey of Career Development (SCD), and the Career Maturity Inventory (CMI), among others have shown some promise as outcome measures, most evaluators have relied principally on self-report questionnaires. As our methods of measuring outcomes become more sophisticated, more carefully controlled evaluational studies will no doubt be conducted. Third, CACG systems are highly complex treatments. Both SIGI PLUS and DISCOVER contain in excess of ten hours of interactive content that may be used over a period of several months, perhaps even years. Clearly, such complex treatments do not lend themselves to "quick and dirty" evaluations.

Despite these obstacles a number of efforts have been made to evaluate CACG systems. Using self-report pre/postquestionnaires, Chapman, Katz, Norris, and Pears (1977) found significant differences between SIGI users and controls on multiple dimensions including: knowledge of values, occupational exploration, definiteness of career plans, knowledge of occupations, and so on. Other studies of both SIGI and DISCOVER using predominantly self-report questionnaires have reported similar findings (Rayman, Bryson, & Bowlsbey, 1978; Sampson & Stripling, 1979). Devine (1976), Risser and Tulley (1977), Pyle and Stripling (1976), and Rayman et al. (1978) used more sophisticated outcome measures (The Career Maturity Inventory Attitude and Competence scales and the Career Development Inventory) in an attempt to determine both main effects as well as interaction effects. Unfortunately the findings from these and other similar effects studies have been inconsistent or nonsignificant.

In one of the better conceived effects studies to date Garis and Harris-Bowlsbey (1984) randomly assigned subjects to four groups: (a) a DISCOVER use only group, (b) an individual counseling group, (c) a DISCOVER and individual counseling group, and (d) a wait-list control group. The Survey of Career Development (Rayman, 1977), a 10-item confidence and progress in educational/career planning questionnaire, a behavior log and the Career Development Inventory (Super, Thompson, Lindeman, Jordaan, & Myers, 1981) were all used as outcome measures. The results of the study yielded the following conclusions:

- All treatment groups showed positive effects in self-rated educational/career planning progress, on all scales of the Survey of Career Development and on the Career Planning and Career Exploration scales of the Career Development Inventory.
- DISCOVER use alone and individual career counseling alone were equivalent in exerting a positive influence on subjects' self-rated progress in educational/career planning.
- The combined DISCOVER/counseling treatment produced stronger effects on career planning progress than either of its components used separately.

Although elements of the design of this piece of research might serve as useful models for subsequent effects studies, it too had serious methodological flaws.

Recently other researchers have begun to compare the effects of DISCOVER with those of SIGI and SIGI PLUS (Buglione & DeVito, 1986; Garis & Niles, 1988; Peterson, Ryan-Jones, Sampson, Reardon, & Shahnasarian, 1988). Unfortunately, the results of these studies have been inconclusive and the studies themselves have been marred by serious methodological flaws. In summary there is little that can be said with certainty beyond Cairo's (1983) review of the evaluational literature for the special issue of *The Counseling Psychologist* on computer-assisted counseling:

At best it is possible to state that there is some evidence to suggest that:

1. Computer-assisted counseling and guidance systems promote a greater awareness of the need for planning, increase concern with vocational choice, and facilitate users' ability to relate information about themselves to potential occupations;
2. users learn more about career exploration resources, including those from which they can learn about educational opportunities, about occupations and about themselves;
3. users acquire relevant information about educational and occupational alternatives;
4. the number of occupational alternatives under consideration is generally increased as a result of interactions with computer-assisted counseling and guidance systems;
5. users sometimes increase the appropriateness of their occupational preferences, making them more congruent with personal attributes;
6. in contrast to what early developers of computer-assisted counseling and guidance systems anticipated, counselors do not, for the most part, report feeling threatened, but rather view systems as welcome additions to the range of career guidance services that can be provided to students; and
7. users report that systems are understandable, helpful in facilitating career development, and enjoyable to use. (p. 276)

Although the admonitions of Johnston et al. (1988) ("Caveat Emptor") may sound sensational, extant CACG systems have largely escaped the psychometric scrutiny that one expects in professionally marketed assessment devices and treatments. The issue of careful evaluation must become the major agenda of the fifth generation of CACG development.

INTEGRATING CACG INTO THE FABRIC OF THE CAREER COUNSELING PROCESS

Common sense and the limited research on the subject suggest that integrating CACG as one component part of a comprehensive career counseling and guidance system is likely to be the best and most powerful way to utilize such a system. Clearly, some guidance content is better delivered by an individual counselor, some in groups and still other in paper-and-pencil form. Additionally, individual user learning-style preference is a key issue. Some studies suggest that a combination of the computer and individual counseling is best (Garis & Harris-Bowlsbey, 1984), but there appear to be several reasons why CACG systems are seldom well integrated.

1. *Reason #1.* Often CACG is seen as a way to "stretch" resources. The computer is seen by administrators as a way to provide guidance and information to users without incurring increased personnel costs. A CACG system requires less space than a counselor, does not need a phone, demands no benefits, creates no potential personality problems, and never demands a raise. This line of thinking also often carries with it the assumption that the CACG system can simply be plugged in and forgotten about. Usually when this approach is used, CACG systems are forgotten about—by everyone including those they were intended to serve. When this happens it is not unusual to see hardware intended for the delivery of CACG being used for word processing or computer games. CACG will not work unless the counseling staff is committed to its success. In those institutions where CACG has enjoyed its greatest success, there is nearly always one counselor, "a prime mover," who has devoted enormous time, energy and dedication to insuring that success.

2. *Reason #2.* Many counselors remain stubbornly resistant to using computers in support of the counseling enterprise. They regard counseling as that most personal of all human interactions, something that simply cannot be done by machine. In addition they often feel threatened by a computer system that in some respects may be more competent then they are. These forms of resistance can be overcome with a carefully planned and sensitively delivered counselor training program.

3. *Reason #3.* Cost remains a key concern in most settings. Even though the cost of providing CACG is generally lower than delivering the same content via one-to-one counseling, group counseling, or the curriculum, CACG is still more costly than doing nothing. Unfortunately, "nothing" is regarded by some school districts and institutions as a viable option. As in the case of most software packages, the failure of CACG can often be attributed to an unwillingness on the part of administrators to allocate the necessary resources for adequate training.

4. *Reason #4.* Vendor support has improved in recent years but the quality of vendor support still leaves much to be desired. Now that the content of the major systems has reached a degree of stability, it is time for vendors to commit to a new heightened level of support including the provision of step-by-step strategies for integrating their products.

The differing philosophy behind DISCOVER and SIGI PLUS has had an impact on the degree to which each lends itself to integration into the ongoing career counseling and guidance process. In its earliest versions SIGI was quite obviously designed to be a "stand-alone" system. There was little attempt to provide "bridges" to other elements of the counseling process. There were no "crosswalks" from the SIGI occupational data file. There were no suggestions within the system that certain portions of the content might better be accomplished "off-line." There was no opportunity to modify text locally, and so forth. To some extent this was an early strength of the system. The "turn-key" philosophy with respect to the software and hardware of SIGI kept the control and integrity of the process in the hands of SIGI developers. This insured a "higher quality" product. Unfortunately, it also discouraged innovation and integration and failed to acknowledge that user suggestions and modifications might have value.

DISCOVER, in contrast was almost too responsive to user suggestion. The early mainframe version attempted to be all things to all people. There were "crosswalks," opportunities to modify text and data files locally, options to enter test scores from off-line assessment devices, and whistles and sirens for everyone. Unfortunately, in this attempt to accommodate and integrate, DISCOVER became a complicated almost cobbled system that was confusing to users and threatening to counselors.

Fortunately both SIGI and DISCOVER have made great strides toward facilitating integration by redesigning and modifying their systems over the past decade. DISCOVER has been streamlined and simplified to great effect. It still has the most obvious commitment to integration as evidenced by the presence of many more crosswalks and a fairly comprehensive section in the professional manual addressing integration. In this manual four general models for providing career guidance are outlined including:

- one-to-one counseling and DISCOVER,
- group counseling/guidance/workshop and DISCOVER,
- curriculum and DISCOVER, and
- DISCOVER alone.

The models lay out in explicit fashion strategies that call for the integration of DISCOVER into the ongoing career counseling and guidance program and even provide rough estimates of the cost of various integration strategies. Finally, DISCOVER has developed a career planning workbook, a film, and other "off-line" materials to be used in conjunction with the system.

THE PAST AND THE FUTURE: CONTRIBUTIONS
AND POSSIBILITIES

The simplistic view of CACG would be that it is nothing more than a new delivery medium and as such it has limited potential to impact the field of career counseling and guidance in any substantive way. The reality is that CACG has had a substantive impact and it will continue to do so.

The Systems Approach

Perhaps the greatest single contribution of the CACG movement has been the impetus it has provided to look at the career counseling process in a logical and systematic way. The early computerized career information systems, in keeping with a long held Department of Labor philosophy placed total emphasis on career information, its careful collection, systematic storage, and retrieval. The CIS systems made a valuable contribution to the field but their impact pales compared to the impact that CACG systems like SIGI and DISCOVER have had in reinforcing to the profession the "process" nature of career counseling. Quality occupational information, no matter how it is delivered, provides a necessary but insufficient condition for quality career development and choice. Such information without self-understanding, without an understanding of how to bridge the gap between self-information and occupational information, without an adequate knowledge of decision making and implementation strategies has little value. The implementation of CACG systems (principally SIGI and DISCOVER) that approach the career planning process in this way have provided valuable "process" role models to counseling practitioners throughout the nation. This contribution has been both far reaching and important not just to system users but to career counseling professionals whose counseling strategies and styles have been shaped and reinforced by the systematic process model demonstrated by both SIGI and DISCOVER.

Direct Client Benefits

Despite the fact that the vast majority of Americans still do not have the opportunity to utilize CACG systems, millions of students and adults have taken advantage of CACG in the last two decades. In many of these cases CACG may have been the only form of career counseling or guidance received. Although systems have not been as widely distributed as one might hope, (and certainly not as widely as developers and vendors would like!) their direct impact on millions of clients has been real.

Liberating Effect

Both computerized-information systems (CIS) and computer-assisted career guidance systems (CACG) have had a profound liberating impact by freeing career counseling professionals from some of the drudgery that once attended the maintenance and updating of occupational and educational data files. The quality and timeliness of these massive data files is still far from perfect, but tremendous strides have been made. Accurate, timely occupational and educational information is more readily available now than ever before thanks principally to the CIS movement. At the same time counselors have more time available to deal with client problems that require human sensitivity.

Although the past contributions of the CIS and CACG movements have been significant, the possibilities for the future are even more exciting. J. Harris-Bowlsbey (personal communication, January 7, 1989), who has been involved in both CIS and CACG development for more than two decades, does not see much change in the content of CACG systems in the foreseeable future. Both SIGI PLUS and DISCOVER have evolved to embrace much of what has utility from among existing career development and vocational choice theories. Subtle changes and on-going "fine tuning" of existing systems will continue, but revolutions in content seem unlikely. But if the message remains the same, those receiving the message will change radically. There will be tremendous broadening of the populations who interact with CACG systems. This broadening will include:

1. *A greatly expanded age range of clients.* Today the bulk of CACG users are high school and college students. CACG systems will be developed to extend the age range in both directions. Systems for junior high are currently under development. Similarly, adult systems, systems for use in organizations, and retirement systems will greatly extend the age range of the populations being served.

2. *A greatly expanded range of types of institutional sites or locations.* Currently, most CACG systems are located in educational institutions. High schools and colleges will continue to be important users of CACG, but in the next decade the demand for organizational CACG systems will increase markedly as more and more businesses and industries acknowledge the need for ongoing career development programs. Similarly, libraries, prisons, and shopping malls will become common sites for the delivery of CACG.

This combination of expanded age range and delivery sites will necessitate the development of subsystems to meet the unique needs of the populations being served. Although life-span theories of career development readily support this trend, current CACG systems are not flexible enough to accommodate the extremes of diversity represented by these expanded populations.

3. *New technology.* One key to new developments will be new technology probably in the form of the compact laser disc. Such discs, similar to currently used audio compact discs will support significant innovation in terms of high resolution graphics, full motion video and enhanced sound capabilities. The laser disc and other innovations will play a key role in the development of subsystems to meet the career development needs of the expanded populations just described. In its current form, CACG is principally a written medium heavily dependent on user reading skill. The aural and visual dimensions that will become available through the utilization of new technology offer great promise for users with hearing, reading, and other deficiencies and/or disabilities.

This broadening of the populations who have access to CACG systems will necessarily be accompanied by changes in vendor services, if CACG systems are to achieve anything close to their potential impact. The most obvious of these changes will be:

1. *Greatly Enhanced Vendor Services.* If institutions are to effectively utilize CACG systems the major vendors will need to develop far more elaborate support networks. Some suggestions to enhance vendor support might include:

a. Establish toll-free hotlines to assist institutional lessees with hardware and software problems.

b. Make available consultant teams who can travel to user cites to conduct in-service training programs and teach counselors and administrators how to effectively use and integrate the systems.

c. Provide consultant and resource support for the effective evaluation of systems.

d. Disseminate evaluation results to users via vendor newsletters.

e. Provide more effective "crosswalks" to noncomputerized materials and informational sources (including those produced by competitors).

f. Develop more elaborate and detailed professional manuals that include validity, reliability, and normative information on ALL of the surveys, assessment devices, and other standardized treatments that are embedded in the systems.

g. Develop additional compatable "off-line" guidance materials that enhance and support the "on-line" programs.

2. *A reduced number of vendors.* CACG like other commercially available software will undergo a further shakedown of vendors. Because of the cost of production, the necessity to maintain and update massive data files, and the increased demand for enhanced vendor support, there are likely to be few survivors beyond DISCOVER, SIGI PLUS and GIS. Indeed, by the mid-1990s, competition in the CACG field is likely to be a two horse race.

3. *Improved data file quality.* The quality of the data files that support both CIS and CACG systems remains an important issue. Although nationally developed data files for most CISs have improved markedly in the last decade, they still leave much to be desired. Locally developed files remain an embarrassment in many cases. In the words of Krumboltz (1985), "The computer can and does print out falsehoods without becoming any more conscience stricken than a pencil!"(p. 165).

In summary the use of computers in career counseling has had a short but very impressive history. The next generation of systems will be marked by enhanced quality assurance and vendor support, mass distribution, and utilization, and an increased focus on the evaluation of the global effects of systems as well as on the effects of individual subsystems. The growth, exploration and developmental stages are behind us. As CACG enters the maintenance stage, the emphasis must be on rigorous evaluation and quality assurance. If not, decline will surely follow.

ACKNOWLEDGMENTS

I am grateful to Barbara Blakeslee Rayman and Diane L. Davis for their critical review of an earlier draft of this chapter.

REFERENCES

Association of Computer-Based Systems for Career Information. (1982). *Handbook of standards for computer-based career information systems.* Eugene, OR: ACSCI Clearinghouse.

Bowlsbey, J. H., Rayman, J. R., & Bryson, D. L. (1976). *DISCOVER field trial report.* Westminster, MD: DISCOVER Foundation.

Bloch, D. P., & Kinnison, J. F. (1989). A method for rating computer-based career information delivery systems. *Measurement and Evaluation in Counseling and Development, 21,* 177–187.

Buglione, S. A., & DeVito, A. J. (1986). Computers in career guidance. *Computers in Psychiatry/Psychology, 8,* 18–25.

Cairo, P. C. (1983). Evaluating the effects of computer-assisted counseling systems: A selective review. *The Counseling Psychologist, 11,* 55–59.

Chapman, W., & Katz, M. R. (1981). *Survey of career information systems in secondary schools: Final report of study 1.* Princeton, NJ: Educational Testing Service.

Chapman, W., Katz, M., Norris, L., & Pears, L. (1977) *SIGI: Field test and evaluation of a computer-based system of interactive guidance and information* (2 vol.). Princeton, NJ: Educational Testing Service.

Chapman, W., Norris, L., & Katz, M. (1973). *SIGI: Report of a pilot study under field conditions.* Princeton, NJ. Educational Testing Service.

Devine, H. G. (1976). The effects of a computer-based career counseling program on the vocational maturity of community college students (Doctoral dissertation, University of Florida, 1976). *Dissertation Abstracts International 36,* 7865A.

Franklin, P. F. (1979). *Educational information and advisement services: A resource guide for creating local services and building statewide networks.* Washington, DC: U.S. Government Printing Office.

Garis, J., & Harris-Bowlsbey, J. (1984). *DISCOVER and the counselor: Their effects upon college student career planning progress.* Iowa City, IA: The American College Testing Program.

Garis, J. W., & Niles, S. G. (1988). *Comparing the effects of SIGI, DISCOVER, and a career planning course on undecided university students* (Report #20). University Park, PA: Career Development and Placement Services.

Ginzberg, E., Ginsburg, S. W., Axelrad, S., & Herma, J. L. (1951). *Occupational choice: An approach to a general theory.* New York: Columbia University Press.

Harris, J. (1968). The computerization of vocational information. *Vocational Guidance Quarterly, 17,* 12–20.

Harris, J. (1970). Can computers counsel? *Vocational Guidance Quarterly, 18,* 162–164.

Harris, J. E. (1972). *Analysis of the effects of a computer-based vocational information system on selected aspects of vocational planning.* Unpublished doctoral dissertation, Northern Illinois University, DeKalb, IL.

Harris-Bowlsbey, J. (1984). The computer and career development. *Journal of Counseling and Development, 63,* 145–148.

Holland, J. L. (1970). *The self-directed search: A guide to educational and vocational planning.* Palo Alto, CA: Consulting Psychologists Press.

Holland, J. L. (1973). *Making vocational choices: a theory of careers.* Englewood Cliffs, NJ: Prentice-Hall.

Impellitteri, J. T. (1967). A computerized occupational information system. *Vocational Guidance Quarterly, 15,* 262–264.

Impellitteri, J. T. (1968). *Computer-assisted occupational guidance: The development and evaluation of a pilot computer-assisted occupational guidance program.* University Park, PA: Vocational Education Department.

Johnston, J. A., Buescher, K. L., & Hepner, M. J. (1988). Computerized career information and guidance systems: caveat emptor. *Journal of Counseling and Development, 67,* 39–41.

Katz, M. R. (1954). *A critical analysis of the literature concerning the process of occupational choice in high school boys* (Harvard Career Studies, No. 6). Cambridge, MA: Harvard University.

Katz, M. R. (1963). *Decisions and values: A rationale for secondary school guidance.* New York: College Entrance Examination Board.

Katz, M. R. (1966). A model of guidance for career decision making. *Vocational Guidance Quarterly, 15,* 2–10.

Katz, M. R. (1974). Career decision-making: A computer-based system of interactive guidance and information (SIGI). In *Measurement for self-understanding and personal development, Proceedings of the 1973 Invitational Conference* (pp. 43–69). Princeton, NJ: Educational Testing Service.

Katz, M. R., & Shatkin, L. (1983). Characteristics of computer-assisted guidance. *The Counseling Psychologist, 11,* 15–31.

Krumboltz, J. D. (1985). Presuppositions underlying computer use in career counseling. *Journal of Career Development, 12,* 165–170.

McKinaly, B. (1984). Standards of quality in systems of career information. *Journal of Counseling and Development, 63,* 149–152.

McKinlay, B., & Franklin, P. L. (1975). *Education components for a career information system: Final project report.* Eugene, OR: Career Information System.

Minor, F. J. (1970). An experimental computer based educational and career exploration system. In D. E. Super (Ed.), *Computer assisted counseling* (pp. 37–45). New York: Teachers College Press, Columbia University.

Myers, R., Thompson, A., Lindeman, R., Super, D., Patrick, T., & Friel, T. (1972). *Educational and career exploration system: Report of a two-year trial.* New York: Teachers College, Columbia University.

Norris, L., Shatkin, L., Schott, P. S. & Bennet, M. F. (1985). *SIGI PLUS: Development and field test of the computer-based system of interactive guidance and information . . . plus more.* Princeton, NJ: Educational Testing Service.

Parsons, F. (1909). *Choosing a vocation.* Boston: Houghton Mifflin.

Peterson, G. W., Ryan-Jones, R. E., Sampson, J. P., Reardon, R. C., Shahnasarian, M. (1988, April). *A comparison of the effectiveness of three computer-assisted career guidance systems: DISCOVER, SIGI, and SIGI PLUS.* Paper presented at the annual meeting of the American Educational Research Association, New Orleans, LA.

Pyle, K. R., & Stripling, R. O. (1976). The counselor, the computer and career development. *Vocational Guidance Quarterly, 25,*(1), 71–75.

Rayman, J. R. (1977). *The survey of career development.* University Park, PA: Career Development and Placement Services.

Rayman, J. R., Bryson, D. L., & Bowlsbey, J. H. (1978). The field trial of DISCOVER: A new computerized interactive guidance system. *Vocational Guidance Quarterly, 26,* 349–360.

Rayman, J. R., Bryson, D. L., & Day, J. B. (1978). Toward a systematic computerized career development program for college students. *Journal of College Student Personnel, 19,* 202–207.

Rayman, J. R., & Harris-Bowlsbey, J. H. (1977). DISCOVER: A model for a systematic career guidance program. *Vocational Guidance Quarterly, 26,* 3–12.

Risser, J., & Tulley, J. (1977). *SIGI project research summary report.* Pasadena, CA: Pasadena City College.

Roe, A. (1957). *The psychology of occupations.* New York: Wiley.

Sampson, J. P., & Reardon, R. C. (1988). *General issues bibliography.* Tallahassee, FL: Center for the Study of Technology in Counseling and Career Development.

Sampson, J. P., Reardon, R. C., & Ryan-Jones, R. E. (1988a). *DISCOVER bibliography.* Tallahassee, FL: Center for the Study of Technology in Counseling and Career Development.

Sampson, J. P., Reardon, R. C., & Ryan-Jones, R. E. (1988b). *SIGI PLUS and SIGI bibliography.* Tallahassee, FL: Center for the Study of Technology in Counseling and Career Development.

Sampson, J. P., & Stripling, R. O. (1979). Strategies for counselor intervention with a computer-assisted career guidance system. *Vocational Guidance Quarterly, 27* (3), 230–238.

Super, D. E., (1957). *The psychology of careers.* New York: Harper & Row.

Super, D. E., Thompson, A. S., Lindeman, R. H., Jordaan, J. P., & Myers, R. W. (1981).

The career development inventory. Palo Alto, CA: Consulting Psychologists Press.

Tiedeman, D. V., & O'Hara, R. P. (1963). *Career development: Choice and adjustment.* New York: College Entrance Examination Board.

Tiedeman, D. V. (1970). Comprehending epigenesis in decision-making development: The information system for vocational decisions. In D. E. Super (Ed.), *Computer assisted counseling* (pp. 23–36). New York: Teachers College Press, Columbia University.

8

A Summary and Integration
of Career Counseling Approaches

W. Bruce Walsh
Ohio State University

In the preceding chapters, a review of the major approaches to career counseling were presented. In this chapter the approaches to career counseling are listed across the horizontal dimension in Table 8.1 and summarized down the vertical axis that elaborates the significant features along which they may be described and differentiated. The model of an approach to career counseling as noted by Crites (1981) defines its theoretical framework and conceptual outline. According to Crites (1981), it encompasses three principal chronological stages of any career counseling contact. In the beginning stage a diagnosis of the client's problem is typically made. In the middle stage the process of intervention with the client is carried out. In the ending stage the outcomes of the counseling experience are reviewed and evaluated by the client and counselor.

The methods of career counseling are more pragmatic than theoretical and attempt to translate the model into operational terms (Crites, 1981). They include the interview techniques used by the counselor, the test-interpretation procedures engaged in by the client and counselor, and the acquisition and use of occupational information.

In 1981 Crites used this model and methods of career counseling to define the unique parameters of a given career counseling approach and provide a schema for synthesizing the approaches (trait-and-factor, client-centered, psychodynamic, developmental, and behavioral). In combination, the model and methods of career counseling serve to effectively summarize the unique parameters of the career counseling approaches. It is within this context that I have used this schema to

TABLE 8.1
Summary and Integration

	Trait–Factor (Rounds & Tracey)	Person-Centered (Bozarth & Fisher)
Diagnosis	Different courses of treatment are a function of level of client information processing, client motivation, and relative progress in the counseling process.	There is an initial emphasis on a certain area of client concern, that of work. As noted by Patterson (1964), this choice of emphasis is made by the client. The locus of control remains with the client and there is a lack of treatment planning.
Process	Person environment context (fit of person with an optimal career); rational problem-solving process; facilitate the compilation of declarative knowledge (facts) into procedural knowledge (integrated procedure). This follows a four-step process of information processing: encoding, goal setting, development of plans and pattern matching, and action.	The counselor creates a psychological climate in which the client can evolve a personal identity, decide the vocational goal that is fulfillment of that identity, determine a planned route to that goal, and implement that plan.
Outcomes	Goal of counseling is to provide the client with information to assist the rational decision-making process.	The focus in the model is the person-to-person interaction that promotes self-discovery by the client and implementation of the personal identity (self-concept) in a fulfilling occupational role.
Interview Techniques	Emphasizes assessment and actuarial methods; use of valid and reliable information is stressed; nonquantitative clinical information is collected to make a complete picture of the client.	The counselor relates with genuineness, unconditional positive regard, and emphathy. The locus of control remains with the client.
Test Interpretation	Vocational interests, work vlaues, and cognitive abilities are stable and show valid relationships with career outcome criteria.	The counselor may use testing exercises, however, it is not to provide the client with a ready-made identity, but to clarify and illuminate the client's own view of self.
Use of Occupational Info	Use of valid and reliable information is stressed.	The career counselor has certain career information and skills available to the client through which a career goal can be implemented. There is a large informational component not present in therapy.

(Continued)

TABLE 8.1 *(Continued)*

	Psychodynamic (Watkins & Savickas)	Developmental (Jepsen)
Diagnosis	A structural interview may be used to assess life themes; the counselor asks the client a predetermined set of questions designed to elicit life-theme material.	The purpose of the appraisal is to derive a comprehensive and accurate picture of the client's career development. Three aspects of the client's situation are appraised: person, problem, and prognostic appraisal.
Process	The counselor seeks to explain the client to the client by making intelligible interconnections among the episodes of the client's life. To do this, counselors may summarize their understanding of the client's life theme to answer the subjective assessment question, "What is the person trying to do?" and the objective assessment question, "Which abilities and interests can the client use to continue to do this in the world of work?"	Process includes several elements: counselor–client collaboration, a thorough appraisal, dynamic description of the client's career development processes are constructed using the appraisal data, interpretations of the descriptions lead the client to discover new meanings and possibilities for action.
Outcomes	To help clients find socially viable and personally suitable vocational opportunities to develop their life themes and grow through work.	Overarching goal of enhancing client career development. Stated differently, counseling is designed to aid the client in utilizing personal attributes to achieve self-determined objectives and to exercise influence on the nature of future choices.
Interview Techniques	Interpretation is used to facilitate self-exploration of life themes in relation to future goals and present decision making and to encourage clients to act based on how things look to them.	The interpretation process is essentially arranging and organizing the discovery of new cognitive and affective associations among the appraisal data or between the data and elements of client's tacit knowledge based on their experience.

(Continued)

265

TABLE 8.1 *(Continued)*

	Psychodynamic *(Watkins & Savickas)*	*Developmental* *(Jepsen)*
Test Interpretation	Structured interviews, projective techniques, autobiographies, and card sorts are presented as assessment techniques. These techniques deal with the person directly as compared to actuarial assessment techniques that deal with the person via social comparisons.	The discovery of new career insights is achieved through both inductive and deductive reasoning processes. Inductive reasoning is applied when appraisal data are arranged according to rules emerging from the client's own thoughts and feelings. Deductive methods of achieving insights involve applying concepts from career development theory.
Use of Occupational Info	Very little said about occupational information. Does not seem to be a significant ingredient. Information on personality styles, interests, and abilities will facilitate client development of life themes and growth through work.	Occupational information is not emphasized.

	Social Learning *(Krumboltz & Nichols)*	*Social Psychological* *(Dorn)*
Diagnosis	In career intervention a counselor must evaluate the accuracy, completeness and coherence of the client's informational system.	Treatment is determined by identifying career myths (ineffective career development attitudes).
Process	Understanding client goals and helping the client clarify goals and resolve goal conflicts is an important part of information giving and problem solution.	The process of assisting in abandoning existing attitudes and formulating new attitudes about career development is a process of persuasion.
Outcomes	Defining a client's set of core goals can help a counselor understand a client's most potent motives. When people pursue their goals, they experience feelings of interest, excitement, satisfaction, and meaningfulness.	Client attitudes lead to specific behavior and if these attitudes are ineffective then it becomes necessary for new attitudes to be formulated so that new behavior can be utilized.

(Continued)

TABLE 8.1 *(Continued)*

	Social Learning *(Krumboltz & Nichols)*	*Social Psychological* *(Dorn)*
Interview Techniques	Counselor reinforcement of desired client reponses is an important interview technique. Other techniques include social modeling and the acquisition of decision making skills.	There are five specific social power bases the counselor can establish that generate technique. These are expert, referent, legitimate, informational, and ecological.
Test Interpretation	The Career Beliefs Inventory is used to identify beliefs and presuppositions that may interfere with people's ability to achieve their goals. In general, test use is not that frequent given that the focus is on behavior.	The Survey of Career Attitudes consists of statements about the career development process that are assessing ineffective career development attitudes.
Use of Occupational Info	Career exploration is important. Career kits have been developed that are useful in stimulating career exploration and decision making.	Informational power results from the counselor's familiarity with informational resources that the client will find to be helpful.

	Computers *(Rayman)*
Diagnosis	The computer and its associated devices are capable of carrying on a structured interview with a client. These interviews are different for different people.
Process	The combination of the capability for interactive dialogue and the on-line administration of a variety of assessment devices allows the computer to provide alternative and individualized treatment to clients based on a prescriptive analysis of their needs.
Outcomes	CACG systems promote a greater awareness of the need for planning, increase concern with vocational choices, and facilitate users' ability to relate information about themselves to potential occupations.
Interview Techniques	The computer is capable of carrying on a structured interview with a client.

(Continued)

TABLE 8.1 *(Continued)*

	Computers (Rayman)
Test *Interpretation*	The computer is capable of administering instruments (interest inventories, personality inventories, ability measures, skill inventories, values inventories, etc.) and providing individualized, standardized interpretation to the client.
Use of *Occupational* *Info*	CACG systems do an excellent job of providing the client with quality occupational information, clients also learn what skills are needed in an occupation, whether they have those skills, and the educational and training requirements.

summarize and elaborate the significant features of the career counseling approaches discussed in this volume.

MODEL

As noted earlier, the model of an approach to career counseling elaborates its theoretical framework and conceptual outline (Crites, 1981). In general, it suggests that the career counseling encounter involves three chronological stages. Usually the beginning stage involves some kind of diagnosis of the client's problem. The middle stage is primarily concerned with the process of intervention. In the final stage, the outcomes of the counseling experience are reviewed and evaluated by the client and counselor.

Diagnosis

There seems to be considerable variability on the parameter of diagnosis and the type of diagnosis which should be made. All but one of the approaches discussed in this book would support the value of diagnosis in identifying and solving the client's problems. The exception of course is the person-centered approach where as noted by Patterson (1964), the choice of emphasis is made by the client. Stated differently, the locus of control remains with the client and there is a lack of treatment planning. One could argue, as Crites (1981) has, that all clients have the same problem from the perspective of the person-centered approach, and that in fact they do diagnose but not differentially. In any event, as noted by Bozarth and Fisher (chapter 2), the locus of control remains with the client and the choice of emphasis is made by the client.

The remaining six approaches to career counseling as previously noted, support the value of a diagnosis but vary on the type of diagnosis that should be made. For example, the trait-and-factor approach is primarily concerned with making a differential diagnosis. What is the client's career decisional problem? Different courses of treatment are a function of level of client information processing, client motivation, and relative progress in the counseling process (Rounds & Tracy, chapter 1). Differential diagnosis is a significant aspect of the problem-solving process. The psychodynamic approach is more concerned with dynamic diagnosis. The focus tends to emphasize why the client has the problem. According to Watkins and Savickas (chapter 3), diagnostic data may involve the use of a structured interview to assess the client's life themes. The counselor asks the client a predetermined set of questions designed to elicit life-theme material. Illustrations are the Individual Psychology Life Style Inventory and the Life Script Questionnaire. A number of projective techniques have also been adapted for career counseling (i.e., the Adlerian Early Recollection Technique, the Vocational Adaption of the TAT, autobiographies, and card sorts). According to Watkins and Savickas (chapter 3), four types of clients seem to benefit most from psychodynamic treatment: indecisive and unrealistic clients; difficult clients; adult clients (mid-career changers, displaced homemakers, discharged employees); and culturally different clients. In developmental career counseling (Jepsen, chapter 4), an attempt is made to derive a comprehensive and accurate picture of the client's career development. Three aspects of the client's situation are appraised: person appraisal, problem appraisal, and prognostic appraisal. The diagnostic process is differential and dynamic suggesting three types of problems that markedly impede successful development: Behavior is problematic because it is dysfunctional; dysfunctional behavior is not present but is anticipated; and behavior is functional and socially appropriate but less than optimal. In the social learning approach (Krumboltz & Nichols, chapter 5), the diagnostic process is more dynamic attempting to explain how people come to be employed in a variety of occupations and to suggest interventions that might help people make satisfactory career decisions. As noted by Krumboltz and Nichols, the Career Beliefs Inventory may be used to identify beliefs and presuppositions that may tend to interfere with the client's ability to achieve their goals. It is also important that the counselor evaluate the accuracy, completeness, and coherence of the client's information system. In the social psychological approach (Dorn, chapter 6), differential treatment is determined by identifying career myths (ineffective career development attitudes). The Survey of Career Attitudes is one assessment that may be used to identify career myths. In the computer approach to career counseling, differential diagnosis is used to identify the career decisional problem. Available systems are used to simulate a counseling interview through the use of prestructured programs. As noted by Rayman (chapter 7), these interviews are different for different people based on client selection or a computer decision based on the client's possession or nonpossession of a combination of prescribed variables.

In summary, six of the seven approaches to career counseling discussed in this volume use some form of diagnosis in identifying and solving the client's problems. The viewpoints vary on the type of diagnosis that is made, but in general tend to be differential and dynamic in nature. Differential diagnosis tends to be primarily concerned with the content and the what of the problem. What is the client's problem? Dynamic diagnosis is more concerned with the why of the problem. Why does the client experience this problem? This differential and dynamic diagnostic information is then used to develop an appropriate course of treatment.

Process

The process in career counseling is primarily concerned with the interview interaction between client and counselor. As noted by Crites (1981), all the approaches implicitly, if not explicitly, indicate that stages occur in the process of career counseling. The stages tend to be primarily problem-solving oriented and in general are defined as follows: problem definition, data collection, intervention and interpretation, and resolution of the problem. In general, the process may involve one interview or several interviews. The counseling relationship and communications tend to be key ingredients in the counseling process for all of the approaches to career counseling. I also observe that the career counseling process varies by approach on a number of Corsini's (1981) dimensions (control, awareness, temporality, range, focus, and view of humans). The process of each career counseling approach is discussed here.

In their discussion of trait-and-factor theory, Rounds and Tracy define career counseling as a problem-solving process that emphasizes diagnosis, assessment, and actuarial methods guided by one or more person environment fit models of occupational choice and work adjustment. They view counseling as a rational, problem-solving process in a person-environment context. The process involves rationally fitting the person with an optimal career. An attempt is made to facilitate the compilation of declarative knowledge (facts) into procedural knowledge (integrated procedure). Thus, information processing along with rational problem solving occupies a central place in this model. Key aspects of information processing are encoding, goal setting, development of plans and pattern matching, and action. In general, the process tends to be more therapist-centered and reasoning and meaning are used to develop new perception, thinking patterns, and self-awareness.

The person-centered approach varies some from the other approaches on the process variable. As noted by Bozarth and Fisher, the locus of control remains with the client and there, in general, is a lack of treatment planning. The counselor attempts to create a psychological climate in which the client can evolve a personal identity, decide a vocational goal that will fulfill that identity, determine a planned route to that goal, and implement that plan. The counselor's trust in the client's actualizing tendency keeps the emphasis on the dynamic, spontaneous person-to-person relationship. The process is client-centered and focuses on feelings and emotions. General adjustment is emphasized and the client is viewed as a being in the process of becoming.

The psychodynamic theories conceptualize people as somewhat neurotic and consider overcoming neurosis to be the most important life problem that faces each person (Watkins & Savickas, chapter 3). Understanding self deals with turning neurotic symptoms into strengths and understanding how the client is like others deals with turning personal strengths into social contributions. To bring this about, the counseling process involves the counselor attempting to explain the client to the client by making intelligible interconnections among the episodes of the client's life. To do this, the counselor summarizes his or her understanding of the client's lifestyle to answer the subjective assessment question, "What is the person trying to do?" And the objective assessment question, "Which abilities and interests can the client use to continue to do this in the world of work?" The process tends to be therapist centered and focuses on the unconscious and the conscious. General adjustment is again important and the client is viewed as a reactive being in depth, reacting to drives, needs, and motives.

The developmental career counseling process involves several elements: (a) counselor–client collaboration; (b) a thorough appraisal; (c) dynamic descriptions of the client's career development processes are constructed using the appraisal data; and (d) interpretations of the descriptions lead the client to discover new meanings and possibilities for actions. As noted by Jepsen, these career ideas may be differentiated into different levels of complexity suggestive of counselor interventions, that is, single concept (planning), new system of concepts (ideas vs. things), or meaning schemes such as a life theme or style. The discovery of new career insights, according to Jepsen, is achieved through both inductive and deductive reasoning processes. The change agent is cognitive mastery. Reasoning and meaning are used to develop new career perceptions. The client is viewed as a being in the process of becoming (growing and developing).

Social Learning theory, according to Krumboltz and Nichols, defines decision making as the process of selecting goals, determining strategies to attain them, and maintaining progress toward those goals. According to Krumboltz and Nichols, in career counseling, understanding client goals and helping the client clarify goals and resolve goal conflicts is an important part of information giving and problem solution. The process tends to be therapist centered with a focus on conscious awareness. Antecedent conditions are important because it is believed that through experience, observation, and thought, one develops an organized system of desired and undesired consequences. The focus of the process tends to be on behavior. The client acts to bring about desired consequences and avoid undesired outcomes. The process involves the learning, modification, management, and control of behavior. The individual is viewed as a reactive being.

The social psychological approach (Dorn, chapter 6) posits that the process of assisting clients in abandoning existing attitudes and formulating new ones about career development is a process of persuasion. Motivated clients are influenced by counselors perceived to be expert, trustworthy, and socially attractive. Dorn also suggests that counselors are influenced by self-presentational strategies that clients employ. Some of these are facework, ingratiation, supplication, self-promotion, and intimidation. Dorn notes that clients are perceived by counselors as more motivated and attractive when they assume responsibility for their presenting concerns. The focus of this process is clearly on cognition (attitudes) that are primarily conscious. Clients formulate new perceptions and thinking patterns that contribute to more effective career behavior. Client's degree of motivation contributes to perceived counselor social power and client change.

Computer-assisted career guidance (CACG) systems offer a counselor-free approach to career counseling. They combine the capability for interactive dialogue and the online administration of a variety of assessment devices that allow the computer to provide alternative and individualized treatment to clients based on a prescriptive analysis of their needs. Career Development Theory has played a significant role in the development of CACG systems since inception. Perhaps the greatest single contribution of the CACG movement has been the impetus it has provided to look at the career counseling process in a logical and systematic way (Rayman, chapter 7). In general, the computer-assisted guidance systems are able to store enormous amounts of information, interact with clients, and give fairly immediate individualized feedback.

In summary, as noted, the basic unit of process in career counseling is the interview interaction between client and counselor (Kiesler, 1973). In general, all of the approaches to career counseling suggest implicitly if not explicitly that the counseling process is made up of certain stages. These process stages usually involve problem definition, data collection, intervention and interpretation, and problem resolution. Communication and relationship (with the exception of the computer-based systems approach) are key ingredients to the counseling process. I also see that the counseling process of each approach varies considerably with respect to the dimensions of control, awareness, temporality, range, focus, and view of humans.

Outcomes

As noted, the three principal stages of any career counseling encounter involve the following: the beginning stage (statement of the problem or diagnosis); the middle stage that involves data collection and intervention; and the final stage, when the outcomes of the experience are assessed by the client and the counselor. Stated differently, the expected outcomes of career counseling as noted by Crites (1981) are mainly implied by the diagnosis of a client's problem. Whatever the client's problem, the major approaches to career counseling are primarily concerned with its solution. It is anticipated that the type of career counseling intervention that the client and the counselor collaboratively agree on will lead to improved client-coping behavior and resolution of the problem. As noted by Grummon (1972), outcomes of career counseling are part of, and emerge from, the process.

In the trait–factor approach, Rounds and Tracy indicate that the goal of counseling is to provide the client with information to assist the rational decision-making process. The agent of change is cognitive mastery. During the career counseling process the client learns a person–environment fit model as a basis for present and future problem solving and decision making.

In the person-centered approach (Bozarth & Fisher, chapter 2), the focus is on the person-to-person interaction that promotes self-discovery by the client and implementation of personal identity (self-concept) in a fulfilling occupational role. However, as we have previously noted, the locus of control remains with the client. The relationship is the key ingredient.

The goal of psychodynamic career counseling (Watkins & Savickas, chapter 3) is to help clients find socially viable and personally suitable vocational opportunities to develop their life themes and grow through work. The counselor seeks to explain the client to the client by making intelligible interconnections among the episodes of the client's life. Thus, the counseling process is not only concerned with career adjustment, but also personal and general adjustment. Enhancing personal adjustment is a desirable outcome of psychodynamic career counseling. As noted by Crites (1981), if a client learns to cope with her or his career problem, it is likely that she or he will be better able to cope with other problems.

In developmental career counseling (Jepsen, chapter 4), the overarching goal is one of enhancing client career development. Intermediate goals (Savickas, 1984), depending on the client's situation, include Career Maturity 1 (CM1) and Career Maturity 2 (CM2). CM1 is an estimate of the client's actual degree of progress relative to expected degree of progress on particular developmental tasks. What is the client's degree of career development on a given developmental task? CM2 is primarily concerned with how well the client is dealing with the full array of career developmental tasks. Stated differently, counseling is designed to aid the client in utilizing personal attributes to achieve self-determined objectives and to exercise influence on the nature of future choices. As noted by Crites (1981), the emphasis is on the choice process, not the choice content. The client acquires and develops a way of coping with career problems that is not time or content bound (Crites, 1981). An expected outcome is that clients will develop an approach to the decision-making situations of life.

The social learning approach (Krumboltz & Nichols, chapter 5) is primarily concerned with defining a client's set of core goals that will help a counselor understand the client's most potent motives. When people pursue their goals according to Krumboltz and Nichols, they experience the feelings of interest, excitement, satisfaction, and meaningfulness. Decision making is the process of selecting goals, determining strategies to attain them, and maintaining progress toward those goals. Thus, similar to the developmental approach, the social learning approach is primarily concerned with the acquisition of decisional skills and the choice process. The client acquires coping behaviors to deal with career problems that are not time or content bound (Crites, 1981).

The social psychological approach (Dorn, chapter 6) is primarily concerned with attitude change. The thinking is that client attitudes lead to specific behaviors and if these attitudes are ineffective then it becomes necessary for new attitudes to be formulated so that new behavior can be utilized. Dorn suggests that the process of assisting clients in abandoning existing attitudes and formulating new ones about career development is a process of persuasion. The client is persuaded to formulate new perceptions and thinking patterns. Stated differently, effective and realistic career attitudes will lead to more effective and realistic career behavior.

The computer-assisted career guidance (CACG) systems in general tend to promote a greater awareness of the need for planning, increasing concern with vocational choice, and facilitating the user's ability to relate information about themselves to potential occupations. As noted by Rayman, common sense and limited research suggest that integrated CACG as one component part of a comprehensive career counseling and guidance system is probably the best and most powerful way to utilize such a system. CACG systems do an excellent job of providing the user or client with quality information. This is probably the computers most obvious strength.

In summary, the different approaches to career counseling suggest a number of desired outcomes. A generally recognized goal by all the approaches is to assist the client in making a career choice. This is a goal accepted by all of the approaches to career counseling. A second goal accepted by a number of the approaches is the general enhancement of personal adjustment. Mounting evidence indicates that there is a relationship between career adjustment and personal adjustment. As noted by Crites (1981), if a client learns to cope with career problems, it is likely that he or she will be better able to cope with other problems. A third goal emphasized by some of the approaches is primarily concerned with decisional skills and the choice process. As an outcome of these approaches, the client develops coping behaviors in order to deal with career problems that are not time or content bound. The client develops coping behaviors that may be used to deal with the general situations of life. Finally, as noted by Crites (1981), all of the major approaches to career counseling support the humanistic value that their common goal is to further the development or growth of clients toward being more fully functioning individuals. More fully functioning vocationally, socially, personally, and intellectually.

METHODS

The purpose of the methods of career counseling is to translate the model into operational terms (Crites, 1981). In career counseling, the methods include the interview techniques used by the counselor, the test-interpretation procedures engaged in by the counselor and client, and the use of occupational information (Crites, 1981). The model is operationalized by the methods of career counseling and both serve to define the significant characteristics of a given approach to career counseling.

Interview Techniques

The model of career counseling (diagnosis, process, and outcomes) is a function of the interview techniques used by the counselor. In general, the interview techniques that are used in the various stages of the career counseling process range on a continuum from being more direct to less direct. In the beginning stages of the career counseling process, nondirective techniques that are relationship oriented tend to facilitate problem exploration and clarification. The middle stage of the process involves considerable use of the more direct technique of interpretation. Meaningful data is interpreted to the client within the context of the intervention. In the final stage of the career counseling process the counselor is more active and the techniques more directive. Client responses are rationally reviewed and reinforced. Interview techniques of the various approaches are discussed here.

The trait–factor approach, as noted by Rounds and Tracy, emphasizes assessment and actuarial methods and the use of reliable and valid information. Nonquantitative clinical information is also collected to make a complete picture of the client. Interpersonal influence processes are used. In general, the techniques used in this approach tend to be fairly direct and focus on planning, being rational, problem solving, and informational.

In the person-centered approach (Bozarth & Fisher, chapter 2), the counselor relates with genuineness, unconditional positive regard, and empathy. Reflection of both meaning and feeling along with restatement are client-centered responses available to the counselor. These kinds of nondirect relationship responses tend to facilitate client self-exploration. Stated differently, the counselor attempts to create a psychological climate in which the client can evolve a personal identity.

In the psychodynamic approach (Watkins & Savickas, chapter 3), the counselor uses interpretation methods that help clients recognize who they are and accept themselves. Interpretation is used to facilitate self-exploration of life themes in relation to future goals and present decision making and to encourage clients to act based on how things look to them. In addition, autobiographies and card sorts are assessment techniques that attempt to combine interview and projective techniques.

The autobiography technique uses an open-ended statement to elicit personal scenarios of the past, present, or future. Card sorts use stimulus materials to evoke client's view about themselves and work. The developmental career counseling approach is also primarily operationalized using an interpretive process. As noted by Jepsen the interpretation process is essentially that of arranging and organizing the discovery of new cognitive and affective associations among the appraisal data or between the data and elements of the client's tacit knowledge based in their experience. According to Jepsen, inductive and deductive reasoning processes are used in this interpretive process. However, Jepsen points out that in general counseling techniques and methods are more effective when adapted to the client level of development. The social psychological approach (Dorn, chapter 6) uses verbal interpretation to assist the client with some understanding about experience. According to Dorn, interpretation provides clients with a greater sense of control over their circumstances. Dorn notes that other techniques may be generated by various social power-based variables: expert, referent, legitimate, informational, and ecological.

The social learning approach (Krumboltz & Nichols, chapter 5) suggests that people acquire their preferences for various activities through a variety of learning experiences. The influence of positive and negative reinforcement from direct performance trials is an important determinant of behavior and self-concept. Within this context, counselor reinforcement of desired client responses is an important interview technique. Other techniques include social modeling and the acquisition of decision-making skills.

In summary, as noted earlier, the different models of career counseling are operationalized or made real through their interview techniques. In the early stages of the career counseling process, the person-centered nondirective relationship techniques seem to be the most appropriate. The counselor is genuine, accepting, and understanding. The counselor attempts to create a psychological climate that tends to facilitate client self-exploration. The middle stage of career counseling is primarily characterized by interpretational processes suggested by the psychodynamic, developmental, and social psychological approaches. The interpretive process focuses not only on career choice, but the enhancement of personal and general adjustment. In the final stage of career counseling, problem solution and the acquisition of coping behaviors is furthered by the counselors becoming more active and the techniques more directive. In this stage the review and reinforcement techniques of the trait-and-factor and social learning approaches are relevant. Counselor reinforcement of desired client responses is important. The use of computer-assisted career guidance systems can also be very valuable in this stage and facilitate the client's ability to relate information about self to potential occupations.

Test Interpretation

From the beginning, the core of trait-and-factor career counseling has been test interpretation. As noted by Rounds and Tracy, trait-and-factor career counseling is best thought of as a problem-solving approach that emphasizes diagnosis, assessment, and actuarial methods guided by one or more person–environment fit models of occupational choice and work adjustment. Within this context, Rounds and Tracy indicate that vocational interests, work values, and cognitive abilities are stable and show valid relationships with career outcome criteria. They further emphasize the tradition of the trait-and-factor approach by noting that counselors who do not avail themselves and their clients of this valuable information do a disservice to their clientele. When person-centered counseling emerged in the 1950s relationship variables were emphasized in the career counseling process. As noted by Crites (1981), the emotional side of decision making was emphasized. Diagnosis and testing, as viewed by the person-centered approach, was too controlling and not client-centered. Bozarth and Fisher suggest that the counselor may use testing exercises, however, it is not to provide a client with a ready-made identity, but to clarify and illuminate the client's own view of self. Consistent with Patterson (1964), they further note that the choice of emphasis is made by the client.

In the psychodynamic approach to career counseling Watkins and Savickas emphasize the use of structured interviews, projective techniques, autobiographies, and card sorts as assessment techniques. According to Watkins and Savickas, these techniques deal with the person directly as compared to actuarial assessment techniques that deal with the person via social comparisons. Goldman (1983) noted that these assessment techniques tend to be as much counseling methods as they are assessment techniques. They may be used for assessment or counseling and permit the counselor considerable flexibility in how they present the assessment results to clients. Counselors may use test-interpretation methods or integrate the presentation of assessment results into ongoing counseling dialogue by using responses to assessment questions as counseling leads. Stated differently, tests are interpreted without the tests.

In the developmental approach to career counseling (Jepsen, chapter 4), the discovery of new career insights is achieved through both inductive and deductive reasoning processes. Inductive reasoning is applied when appraisal data are arranged according to rules emerging from the client's own thoughts and feelings. Counselors assist clients in rearranging information in a way they have not done previously using the client's common sense reasoning. From a different perspective, deductive methods for achieving insights involve applying concepts from career development theory. The counselor relies on knowledge of developmental concepts (developmental tasks, life events, social roles, self-concept, etc.) to suggest categories for grouping career and test data. Counselors organize client's career data for interpretation by using the concept definition as the criteria for collating the data. The counselor assumes a much more active role in this process.

In the social learning and social psychological approaches to career counseling, tests are not all that frequently used to assess individual differences in behavior and cognition. Krumboltz and Nichols indicate that in social learning career counseling, understanding client goals and helping the client clarify goals and resolve goal conflicts is an important part of information giving and problem solution. In this process, the Career Beliefs Inventory may be used to identity beliefs that may interfere with a client's ability to achieve their goals. However, in general, test use is not that frequent given that the focus is on behavior. According to Dorn, social psychological career counseling is a social influence process that assists client's in abandoning existing attitudes and formulating new attitudes about career development. Client attitudes lead to specific behaviors and if these attitudes are ineffective then it becomes necessary for new attitudes to be formulated so that new behavior may be utilized. Thus, the focus is on attitude change, but tests may be used to identify career myths (ineffective career development attitudes).

Rayman notes that the computer is capable of administering instruments (interest inventories, personality inventories, ability measures, skill inventories, value inventories, etc.) and providing individualized, standardized interpretations to the client. Subsequently, the results from the client's online assessment may be used to generate a list of occupations based on the client's responses. This clearly is a strength of the computer and a reason for using the computer as one component part of a comprehensive career counseling system.

In summary, all of the approaches to career counseling emphasize that testing is part of ongoing career counseling. The client is very much involved in the process and collaborates with the counselor in the development of greater self-knowledge (Crites, 1981). It is not an isolated activity that takes place outside the counselor–client interaction. Stated differently, testing and test interpretation is an interaction between two people (the counselor and the client). As noted by Crites (1981), testing and test interpretation has a number of positive characteristics. It provides the client with reliable and valid information for making a specific career choice. It models coping behaviors and decisional skills and how they may be used in problem solving. Finally, it contributes to more effective career adjustment and personal adjustment through greater self-understanding and self-confidence.

Occupational Information

The use of occupational information in career counseling is mentioned by most of the approaches, but rarely emphasized. Generally, the intent in the use of occupational information is to increase the client's knowledge of the world of work, more specifically in the career choice areas that the client is considering. Thus, although most approaches to career counseling view occupational information as an important aspect of the career counseling process, very few approaches attempt to follow through on this aspect of the counseling process.

In the trait-and-factor approach, Rounds and Tracy emphasize diagnosis, assessment, and actuarial methods and the use of valid and reliable information. The process is guided by a person–environment fit model that attempts to match the person and the occupational environment. This matching process suggests the need for occupational information to reinforce a choice, resolve indecision between equally attractive alternatives, or reconsider a choice. According to the person-centered approach (Bozarth & Fisher, chapter 2), the career counseling process involves a large informational component not present in therapy. The career counselor has certain career information and skills available to the client through which a career goal may be implemented. The psychodynamic approach to career counseling not surprising emphasizes the person aspects of the process. Watkins and Savickas emphasize the need for information on personality styles, interests, and abilities that will facilitate client development of life themes and growth through work. Very little is said about occupational information. In developmental career counseling (Jepsen, chapter 4), occupational information is not emphasized. However, from an information standpoint deductive methods are used by the counselor to draw on career development theory and assist in organizing client career data. The counselor relies on knowledge of developmental concepts to suggest categories for grouping the client's career data. In the social learning approach (Krumboltz & Nichols, chapter 5), not much is done with printed occupational information, but career exploration is clearly believed to be important. In this approach, career kits may be used in order to stimulate career exploration and decision making. The social psychological approach to career counseling (Dorn, chapter 6) does not say much about the use of occupational information, but views such information as a social power base for the counselor. Informational power results from the counselor's familiarity with information or resources that the client may find to be helpful.

In the use of computers, Rayman has noted that integrating computer-assisted career guidance (CACG) as one component part of a comprehensive career counseling system is likely to be the best and most powerful way to utilize such a system. Clearly, computers carry out a number of tasks well. They generate a list of occupations based on personal assessment. Multiple on-line assessment devices assist the client in establishing linkages between personal interests, values, abilities, skills, and experiences on the one hand, and occupations deemed more likely to fit these personal characteristics on the other. There is no question that CACG systems do an excellent job of providing the client with quality occupational information. In addition, clients learn what skills are needed in an occupation, whether they have those skills, and the educational and training requirements.

SUMMARY

The approaches to career counseling that have been detailed in this volume have been informed by a variety of psychological perspectives as well as by models drawn from other disciplines. Reviewing the range of approaches, it is evident that both differential and developmental contributions have been used to understand career development and vocational behavior. In addition, social learning models, cognitive models, and social psychological models of human behavior have been used to develop meaningful approaches to career counseling. The range and wealth of perspectives has been very satisfying, and it is hoped that future theorizing about career development and counseling continues to be as productive.

The Bureau of Labor Statistics estimates that by the year 2000, the labor force is expected to grow 18%, an increase of 21 million workers. The Bureau further estimates that women and minorities will account for more than 90% of the growth. There will be fewer older workers and fewer younger workers. A significant question that needs to be asked is how will counselors help people prepare for making career choices in the future? We hope that the models and methods of the career counseling approaches described and elaborated in this volume will in some sense help show the way.

REFERENCES

Corsini, R.J. (1981). *Handbook of innovative psychotherapies*. New York: Wiley-Interscience.

Crites, J.O. (1981). *Career counseling: Models, methods, and materials*. New York: McGraw-Hill, Inc.

Goldman, L. (1983). The vocational card-sort technique: A different view. *Measurement and Evaluation in Guidance, 16*, 107–109.

Grummon, D.L. (1972). Client-centered theory. In B. Stefflre & W.H. Grant (Eds.), *Theories of counseling* (2nd ed., pp. 73–135). New York: McGraw-Hill.

Kiesler, D.J. (1973). *The process of psychotherapy*. Chicago: Aldine Press.

Patterson, C.H. (1964). Counseling: Self-clarification and the helping relationship. In H. Borow (Ed.), *Man in a world of work* (pp. 434–459). Boston: Houghton-Mifflin.

Savickas, M.L. (1984). Career maturity: The construct and its measurement. *Vocational Guidance Quarterly, 32*, 222–231.

Author Index

Subject Index